MASTERMIND

MASTERMIND

Over 2,700 questions and answers from the BBC tv
quiz game compiled by Boswell Taylor

TREASURE PRESS

Mastermind was first published in Great Britain in 1973 by the British Broadcasting Corporation
© 1973 Boswell Taylor

Mastermind Two was first published in Great Britain in 1975 by the British Broadcasting Corporation
© 1975 Boswell Taylor

Mastermind Three was first published in Great Britain in 1978 by the British Broadcasting Corporation
© 1978 British Broadcasting Corporation

This one-volume edition first published in 1984 by
Treasure Press
59 Grosvenor Street
London W1

Reprinted 1985

ISBN 0 907812 64 3

All Rights Reserved

Printed in Great Britain by
Richard Clay (The Chaucer Press) Limited
Bungay, Suffolk

Introduction

Most good ideas are invariably simple ones, and I think this is the strength of *Mastermind*. Devoid of all the usual quiz gimmickery it is a simple confrontation of Questioner and Questioned.

How did it all begin? It began in the Quiz Unit office of the Entertainment Department of Outside Broadcasts – a unit that has been responsible for *Television Top of the Form*, *Quiz Ball* and *Transworld Top Team*. We produced also a television version of *Brain of Britain* some years ago, but I had always thought that television ought to be able to produce an intellectual quiz that was entirely original. *Mastermind* gradually took shape from the basic concept of a single contestant with an interrogator firing questions. Many titles were considered but the name Mastermind, an inspiration of *Television Top of the Form* researcher Mary Craig, was eventually decided on.

Luck of course plays a part in any competition and *Mastermind* is no exception, but I think we have achieved with this format a competition that reduces the luck factor to a minimum. To qualify as *Mastermind* material you have to know your chosen subject thoroughly to stand any sort of chance at all. Couple the degree of excellence in a given subject with a sharp, decisive and concise mind and you have the qualifications required to enter for the title Mastermind of the United Kingdom'.

Any television programme, simple or otherwise, requires a great deal of team work, and I would like to pay tribute to my production team, particularly Martin Bell our director, Cherry Cole our hard-working researcher, Janet Evans who is now without doubt the most informed typist in the business, and Philip Lindley our designer; to my engineering colleagues and, of course, the star of the show, Magnus Magnusson who has so adroitly developed an art of gentle interrogation. This team has worked hard together to make the series a success.

Bill Wright, Executive Producer

CONTENTS

Mastermind Book Two 165

MASTERMIND
BOOK ONE

General Knowledge 1

1 Who designed the 'bouncing bomb' used by the 'Dam Busters' to destroy the Ruhr dams in World War II?

2 What is the name of the bell used at Lloyd's in London?

3 In what year did Mussolini invade Ethiopia?

4 Which group of people were emancipated in Britain in 1829?

5 At one time a member of Diaghilev's Company, she became Director of the Royal Ballet. Who is she?

6 He was the author of *The Shortest Way with Dissenters* and *A Journal of the Plague Year*. Who was he?

7 The Roman goddess of agriculture who bore a daughter by Jupiter is identified with the Greek goddess Demeter. What is her name?

8 What are the names of the two large towers of the Palace of Westminster?

9 Who was the founder of the German 'Christian Democratic Party'?

10 Which (contemporary) composer first used the Dodecaphonic Scale in his later works?

11 The yield of an oil well is measured in barrels. How many gallons are there to a barrel?

12 What special gift did Jean Baptiste Tavernier present to King Louis XIV of France?

13 Why do Tibetan priests search for a boy after the death of the Dalai Lama?

14 In what part of the world would you find a Gamelan Orchestra?

15 His first play was *The Room* in 1957 and his other works include *The Servant*. What is his name?

16 What is natation?

17 What is the name of the Rake in *The Rake's Progress*?

18 In the theatre, what would you be doing if you were 'papering the house'?

19 Goethe wrote about him; Berlioz, Wagner and Liszt all composed music about him. Who was he?

20 What is the capital of Nepal?

Twentieth-century English Literature

Set by Boswell Taylor

21 What book, modelled on Homer's *Odyssey*, tells the story of a day in Dublin?

22 *Man of Property* is the first book in Galsworthy's trilogy *Forsyte Saga*, what is the last?

23 What is the name of the large island which is the setting for Conrad's *Almayer's Folly* and *An Outcast of the Islands*?

24 D. H. Lawrence adopted the phoenix as a personal symbol. What bird is named in the title of his first novel?

25 What twentieth-century novel has as its epigraph the words 'only connect . . .'?

26 Alec Waugh, brother of Evelyn, wrote a first novel about life at a public school, what was it?

27 What is the connection between Lady Ariadne Utterwood and Mrs Hesione Hushabye?

28 Which modern novel ends with the words 'She walked rapidly in the June sunlight towards the worst horror of all'?

29 Who was the predecessor of Cecil Day-Lewis as Poet Laureate?

30 What poet wrote this epitaph for his own grave: 'cast a cold eye, on life, on death. Horseman, pass by!'?

31 How did Edward Ponderevo make his fortune?

32 What is the title of Shaw's five-part play which is supposed to trace the entire history of mankind?

33 Where do you find Willy Nilly, Organ Morgan and Bessie Bighead?

34 Justine, Balthazar, Mountolive, what's the fourth?

35 What is the real name of the British Intelligence Officer who created *The Spy who Came in from the Cold*?

36 What is the title of the book published in 1954, which is a black parody of Ballantyne's *Coral Island*?

37 What were the first names of Dame Edith Sitwell's famous brothers?

38 Who wrote the wartime book *The Last Enemy*?

39 Who were Priestley's 'Good Companions'?

40 What is the name of the Tibetan mountain retreat described by James Hilton in *The Lost Horizon*?

National Flags Past and Present

Set by I. O. Evans

41 What flags were raised above the summit of
Mount Everest by Hillary and Tensing in 1953?

42 We all know the Stars and Stripes, but what were
the Stars and Bars?

43 What emblems are used, and where, for the Red
Cross Flag?

44 How many stripes appear on the National Flag of
Greece, and why?

45 What is the translation of the Arabic script on the
flag of Saudi Arabia?

46 Explain how a certain national flag was inspired by
an Aztec legend.

47 Which was the first flag to reach the Moon?

48 Which flag of a foreign region resembles a British
Ensign in having the so-called Union Jack in its
canton and what is the design on the remainder of
the flag?

49 What were the colours of the original flag of the
Netherlands and why were they varied?

50 What flag bears a representation of St George
slaying the Dragon?

51 How is the State Flag of East Germany
distinguished from the National Flag of West
Germany?

52 What two National Flags display the 'Sun of May'
and why?

53 Which two flags were the first to reach the South Pole?

54 How are the flags of the constituent Republics of the Soviet Union distinguished from that of the Soviet Union itself?

55 What foreign flag most resembles the British Union Flag and in what respects does it differ from this?

56 The flags of what regions bear emblems of the rising or the setting sun, and why was the latter chosen?

57 What emblem appeared on the American flag flown at the Battle of Concord and what historic British flag does it resemble?

58 Why were the Lilies of France shown in the place of honour in the English Royal Standard?

59 What former National Flag is now used as the House Flag of a shipping line?

60 What is, or was, the Sabah Jack?

IDRISYN OLIVER EVANS: author of *The Observer's Book of Flags* (Warne), and *The Book of Flags* (OUP).

General Knowledge 2

61 He directed *Rembrandt* and *Lady Hamilton* and produced *The Scarlet Pimpernel* and *The Third Man*. Who was he?

62 James I of England presided over an important conference held at Hampton Court in 1604. What did it bring about?

63 What mythological creature was half-man and half-horse?

64 Originally a French eighteenth-century innovation, what is the method of gilding furniture and clocks known as?

65 Rigel and Betelgeuse are two stars in which constellation?

66 Who was the world's first woman Prime Minister?

67 The Adi Granth is a holy book of which religion?

68 What was the sensational discovery of Charles Dawson in Sussex in the early years of the present century?

69 What famous building was built at Alexandria in the region of Ptolemy (308-245 BC)?

70 Ouagadougou is the capital of which country?

71 How many women's colleges are there in Oxford University?

72 Who said: 'Let us never negotiate out of fear. But let us never fear to negotiate.'?

73 King Edward III founded this premier Order in about 1349. What is it called?

74 What is 'The Witch of Wookey'?

75 Of which Canadian Party is Pierre Trudeau the leader?

76 He first came to Europe from America in 1857 and amongst his most famous paintings is a portrait of his mother. Who was he?

77 A village in Huntingdonshire is famous for its cheese. What is its name?

78 In Greek Legend who was Pygmalion?

79 What is majolica?

80 What is the largest organ in the human body?

Grand Opera

Set by Harold Rosenthal

81 What is the English translation of the title of the opera 'Die Verkaufte Braut'?

82 Who composed the opera 'Oedipus Rex'?

83 What does the word 'Opera' mean?

84 From which author's story was the opera 'Barber of Seville' taken?

85 Mussorgsky's 'Boris Godunov' was based on a play by whom?

86 Where was 'Das Rheingold' first performed?

87 Who was Helen Mitchell?

88 The songs 'Once there lived a king in Thule' and 'Forever Thine' come from which opera?

89 Name the first opera ever performed.

90 Where was the first public opera house opened?

91 What famous opera house stands on the site of a church?

92 How many Rossini operas have the same overture?

93 How many conquests did Don Giovanni make in Spain, according to Leporello's cataloguing?

94 When audiences acclaimed Verdi with the shouts 'Viva Verdi what political significance did these words have?

95 How many Walküres were there?

96 What was the 'mystic gulf'?

97 Who was Uncle Greifenklau?

98 What famous opera takes place while another opera is supposed to be played off stage?

99 By what name is June Gough better known?

100 Who was Gualtier Malde?

HAROLD ROSENTHAL: Editor of *Opera*, writer on music, formerly archivist at the Royal Opera House, Covent Garden.

Astronomy 1

Set by Patrick Moore

101 Which planet was discovered in 1930?

102 What is the Cassini division?

103 What would happen to the moon of a planet if it passed the Roche limit?

104 The Trojans are groups of asteroids that move in the same orbit as one of the planets. Which planet?

105 How many moons has Saturn?

106 Mercury orbits the Sun once every 88 days. How long does it take for Mercury to rotate once on its axis?

107 What is a pulsar?

108 What planet is known as the Horned Planet?

109 Who discovered the planet Uranus?

110 Which planet has the least density?

111 For what was Flamsteed famous?

112 Fred Hoyle put forward a theory of creation. What did he call it?

113 Where, today, would you expect to find Hell, Julius Caesar, Birmingham, Billy, Ptolemaeus and Archimedes?

114 On 25 October 1973 the planet Mars was at opposition. What precisely does this mean?

115 What was the name of the great Dutch astronomer who discovered a supernova in 1572 and who drew up a famous star catalogue?

116 The lunar craters, Gassendi, Hippalus, Doppelmayer, Vitello and Lee lie around the border of a well-defined sea or Mare. Name the Mare.

117 Only three external galaxies are clearly visible with the naked eye. Which of them can be seen from the latitude of London?

118 What is the significance of the apparently chaotic sequence of letters W, O, B, A, F, G, K, M?

119 What is particular about the orbit of Pluto?

120 Of the following ten stars, nine are long-period variables and the tenth is irregular. Name the irregular variables from: W Lyrae, R Leonis, R Arietis, R Coronae Borealis, U Herculis, R Cygni, U Orionis, S Corona Borealis, Omicron Ceti, Chi Cygni.

PATRICK MOORE: Well-known television personality, author, and expert on astronomy.

General Knowledge 3

121 At the mouth of which river is Dublin situated?

122 Isobars are lines joining places with the same atmospheric pressure. What are isotherms?

123 Women's events made their first appearance in this competition in 1928. Which competition?

124 Stalingrad is now known as Volgograd, what was its original name?

125 What is a line of iambic hexameter called?

126 He became William the Conqueror's Archbishop of Canterbury in 1070. Who was he?

127 The Dutch have a plan to prevent the North Sea inundating the South-western lowlands. What is the plan called?

128 What is an acrostic?

129 From what fruit is the liqueur known as Kirsch distilled?

130 If you had a cadaceus, what would it be?

131 What battle is sometimes called the 'Battle of the Three Emperors'?

132 Most people understand Utopia to mean an impossibly ideal place or state of affairs. What does this word, derived from the Greek, literally mean?

133 His name in particular has become synonymous with political double dealing and intrigue. Who was he?

134 What unique find was made by a Bedouin shepherd boy in a cave in the Wadi Qumran (Qumran Valley)?

135 The lakes of Grasmere, Hawes Water and Rydal Water all lie within which English county?

136 What are the Roman numerals for 400?

137 Who led the 'Huns' of the fourth century AD?

138 Men and women of ancient Greece wore a similar garment. What was it called?

139 In nautical terms, what name is given to the upper edge of a ship's side?

140 Convallaria Majalis is the national flower of Sweden. What is its more common name?

Classical Mythology
Set by Dr Wolfgang Liebeschuetz

141 What was Paris, prince of Troy, doing when the three goddesses, Hera, Aphrodite, and Athena asked him to judge which of them was the fairest?

142 For how long was Troy besieged by the Greeks?

143 How did Achilles die?

144 Why did Orpheus fail to bring back Eurydice from the underworld?

145 What are the names of the couple who survived to re-people the world in the Greek version of the flood legend?

146 Which Greek heroine took poison so that her husband might live?

147 Why did Heracles agree to hold up the heavens?

148 Which Greek heroine was hatched from an egg?

149 Which Greek queen played the role of 'Potiphar's wife' to her step-son?

150 Parts of what animals made up the Chimaera?

151 How does Greek religion suggest a connection between commerce and thieving?

152 The Greeks explained the annual return of spring by the story of a rape. Who was the victim?

153 For what offence was Prometheus chained to the Caucasus?

154 What was Oedipus' (correct) answer to the riddle of the Sphinx?

155 Why did the women of Lemnos live without men when the Argonauts arrived?

156 Which level of stratification on the excavated site of Hissarlik is now thought to represent the Troy destroyed by Agamemnon's army?

157 Name the Victorian rediscoverer of the site of Troy.

158 What was the duty of Triptolemus?

159 'A little learning is a dangerous thing, drink deep, or taste not the Pierian spring' (Pope). What was the Pierian spring?

160 The straits leading from the sea of Marmora into the Black Sea are known as the Bosporus. What does the name mean and/or why was it given?

DR WOLFGANG LIEBESCHUETZ: of the Department of Classics, Leicester University.

History of Music 1550-1900

Set by Boswell Taylor

161 By what name is Handel's aria 'Ombra mai fu', composed for his opera *Xerxes*, better known?

162 What is 'opera bouffe'?

163 What is 'The Forty-Eight'?

164 What was the opera that was written for a Chelsea girls' school run by the dancing master, Josias Priest?

165 What form did Mozart's 'Haffner Symphony' take before it became the work we know today?

166 What was the sprightly music often paired with the pavane in the sixteenth century?

167 What is the nickname of Chopin's piano sonata in B flat minor?

168 Who was the Master of the King's Band who composed 'Heart of Oak' to commemorate the British victories in 1759?

169 What is the title of the tunes you play with two fingers on the piano, of which variations have been composed by Borodin, Rimsky-Korsakov and Liszt?

170 What is the title of the operetta that Sullivan composed without Gilbert to a libretto by F. C. Burnand?

171 Who is the heroine of Beethoven's opera *Fidelio*?

172 Many plantation songs, including *The Old Folks at Home* and *Camptown Races*, were composed by whom?

173 What is the generic title of the thirty-six pieces Mendelssohn composed for the piano, among which are three Venetian songs?

174 Why is Schubert's Quintet in A major known as the 'Trout Quintet'?

175 Where did Weber, against considerable opposition, establish a theatre devoted to the performance of opera in German?

176 What music did Beethoven dedicate to the Russian Ambassador in Vienna in 1806?

177 In which city was the first public performance of Handel's *Messiah*?

178 What is the name, meaning 'a pie', which is given to an operatic work such as *Love in a Village*?

179 What island is the setting for Bizet's *The Pearl-Fishers*?

180 Who wrote the drama of French rural life *L'Arlésienne*, for which Bizet composed the incidental music?

General Knowledge 4

181   What is the name of the Greek God of the winds?

182   Victoria Woodhull was the first woman candidate for what office?

183   What is the subtle difference between assault and battery?

184   If you were in a Hummum what would you be most likely to be doing?

185   Born in Stockholm, she first won international fame in a Swedish film *Gosta Berling* in 1924. Who was she?

186   What did William Miller prophesy would happen in 1843?

187   'If all knew what others say about them there would not be four friends in the world' was written by whom?

188   The Norwich School of Painting was founded by whom?

189   Arthur Fitzgibbon was awarded the Victoria Cross in 1861. What was unique about the award?

190   Moscow's church of St Basil the Blessed owes its existence to whom?

191   What is the connection between the Farne Islands and eiderdowns?

192   Who founded the Ballet Russe?

193   Juan Sebastian de Cano commanded a ship called the *Vittoria*. What did he achieve in her?

194 Which is the longest river in France?

195 What is the largest known fish in the sea?

196 What name is given to the art and practice of bell ringing?

197 In history, who was 'Hotspur'?

198 The first Dimbleby Lecture was given on BBC television on 31 October 1972. Who delivered it?

199 What is now understood by the phrase 'crossing the Rubicon'?

200 Whose plays fall into two categories, 'pièces noires' and 'pièces roses'?

British Politics Since 1900
Set by Dr David Butler

201 What election in this country yielded the biggest majority?

202 When and why did the Duke of Devonshire resign from the Cabinet?

203 What was 'Mr Balfour's poodle'?

204 How many Parliaments in this country lasted less than a year?

205 Who was Prime Minister for the longest continuous period in this century?

206 What office did Winston Churchill hold for the longest continuous period?

207 When did nationalisation of steel first come into force?

208 When did the Leader of the Opposition first get an official salary?

209 Who brought about a 'bonfire of controls'?

210 Who agreed that who was 'the best Prime Minister we have'?

211 Who said of whom that they were aiming for 'power without responsibility—the prerogative of the harlot throughout the ages'?

212 When did Clement Attlee become Leader of the Labour Party?

213 Who was the first Minister of Technology?

214 When were Life Peers first created?

215 Who introduced Premium Bonds?

216 Why did Sir Samuel Hoare resign from the Cabinet?

217 Who was the first man to resign his peerage?

218 What was the basis for the phrase 'Selsdon Man'?

219 What was the biggest single change in the parity of the pound in this century?

220 What was the Fulton Report?

Dr DAVID E. BUTLER, M.A., D.Phil.: Fellow of Nuffield College, Oxford. Author of: *The British General Election of 1951*, *The Electoral System in Britain, 1918–1951*, *The British General Election of 1955*, *British Political Facts, 1900–1969* etc.

English Costume

Set by Margaret and Boswell Taylor

221   What city is associated with the bright green cloth traditionally worn by Robin Hood?

222   What were 'pomanders'?

223   Who is usually given the credit for inventing 'bloomers'?

224   According to Dickens, Mrs Peerybingle wore 'pattens'. What were these pattens and why were they worn?

225   Still with Dickens, what is a 'Dolly Varden'?

226   Sartorially, what is the difference between a 'Blücher' and a 'Wellington'?

227   Chopin played it. Women wore it. What was the polonaise that women wore in the eighteenth century?

228   The 'liripipe' was not a musical instrument. What was it?

229   In the sixteenth century, how would you have used a 'mocket'?

230   What is a 'billycock'?

231   In the 'naughty nineties', what was a 'gibus'?

232   Sir Walter Scott wrote 'The huntsmen twitched their mauds'. What were their mauds?

233   In the Tudor period a young man might have the choice between wearing 'Spanish slops' or 'Venetians'. What kind of garment were these?

234 In some of the portraits we have of him,
Shakespeare wore a 'whisk'. What was this?

235 What was known as 'incardine satin'?

236 What was the alternative name that was better
suited to the bakery than the hatters for the 'high
Burgundian hat' worn in the fifteenth century?

237 What did a sprig of palm in a traveller's hat in
Chaucer's time signify?

238 From what article of wear do we get the word
'sabotage'?

239 In the Dark Ages a peasant might wear a felt hat
of any colour except yellow. What was the special
category of person who was obliged to wear a
yellow hat?

240 To a Victorian, what article of clothing was a
'bertha'?

Words

Set by Gillian Skirrow and Bill Wright

241 What is a palindromic word?

242 What is a syllogism?

243 What is the origin of the word 'language'?

244 What does this Latin phrase mean; Ad Valorem?

245 What is syntax?

246 What are cognates?

247 The word 'cab' is a shortened version of what?

248 What is homoeopathy?

249 What is the derivation of the word 'recalcitrant'?

250 What is a diacritical mark?

251 What is the derivation of 'aftermath'?

252 What is neologism?

253 What is the derivation of 'assassin'?

254 What does the word 'maundy' mean?

255 What do the words Bar Mitzvah mean?

256 What is the derivation of the word 'ballot'?

257 The small Australian animal is known as a 'koala'. What does 'koala' mean?

258 What is the derivation of the word 'candidate'?

259 What is the derivation of the word 'salary'?

260 What is the derivation of the word 'sandwich'?

General Knowledge 5

261 Lake Erie and Lake Ontario are linked by which canal?

262 'Bailiwick' is a feudal term denoting the limits of a bailiff's jurisdiction. Where is the term still in use today?

263 The American Civil War of 1861 was in the main precipitated by what event?

264 Yabusame is a Japanese version of which sport?

265 Who invented the diesel engine?

266 Which breed of dog is considered to be the tallest?

267 Who was the first of the Lancastrian Kings?

268 The word 'Weald' is the Old English for – what?

269 University College, Cambridge, is to change its name to what?

270 To whom was Churchill referring when he said 'There he stalks, that Wuthering Height'?

271 He lost his head after arranging a marriage between Henry VIII and Anne of Cleves. Who was he?

272 *The Book of Common Prayer* was introduced in 1549 by whom?

273 Who was the author of the collection of short stories entitled *Mortal Coils*?

274 Which character in Shakespeare's *Richard II* described England as 'This precious stone set in the silver sea'?

275 When was the term 'Concentration Camp' first used?

276 What is the name of the Danish Prime Minister who resigned after his country's referendum on the Common Market?

277 He was born Jean Chauvin in Picardy in 1509. By what name is he remembered?

278 What is the English word for the Italian 'Zingaro'?

279 The hero of a Babylonian epic offended the goddess Ishtar and was punished. How was he punished?

280 Baron Passfield helped to found the London School of Economics. By what other name was he known?

British Moths
Set by L. Hugh Newman

281 Which is the most common migrant moth in this country?

282 Which British moth has false eyes in the juvenile stage and turns pink as an adult?

283 Why has the Privet hawk moth been given the generic name of Sphinx?

284 Why is the Peppered moth of special scientific interest?

285 Which British moths contain cyanide?

286 Which British moth has the same colour scheme in the caterpillar stage and as an adult moth?

287 Where was the Waved Black moth first discovered?

288 Which large moth caterpillar has a strong and unpleasant smell?

289 What group of British moths is named after a breed of dog?

290 Which British moth is a silk-spinner, and is related to the tropical silk moths?

291 What British moth was thought to be extinct for nearly a century and was then re-discovered in the East Anglian marshes?

292 Which moth is named after polished metal?

293 What is the deficiency that is common to the Female Winter Moth, the Mottled Umber and the Vapourer?

294 In what way is it true that the Death's Head moth has a voice?

295 What is the common feeding habit of the caterpillars of Clearwing moths?

296 What is the group of British moths named after an almost extinct type of domestic servant?

297 How is it possible for male moths to locate females in the dark?

298 In the lepidopteral sense, why is the small Puss moth caterpillar not a kitten?

299 What kind of weather do moths prefer for their noctural jaunts?

300 In what way is the male Ghost moth ghostlike?

L. HUGH NEWMAN, F.R.E.S.: Managing Director, Butterfly Farm. Author of: *Butterfly Farmer* (Phoenix House), *British Moths in their Haunts* (Edmund Ward), etc.

English Literature

Set by Boswell Taylor

301 Who was the fifteenth-century jail-bird who wrote a classic romance of knighthood?

302 Who was the Shakespearian heroine who disguised herself as Ganymede after 'Jove's own page'?

303 What is the title of the important book on education written by Queen Elizabeth the First's childhood tutor?

304 Who was the titled recipient of Dr Samuel Johnson's famous letter upon his patronage?

305 There were two main contributors to the first numbers of *The Tatler* and *The Spectator*. One was Sir Richard Steele, who was the other?

306 What is the literary term introduced into our language by John Lyly?

307 What famous nineteenth-century novelist attempted to clear off a debt of more than £100,000 with a succession of novels?

308 What is the real name of the village of Cranford?

309 Christopher Marlowe and John Donne each begin a poem with the identical first line. What was that line?

310 What is the title of the novel that Henry Fielding wrote as a parody of Richardson's *Pamela*?

311 What is the book in which Charles Dickens attacked the lust for money through inheritance and the Chancery Court?

312 What is the reasoning in the choice of 'Erewhon' as the title of Samuel Butler's satire?

313 Of what school were Stalky and Co. pupils?

314 Who was the author of *Curiosa Mathematica* and *Notes on the First Two Books of Euclid?*

315 Wycherley and Congreve were two of the main writers of comedies of manners, who was the third?

316 Who did Thomas Thorpe, the publisher, claim to be 'the onlie begetter of these insuing sonnets'?

317 What was the political position ultimately achieved by the author of *Coningsby?*

318 What famous work had its genesis in a back room of Tom Davies's bookshop at No. 8 Russell Street, Covent Garden?

319 Who is Edgar Allan Poe's detective, said to have been the first of a prolific line of fictional detectives?

320 What were the actual names of the authors who wrote as Currer, Ellis and Acton Bell?

Tudor History

Set by John D. Bareham

321 Who was the royal officer sent by Henry VII to govern Ireland for him (his name was given to the laws which settled the relationship between the English and Irish Parliaments of the time)?

322 Which famous Netherlands' writer and philosopher came to lecture in Oxford in 1498?

323 One of the so-called Commonwealth Men, John Hales, was the moving spirit behind a commission in 1548 which investigated an important social and economic problem. What was this problem?

324 Who led a rebellion against Queen Mary Tudor in 1554, partly against the Spanish marriage?

325 What connection is there between Bishops Hooper, Ridley and Latimer, apart from their being Protestants in doctrine?

326 What happened on Evil May Day 1517 in London?

327 Who wrote 'The Assertion of the Seven Sacraments', in 1521, a defence of the Church against Luther?

328 How was English life affected in 1563 by an attempt to encourage seamen and seamanship?

329 When and what was the 'Whip with Six Strings'?

330 Princess Mary Tudor married Louis XII of France. Who was her second husband?

331 With what art or craft do you associate Wynkyn de Worde?

332 Local historians and demographers have reason to be pleased with Thomas Cromwell's instructions to the English parish clergy of 1538. Why?

333 Whose life was Queen Elizabeth I forced to sacrifice to the executioner, in order to save Mary Queen of Scots' life when it was threatened by Parliament and the Council?

334 The traditional Parliamentary tax of the Tudors was the Fifteenth and the Tenth. What was this?

335 Who came back to England in 1548, on leave of absence from Spain, and spent the last ten years of his life teaching the English the art of navigation?

336 What was Sir Christopher Hatton's cognizance, from his coat of arms (remembered most because of his investment in sea voyages)?

337 Professor Hoskins maintains that standard historians of the Tudor period neglect one vital factor causing sixteenth-century discontent. He mentions particularly troubles in 1549–51, during Edward VI's reign. What factor does he stress?

338 A famous Elizabethan miniature painter born about 1547 was the first English-born artist to leave details of his own life and work. Who was he?

339 Professor Scarisbrick has urged a particular theory regarding Cardinal Wolsey's foreign policy. Which is his main theme: (a) Wolsey the servant of Henry VIII; (b) Wolsey hoping to become Pope; (c) Wolsey the Peace-maker?

340 One of the great problems of historians of the Tudor period is to estimate the population of England; no figure is more than an estimate, but there has been much modern research. According to Professor J. C. Russell and Mr Julian Cornwall, about what figure was the population of England at about the end of the reign of Henry VIII (1545–7)?

JOHN D. BAREHAM: Senior History Lecturer, Exeter College.

General Knowledge 6

341 A member of the family *Alaudidae*, Wordsworth wrote a poem in his praise. Who is he?

342 Which author did Hitler and Mussolini acclaim as the master prophet of right-wing authoritarianism?

343 Indonesia was declared a Republic in 1945. Who was its First President?

344 The French gendarme wears a distinctive hat. What is it called?

345 At sea what period of time is covered by the first 'Dog Watch'?

346 They were founded in the reign of Henry VII for the protection of the Royal Person. Who were they?

347 Her first major success was in the film *The Blue Angel*. Who was she?

348 It was designed by Robert Fulton and tried out in the Seine in 1801. What was it?

349 He wrote many of the plays known as 'The Aldwych Farces' in the 1920s such as *Rookery Nook*. Who was he?

350 For what would you use a Wheatstone Bridge?

351 His first novel was *Desperate Remedies* and his last was *Jude the Obscure*. Who was he?

352 What fortunate discovery was made by Jacobus Jonker in 1934?

353 Where did the game squash originate?

354   What do the letters P.V.C. stand for?

355   Among his famous musicals were *The Vagabond King* and *Rose Marie*. Who was he?

356   In sailing, what is a 'jury mast'?

357   Who used the pseudonyms Diedrich Knickerbocker and Jonathan Oldstyle among others?

358   T. S. Eliot wrote, 'He always has an alibi, and one or two to spare; At whatever time the deed took place – Macavity wasn't there'. Who was Macavity?

359   First Baron Tweedsmuir, he was at one time the Governor-General of Canada, and wrote many successful adventure stories. By what name is he better known?

360   In 1877 he constructed the phonograph, which he called 'the Ideal Amanuensis'. Who was he?

Assassinations and Murders
Set by Boswell Taylor

361 How many presidents of the United States have been assassinated?

362 Who is the only British Prime Minister to be assassinated?

363 Where was he assassinated?

364 What was the play that Abraham Lincoln saw the night that he was assassinated?

365 Who is alleged to have been assassinated by Nazi agents on 25 July 1934?

366 Who assassinated the Duke of Buckingham in 1628?

367 In which city did the assassination of Martin Luther King take place?

368 Lee Oswald was accused of shooting John Kennedy, the President of the United States. Who shot Lee Oswald?

369 Who was the king of Yugoslavia who was assassinated in Marseille in 1934?

370 When Archduke Francis Ferdinand was assassinated in 1914, his wife died with him, what was her name?

371 Who assassinated Robert Kennedy?

372 Who was assassinated by a Hindu fanatic as he was on his way to a prayer meeting on 30 January 1948?

373 In the Maybrick case, according to the prosecution what was the source of the poison used by Florence Maybrick to murder her husband?

374 Where was Ronald True when he was arrested for the murder of Gertrude Yates?

375 Whose love letters are said to have led to the murder of her husband and her execution in the nineteen-twenties?

376 Who was the infamous dweller in the notorious No. 10 Rillington Place, North Kensington?

377 Who was the last woman in Britain to be hanged?

378 What was the verdict in the Madeleine Smith trial in the 1850s?

379 What was the unusual defence put forward for Guenther Fritz Podola when he was tried for the murder of Detective Sergeant Purdy?

380 Who was the well-known pathologist who was concerned in both the Seddon case and the Edith Thompson trial?

Visual Arts

Set by Richard Francis

381 Picasso's *Guernica* was a protest about the bombing by Spanish planes of a village. What was the year when the event took place that inspired the painting?

382 Name the artist who was responsible for the windows in the new cathedral at Coventry.

383 Whose political monument which won Grand Prize in an international competition in 1953 caused an aggressive public response?

384 A famous architect died whilst swimming in 1965. He was responsible for the design of *La Tourette* amongst many other famous buildings. Who was he?

385 With which printmaker do you associate *Atelier 17* and new ways of gravure?

386 What is an icon?

387 Over the south door of Sancta Sophia, Constantine presents a model of the city and Justinian one of the church to a figure on the throne. Whom does the figure represent?

388 Completed around 1190, where is a mosaic cycle showing Christ's miracles?

389 A leader of the avant-garde in the 1920s, late in life he took to drawing from earlier masters. A museum is dedicated to his work in Biot. Who was he?

390 *Creation and Crucifixion* won the first prize at the first John Moore's Exhibition at Liverpool. Who was the prizewinner?

391 What was Anthony Caro's connection with the *New Generation*?

392 Who was the first American painter to win the *Venice Biennale*?

393 What is the name of the Byzantine cathedral of Constantinople?

394 Two major exhibitions in 1971 were closed soon after the opening. The first, in New York, was of photographs by Hans Haache; the second, in London, was by another American artist, who was he?

395 Who is the Professor of Sculpture at the Kunstakademie in Düsseldorf?

396 Where would you find the eleventh-century apse mosaic *The Virgin with Apostles*?

397 Which painter since the war do you associate with the iconic image of a flag?

398 What is the subject of the squinch in the dome of the church of Daphni near Athens, where Christ dominates the open space in the vaults?

399 At what date did Iconoclasm end?

400 What is the 'Joshua Roll'?

History of Aeronautics
Set by Charles Gibbs-Smith

401 Who made the first cross-channel flight in an aeroplane?

402 One of the two earliest airborne aeronautical devices was the kite. What was the other?

403 Venice was the first city to be bombed from the air. How was it done?

404 Who first crossed the Channel by air?

405 What was the first machine to attempt to cross the English Channel?

406 What world-famous light aeroplane first flew in 1925?

407 What was the first turbo-jet aeroplane to fly?

408 By what aerodynamic means did the Germans intend to increase the range of their A-4 rocket bomb, popularly called the V-2?

409 In 1931 the RAF won the Schneider Trophy outright. With what machine did they achieve this?

410 The first fatal accident in a powered aeroplane was in 1908. Name one of the two passengers in the plane.

411 What single make of aero-engine was the mainstay of early European aviation?

412 The first aerial passenger service runs were made between 1910 and 1914. Where?

413 By whom was the first parachute jump made from the air?

414 What was the accepted technique of survival in Victorian ballooning?

415 Who flew the first circle in an aeroplane?

416 Why did not the aeronautical drawings and writings of Leonardo da Vinci play any part in inspiring any pioneer in the history of the aeroplane?

417 What was peculiar about the functioning of the tailplane on Otto Lilienthal's standard and later gliders?

418 How was control-in-roll effected in Louis Blériot's successful cross-Channel monoplane?

419 What directly inspired the familiar early configuration of biplane wings and forward elevators?

420 Who was the first man to fit ailerons or elevons to a full-size aircraft?

CHARLES H. GIBBS-SMITH, M.A., F.M.A., F.R.S.A., Chevalier Danish Order of the Dannebrog, Keeper Emeritus, Victoria and Albert Museum. Author: *A History of Flying* (Batsford), *The Aeroplane, An Historical Survey* (H.M.S.O.) etc.

421 In mythology, what were Medusa, Stheno and Euryale collectively known as?

422 Who assassinated Jean Paul Marat?

423 In which country is the temple of Amun at Karnak?

424 Which English composer was a pupil of John Blow and became organist of Westminster Abbey in 1679?

425 What is the basic law of magnetism?

426 What is the meaning of symbiosis?

427 Where would you find a martingale?

428 In which English county do these rivers flow: Teme, Frome, Lugg, Dore, Arrow and Monnow?

429 Joseph Smith founded a religious sect in 1830. What is it called?

430 He edited the 'North Briton', was outlawed, and later became Lord Mayor of London. Who was he?

431 Who founded Oxford University's Christ Church College?

432 What are the Hagiographs?

433 .What family ruled Austria from the thirteenth century to 1918?

434 Who describes his journeys as a young man from his Gloucestershire village to London, and finally Spain and the Civil War?

435 Who followed Friedrich Ebert as President of the Weimar Republic?

436 Stoke, Burslem, Longton, Hanley and Tunstall are collectively known as what?

437 What name is given to the painting medium that uses the yolks of eggs?

438 Boadicea or Boudicca, queen of the Iceni, died in the time of which Roman emperor?

439 Von Reuter ordered the scuttling of the German Fleet in 1919. Where was it scuttled?

440 He was a musician, the son of a poor school teacher, born in Vienna in 1797, and he died there in 1828. Who was he?

Old Time Music Hall

Set by Peter Davison

441 In what year did George Formby senior die?

442 What was Sam Collin's original profession?

443 Who first sang, 'If you want to know the time, ask a P'liceman'?

444 In what year did the Metropolitan finally close?

445 Who was 'The woman who knows'?

446 When did the music hall strike begin?

447 Who tried to close the Empire Promenade in the 1890s?

448 When the Promenade was partitioned off, what man, later a Prime Minister, helped break it down?

449 What performer was shot by his father in a fit of jealousy?

450 Who was 'The Essence of Eccentricity'?

451 What was the name of the music-hall performer who was murdered by her husband in 1910?

452 Who was the mesmerist with whom, in effect, George Robey began his professional career?

453 Who first sang 'It's a long way to Tipperary'?

454 Who was 'John Bull's Girl'?

455 Who, before becoming a university professor, wrote for Marie Lloyd?

456 Who sang a song called 'The Lambeth Walk' at the end of the nineteenth century'?

457   Which music hall was called 'The Royal Academy over the Water'?

458   Who, in 1878, sang in a song 'I ain't a Briton true'?

459   What was the music hall at which George Ridley sang 'Blaydon Races'?

460   What were the subjects of the three songs Dan Leno sang to Edward VII?

Chemistry

Set by R. A. Ross

461 For what is the chemist Newlands remembered?

462 Mendeleev, on the basis of his Periodic Table, predicted the properties of some, at the time, unknown elements. One he called eka-silicon. What was it called when it was discovered?

463 What is the name of the element whose symbol is Pm?

464 Prometheum belongs to a group of elements. What is the group called?

465 The group of fourteen elements called Lanthanides have very similar chemical properties. How is the similarity explained?

466 Relative atomic masses are defined in terms of carbon 12. Why does the carbon in graphite have a relative atomic mass of 12.011?

467 Can you, in theory, have a mole of mice?

468 Approximately, how many mice in a mole of mice?

469 What is the thermicity of the reaction between carbon and oxygen?

470 What is the sign of the enthalpy change for such a reaction?

471 Which is the odd man out of the following list and why: sodium, potassium, barium and cesium?

472 What have haemoglobin, copper tetramine sulphate and potassium ferriferrocyanide in common?

473 What is the crystal structure of sodium chloride?

474　How was sodium first prepared, and by whom?

475　In representing organic compounds we use a line to stand for a bond. This represents two electrons shared. This method does not work for benzene. What is the phenomenon responsible for this failure called?

476　How many different compounds have the formula C H Cl Br F?

477　How are these substances distinguishable?

478　Why does hexene decolorise a solution of bromine?

479　What is the hydrogen ion concentration in pure water?

480　Why is 0.1 mole per litre acetic acid called a weak acid?

History of the English Language
Set by A. A. Evans and Boswell Taylor

481 The prefix 'geo' is derived from the Greek. What was its original meaning?

482 In the consonant shift *k* became *h;* what did *p* become?

483 In the history of the English language what period is covered by 'Old English'?

484 There are several river Avons in England. What did the name 'Avon' mean originally?

485 What is a mutated plural?

486 Why are the uplands of southern England called Downs?

487 What is the special name sometimes applied to Scottish and Irish Gaelic?

488 Madrigals are associated with Elizabethan England, but from which language did the English borrow the word?

489 We took the word 'tea' from the Chinese. From which language did we get 'coffee'?

490 How did the word 'boycott', meaning to have nothing to do with a person, get into the English language?

491 What is the derivation of the word whisky?

492 What were the meanings of the two Greek words that scientists used to make the word *chlorophyll?*

493 What are the elements that make up the word *ampersand?*

494 Who was the Scottish novelist who helped to popularise the use of Scottish words in the early part of the nineteenth century?

495 What name is often given to the series of changes in the long vowels which took place in late Middle English and Early Modern English?

496 What is the derivation of the town-crier's repeated 'Oyez'?

497 Old English script used seven vowel symbols: *a e i o u* and *y* and another one. What was the seventh vowel symbol?

498 Why did Francis Bacon, who had published his *Advancement in Learning* in 1605 in English, have it re-published in Latin later?

499 Why the 'by' in By-law?

500 What would be the most likely pronounciation that a member of the Victorian upper-classes would give to the word we know as cucumber?

General Knowledge 8

501 Where was Hitlers' mountain hideout?

502 Who was the admiral and hydrographer who gave his name to a 'scale' that described the force of winds?

503 In 1519 the *Trinidad*, *San Antonio*, *Concepcion*, *Vittoria*, and *Santiago* made up the fleet of a famous explorer. Who was he?

504 Among the plays he has written are *Photo Finish* and *Romanoff and Juliet*. Who is he?

505 They are ancient Hindu scriptures, written in an old form of Sanskrit. What are they called?

506 What is the mark called that fixes the maximum load line of a merchant vessel in salt water?

507 What is the longest river in Scotland?

508 In Britain the sovereign has three crowns, what are they?

509 Newton was at one time its President and it first received the Royal Charter in 1662. What was it?

510 Which English king was born at Caernarvon Castle in 1284 and ended his life in Berkeley Castle?

511 Can you name two of the pictures illustrated musically by Mussorgsky in his composition *Pictures at an Exhibition*?

512 The Lord Chamberlain's men were a theatrical company. Who was their most famous member?

513 His first play *Catalina* was published in 1850. Who was he?

514 By what name is the painter Domenicos Theotocopoulos, who lived from 1541-1614, better known?

515 Alexei Leonov marked up a first in space exploration. What did he achieve?

516 Who, in Greek mythology, were Clotho, Lachesis and Atropos?

517 His Latin name was Carolus Magnus. Who was he?

518 Vintners mark them on each side, but those belonging to the Crown are unmarked. What are they?

519 In 1572 who observed a nova in the constellation of Cassiopeia?

520 Cardinal John Newman was the author of *The Dream of Gerontius*. Who set it to music?

Sea and Ships

Set by Alan Villiers

521   How many ropes are there in a full-rigged ship?

522   Teodor Nalecz Korzeniowski is associated with the sea. In what way?

523   What was the name by which Drake's famous ship was known before his circumnavigation?

524   Who was the 'doctor' at sea in sailing-ship days?

525   What speed records are held by the clipper-ship *Cutty Sark*?

526   Which was the first true steamship to cross the Atlantic?

527   When was the Suez Canal first closed?

528   What is the name of the first nuclear-powered sea-going vessel?

529   What is the deepest known spot in the world's oceans?

530   What percentage of the earth's surface is covered by the oceans (approx.)?

531   What was the special feature of the British ship *Vulcan* built in 1818?

532   Name the first nuclear-powered merchant ship.

533   What was the name of the first propeller-driven ship to cross the Atlantic?

534   What did Cook's ship have in common with Colonel Scott's Apollo 15 space shot recently?

535 What are the following vessels noted for: *SS Waratah;* the four-masted barque, *Admiral Karpfanger;* the Brazilian battleship *Sao Paulo?*

536 Aboard ship, what is (or was) meant by the term 'Tell-tale'?

537 What was a bald-headed square-rigged ship?

538 How would you set about putting a model ship in a bottle?

539 Why was the non-commissioned officer James Cook selected to command the British *Endeavour* expedition in 1768?

540 Which well-known discoverer turned back from the Coral Sea when on the point of preceding Captain Cook to the discovery of Australia's East Coast?

Medical Science
Set by Professor A. J. Harding Rains

541 What does the abbreviation E.C.G. stand for?

542 How large is the blood volume in an average adult male?

543 What is haemorrhage which takes place 7-14 days after operation or injury called?

544 What is the volume of air normally inspired and expired at each breath called?

545 What is gastrin?

546 What group of organisms may cause gas gangrene and tetanus?

547 Name the skin test for susceptibility or immunity to diptheria.

548 What is scotopic vision?

549 What are the large molecular complexes which form bile acids?

550 What is the second-set phenomenon?

551 What chemical substance is released from the blood platelets?

552 What is the anti-bacterial advantage in sucking a cut finger?

553 Which vitamin may be found in sewage and sludge?

554 When can you hear the sounds of Korotkow?

555 What are Betz cells?

556   What is a Rad?

557   What is an anamnestic reaction?

558   What is an absolute refractory period?

559   What is After-discharge?

560   What are the powerful shock-producing
      polypeptides liberated in the plasma (fortunately
      destroyed rapidly)?

PROFESSOR A. J. HARDING·RAINS, M.S., F.R.C.S.,
Professor of Surgery, Charing Cross Hospital Medical
School.

Antiques

Set by Arthur Negus

561　What was the principal wood used by Thomas Chippendale during the eighteenth century?

562　What is the main difference between pottery and porcelain?

563　Glass paperweights were produced in France, circa 1848 at Baccarat, Clichy and one other factory. Name the factory.

564　What is the present sterling standard of silver required by British Law?

565　Thomas Bolsover invented an efficient substitute for silver about 1745 – what was it called?

566　Shark-skin, often dyed green, was used for covering cases which held scientific instruments. What was this material called?

567　Seventeenth-century needlework with raised padded portions of the design was used on caskets, can you name it?

568　Name the firm that sponsored 'Art Nouveau' in England.

569　What was the original Portland Vase called?

570　Messrs Chippendale, Adam, Hepplewhite and Sheraton gave their names to definite styles of furniture; who are the 'odd ones out' in the four?

571　Early English oak is sometimes inlaid with a white wood – what is it?

572　Only three factories in England make hard-paste porcelain. Newhall in its early days, name the other two.

573 Rosewood is a good hard wood; what other woods from the same genus (Dalbergia) are allied to it?

574 What is fore-edge painting?

575 Can you name the type of clock made of brass during the seventeenth century with hinged side doors, a dome surmount and pierced frets?

576 What is a dummy board figure?

577 Can you name the flower painter who followed William Billingsley at Derby circa 1795?

578 When a picture is painted composed of opaque colours and gum, what term is used to describe it?

579 Describe briefly a *cheveret*.

580 Chests in the sixteenth century were inlaid with conventional representations of buildings – can you give a name to this type?

ARTHUR NEGUS: Well-known television personality and expert on antiques. Author of: *Going for a Song* (BBC).

General Knowledge 9

581 On the hundredth anniversary of American Independence the people of France made a presentation to the American people. What was it?

582 During the First World War the British soldier was known as a 'Tommy': what name was given to the French soldiers?

583 From 1881 Russian Jews and their property were subjected to periodic mob attacks. What were these attacks called?

584 What is the anatomical name for your shoulder blade?

585 In the fictional submarine *Nautilus* who was the Captain?

586 Plymouth, Massachusetts, was founded in the 1600s by what group of people?

587 During the troubles in Cyprus, who was the leader of the movement known as Eoka?

588 Which regiment of the British Army were known as 'Pontius Pilate's Bodyguard'?

589 Who wrote the play *The Passing of the Third Floor Back*?

590 Eamon de Valera founded the Irish Fianna Fail party in 1926. What is the English translation of 'Fianna Fail'?

591 At the Diet of Worms in 1521 what was defended?

592 What are the 'White Horses' of Westbury and Uffington?

593 Who professed his love in these lines: 'I cry your mercy – pity – love! – aye, love! Merciful love that tantalised not...'?

594 Who wrote *Chips with Everything* and *Roots* among other plays?

595 In 1858 Bernadette Soubrious was witness to a supernatural event. Where did it take place?

596 Her real name was Frances Gumm but under what name did she rise to stardom?

597 Who was the soldier/statesman whose picture appears on the back of the English £5 note?

598 Who proved that all falling objects have the same velocity whether large or small?

599 Who were the Kamikaze of the Second World War?

600 The Biblical Solomon was the son of David; who was his mother?

Gardening

Set by Professor Alan Gemmell

601 What is topiary?

602 What is the name of the pollen-producing part of a flower?

603 What is hydroponics?

604 What is a 'piping' and what is it used for?

605 What is the name of a disease which attacks the cabbage and cauliflower family (brassicas) and causes swellings of the roots?

606 How would you prune a newly planted hybrid tea rose bush?

607 What distance below the surface should you sow carrot seed?

608 In gardening what is ph?

609 What is tilth?

610 When do you prune plums?

611 What was the name of the great British landscape gardener of the eighteenth century?

612 What is the art of bonsai?

613 A white frothy liquid is produced on plants by the frog hopper insect, what is it called?

614 If I were marcotting a shaddock what would I be doing?

615 Only one of the following will tolerate a limy soil. Which is it: (a) Camellia indica (b) Pieris forrestii or (c) Erica cinerea?

616 What is the botanical name for African Violet?

617 What does it mean when a potato is said to be 'immune'?

618 What is the meaning of MM106?

619 If the apical (or terminal) bud of a chrysanthemum is removed a number of side shoots or breaks will arise. What is the name of the apical bud on one of these side shoots?

620 If Pitmaston Duchess has 51 how many has Louise Bonne de Jersey?

PROFESSOR ALAN R. GEMMELL: Professor of Biology at Keele University, well-known radio personality in gardening programmes.

Mammals

Set by Dr L. Harrison Matthews

621 Do any female deer normally have antlers, and if so, which?

622 Name two British mammals that hibernate.

623 When a baby kangaroo is born how does it get into the mother's pouch?

624 One of the possums of Australia and New Guinea is called the 'Ring-Tailed Possum'. Why?

625 Which mammal has a natural sun-burn lotion?

626 Name one mammal, other than man, that uses tools.

627 Camels when excited often protrude from the mouth a thing like a pink toy balloon called the palu. What exactly is it?

628 What mammal is the natural host of the myxoma virus?

629 Name one mammal that has a poisonous bite that paralyses small prey.

630 The honey-guide (Indicator) is an African bird. What mammal does it guide to honey?

631 Which mammal has its liver so packed with vitamin A that the liver kills you if you eat it?

632 The walrus makes a musical sound like striking a church bell. How?

633 Which mammals often anoint themselves with foamy saliva when stimulated by a strange odour?

634 What do sea-cows – manatees and dugongs – eat when in the sea (some live in fresh water)?

635 Which mammal carries what is known as a pearl necklace?

636 Two kinds of bats habitually eat fish. Name one of them.

637 How do these bats catch fish?

638 Of all the kinds of antelope only one has been domesticated. Which one?

639 All the toothed-whales have a more or less rounded forehead filled with oily fat called the 'melon'. What is its function?

640 Mammals have a normal body temperature of about 37°C. Apart from hibernating, which normally has the lowest?

Dr L. HARRISON MATTHEWS: Former Director London Zoo.

General Knowledge 10

641 It was a tenth part of a legion and consisted of 600 infantrymen. What was it called?

642 Between 1763 and 1767 two English surveyors drew a line separating the old slave States of America from the free state of Pennsylvania. Who were they?

643 Drosophila have been of great assistance in the study of genetics. What are they?

644 Where did Edward II die?

645 The tradition of summoning MP's by Black Rod from the House of Commons to the House of Lords dates from which event?

646 Which mountain was sacred to Apollo and the Muses?

647 The zenith is a point on the celestial sphere. What is the point directly opposite to it?

648 Who was the originator of the Penny Post?

649 Which former home for disabled soldiers contains Napoleon's tomb?

650 Which famous man's ancestors lived at Sulgrave Manor, Northamptonshire?

651 Brutus and Cassius were defeated at Philippi by whom?

652 Historically, what was the Heptarchy?

653 Which composer wrote works as *Moments Mikrophonie I and II* and *Mixtur* among others?

654 What is the highest peak in Northern Ireland?

655 What is the better known title for the operetta called *The Peer and the Peri*?

656 How did Lord Kitchener die?

657 Who was the Russian physiologist best known for his experimental work on animal behaviour, particularly conditioned reflexes in animals?

658 In which sport are these terms used: 'bull-pen' and 'strike-out'?

659 Usually every human being has twenty-three pairs of these, what are they?

660 $E = MC^2$ is a formula for which theory?

Scandinavian Mythology

Set by Professor Peter Foote

661 Which Eddiac poem appears to reflect a ritual of 'sacred marriage' with Frey (Freyr) as the male partner?

662 From whom are the gods supposed to have learnt the shamanistic kind of magic called *seid* or *seithur*?

663 What is Aurvandil's toe?

664 Whose hearing was so keen that he could hear wool growing on sheep?

665 What does a Norse poet mean when he refers to 'tears of Freyja' and 'hair of Sif'?

666 Which god had the central place in the temple at Uppsala according to Adam of Bremen?

667 Which Danish island and Swedish lake are said to match because of the ploughing of Gefujn?

668 There are two main groups of divinities of Norse mythology, aesir is one of them, what is the other?

669 What is the name of the chief prose source for Scandinavian mythology?

670 What is *Skidbladnir* (or *Skithblathnir*)?

671 Why does a Norse poet call the sky the 'labour of Austri'?

672 Tacitus describes a female divinity who appears to have the same name as one of the Vanir gods; what are their names?

673 Which exploit of Thor's is sculpted on stones at Altuna in Sweden and Hordum in Denmark?

674 Which is counted the more original expression, Ragnarok 'doom of the gods', or Ragnarokk(u)r 'twilight of the gods'?

675 What, in Norse mythology, is counted the equivalent of Noah's Flood?

676 Noise of a cat, spittle of a bird, beard of a woman, breath of a fish, roots of a rock, sinews of a bear were ingredients to make what?

677 After dwarves killed Kvasir how did they explain his death to the gods?

678 How, according to Adam of Bremen, did the Swedes regard Thor?

679 Where have scholars chiefly detected Christian influence on Norse mythology?

680 There are three main divisions of the system postulated by Dumezil and others for Indo-European religion supposedly represented by Norse gods. Sovereign gods and Warrior gods are two, what is the third?

PROFESSOR PETER FOOTE, Professor of Old Scandinavian and Director of Scandinavian Studies, University College, London, Secretary, Viking Society, Chevalier, Icelandic Order of the Falcon. Author: *The Viking Achievement* etc.

Scottish History
Set by Nigel Tranter

681 What is the Battle of Otterburn generally called in England?

682 Who used an arm to bar a door against a King's attackers?

683 What is the link between an Oxford College and an old Dumfries bridge?

684 What does a black bull's head served on a platter mean in Scottish history?

685 When did a force of Spaniards last fight on Scottish soil?

686 What was the name of Rob Roy's wife?

687 What two Scots brothers were monarchs at the same time?

688 Who was captured in a hollow tree on an island?

689 What was the name of the ship which finally bore Prince Charlie from Scotland to France?

690 What part did the Dewars play in old Scotland?

691 What were the Spanish Blanks?

692 What clause, offered by the English in the Treaty of Northampton, was surprisingly ignored by the Scots?

693 What bloody deed was heralded by reports of a stranger with a black cloak and a pot of gold?

694 What was the Trot of Turriff?

695 What was the Brooch of Lorn?

696 Donald, Lord of the Isles, led one side at the Battle of Harlaw in 1411 – who led the other?

697 Who worded the famous Declaration of Independence, 1320?

698 Where did King Charles the Second sign the Solemn League and Covenant?

699 What was the game known as Hurly Hackit?

700 Who were the Joint Guardians who succeeded William Wallace as Guardian of Scotland in 1298?

NIGEL TRANTER: Author of many novels set in Scotland and about Scottish heroes, one of the most recent being *Robert the Bruce*. Now compiling a series *The Queen's Scotland*.

First World War
Set by Bill Wright

701 In what year was poison gas used for the first time?

702 The Germans called it the Siegfried Line, what did the Allies call it?

703 Why are the 'Old Contemptibles' so called?

704 What historical event took place on 28 July 1914?

705 A strategic base for the German fleet in World War 1 once belonged to Britain for over a hundred years. What was it?

706 Where did General Ludendorff and General Hindenburg crush the Russian armies in 1914?

707 In 1917 which King was forced by an ultimatum from the Allies to abdicate in favour of his son?

708 What were Tabloids, Pups and Camels?

709 Which British towns were attacked by the first Zeppelin raid of the war?

710 Which forces were engaged at the Battle of Lemberg?

711 On what plan did Germany base its war strategy?

712 Who was the Turkish War Minister who virtually took command of the troops in the field during the Dardanelles campaign?

713 In 1916 peace proposals were addressed to America and other nations. Who initiated these proposals?

714 The allies established an army at Salonika in October 1915. What was the object of this?

715 Where did a British fleet destroy Vice-Admiral
Maximilian Von Spee's fleet?

716 With what theatre of war would you associate
these place names; Achi Baba, Sari Bair and
Kilid Bahr?

717 Which troops stormed Vimy Ridge in 1917?

718 At which battle were tanks used on a large scale?

719 Whom did the Allies appoint Generalissimo over
the Western Front in 1918?

720 The Japanese delivered an ultimatum to Germany
on 23 August 1914 demanding that Germany
relinquish the leased territory she possessed. Where
was this?

General Knowledge 11

721 What kind of character was 'Gargantua' created by Rabelais?

722 James Loveless, George Loveless, James Hammett, James Brine, Thomas Standfield and John Standfield became known as what?

723 What gets burnt at 'Up-Helly-A'?

724 What did John Stutter start in 1848?

725 What was the name of the standard mathematics book used for over 2,000 years?

726 His pen name was 'Saki'. What was his real name?

727 Henry VI of France gave full freedom of worship to the Protestants in 1598. What was this decree called?

728 Percy Shaw's invention has been a boon to motorists. What was it?

729 Who invented the conspiracy known as the Popish Plot?

730 What in the scientific world is known as Zeta?

731 According to Greek mythology who was the first woman on earth?

732 In musical terms, who was the 'Bringer of Jollity'?

733 What was the function of the Press Gangs of the early nineteenth century?

734 What access did the Polish corridor provide for Poland after the First World War?

735 A famous allegory was written in Bedford gaol. What was the title?

736 Which Queen of England married her brother-in-law?

737 The French call it 'La Tapisseri de la Reine Matilde'. What do we call it?

738 In Roman times gladiators were matched against opponents carrying tridents and nets. What name was given to a trident carrier?

739 Gertrude Ederle of USA achieved a famous first. What was her achievement?

740 Who virtually ruled Florence between 1469 and 1492?

Poetry
Set by Boswell Taylor

741 If a stately Spanish galleon 'had a cargo of
diamonds, emeralds, amethysts, topazes and
cinnamon and gold moidores', what kind of ship
carried 'Tyne coal, road-rails, pig-lead, firewood,
iron-ware and cheap tin trays'?

742 What was the famous anthology that first included
William Wordsworth's 'Lines written above
Tintern Abbey?'

743 Who was the girl that Robert Burns wished to
toast in 'a pint o' wine, An' fill it in a silver tassie . . .'?

744 What was the nickname by which James Hogg
was generally known?

745 Of which bird does Wordsworth ask 'shall I call
thee bird, Or but a wandering Voice'?

746 Who is the modern poet who declared: 'Time held
me green and dying, Though I sang in my chains
like the sea . . .'?

747 What was the relationship between Sohrab and
Rustum in Matthew Arnold's famous peom?

748 What is the pen-name of Christopher Murray Grieve?

749 What was the creature that D. H. Lawrence
mourned because 'Her bright striped frost-face will
never watch any more, out of the shadow of the
cave in the blood-orange rock'?

750 Which of Chaucer's pilgrims asked to be: 'excused
of my rude speche. I lerned nevere rethorik,
certayn; Thyng that I speke, it moot be bare and
pleyn. I sleep nevere on the Mount of Pernaso,
Ne lerned Marcu Tullius Scithero . . .'?

751 What is the title of the poem Edmund Spenser wrote to celebrate his marriage in 1594?

752 What is R. L. Stevenson's own epitaph which is inscribed on his gravestone?

753 Which section is missing from this list of T. S. Eliot's *Four Quartets: The Dry Savages, Burnt Norton, Little Gidding?*

754 Which of Sir Walter Scott's poems is sub-titled 'A Tale of Flodden Field, in Six Cantos'?

755 What is the first line of Wordsworth's sonnet 'Upon Westminster Bridge'?

756 In the poem that begins 'Why should I find Him here And not in a Church', where does Jack Clemo find Christ?

757 What was the name of Oliver Goldsmith's 'Deserted Village'?

758 According to John Milton in an early sonnet what, 'hath time, the subtle thief of youth, stolen on his wing . . .'?

759 What was the happening that made Keats look: 'like stout Cortez when with eagle eyes, he stared at the Pacific'?

760 What modern poet turned a sergeant's instructions on the naming of parts of a rifle into a poem he called 'Lessons of the War – Naming of Parts'?

Astronomy 2

Set by Patrick Moore

761 What is believed to be the main constituent of the Martian atmosphere?

762 What distinguished position has been held by James Bradley, Nevil Maskelyne, and Edmund Halley among others?

763 What spectacular event happened in Siberia in 1908?

764 Name a famous philosopher of classical Greece who maintained that the Earth goes round the Sun, not vice versa.

765 During the last century a planet was said to exist close to the Sun, with its orbit within that of Mercury. What was it called?

766 What is the brightest star in the northern hemisphere of the sky?

767 Name the Astronomer Royal who retired at the end of 1971.

768 Which one of these bodies moves round the Sun in a retrograde direction: Encke's Comet, Pluto, the Earth, Vesta, Halley's Comet, Venus?

769 Name the nearest naked-eye star to the south celestial pole?

770 In which constellation would you find the star Capella?

771 Name the outermost of the five satellites of the planet Uranus.

772 Who was the discoverer of Bennett's Comet?

773 Where in the sky would you find Pleione?

774 What is the name of the largest asteroid?

775 Which of the following types of reflectors gives a naturally erect image: Newtonian, Gregorian, Cassegrain?

776 A modern English amateur astronomer has discovered four comets and three novae. He lives near Peterborough. What is his name?

777 Two German observers compiled the first really good map of the Moon in the 1830s. One was Johann Von Madler, who was the other?

778 In what sea would you look for Archimedes?

779 Which has the higher surface temperature; an S-type star or an O-type star?

780 Name one of the two Australian astronomers who discovered the first radio star.

French Literature

Set by Ronald S. Kirkman

781 What is the name of the miser in Molière's play
L'Avare?

782 With which French Romantic poet is the Lac du
Bourget in Savoy particularly associated?

783 Which was the only comedy written by Jean
Racine?

784 Who is the hero of Stendhal's novel *Le Rouge et
le Noir*?

785 What is the name of the village near Geneva where
Voltaire lived for almost twenty years?

786 Which comedy by Jean Anouilh was adapted into
English by Christopher Fry under the title *Ring
Round the Moon*?

787 Bizet's famous opera *Carmen* is based on a short
story of the same name by a nineteenth-century
French novelist. Who was this writer?

788 Who is the principal character in Henri Troyat's
novel *La Téte sur les Epaules*?

789 Whilst awaiting execution Chénier wrote a number
of satirical and politcal poems. What is their
collective title?

790 The first and third parts of Balzac's *Illusions
Perdues* are set in the same provincial town. What
is this town?

791 In 1964 a French philosopher and writer refused
the Nobel prize for literature. Who is he?

792 Roger Martin du Gard wrote about a French
bourgeois family. What was the title of this series?

793 Ronsard, Du Bellay, Jodelle, Rémy Belleau,
de Baïf, de Tyard and Dorat were all members of a
sixteenth-century literary group. What was the
group called?

794 The trial in 1906 of Mme Blanche-Henriette
Canaby for attempted murder was the basis for a
famous novel – which one?

795 Which of André Malraux's novels was based on
his experience in the Spanish Civil War?

796 The early novels of André Chamson were concerned
with peasant life in an underdeveloped region of
France. Which region?

797 Which poet was imprisoned in 1526 for having
boasted of eating bacon during Lent?

798 Five Arthurian romances in verse were written by
the same author. What is the title of the last of
these, the theme of which was the Holy Grail?

799 An author and poet recently elected to the
Académie Française has written a series of essays
on the natural beauty of rocks and stones. Who is
he?

800 *Roman de la Rose* was begun by Guillaume de
Lorris and completed by another poet. Who was
he?

General Knowledge 12

801 A famous monument was blown up in O'Connell Street, Dublin, in March 1966. To whom was it dedicated?

802 In Greek legend a sculptor and craftsman constructed the labyrinth for Minos. Who was he?

803 His best-known works are *Roderick Random* (1748), *Peregrine Pickle* (1751) and *Humphrey Clinker* (1771). Who was he?

804 A morganatic marriage describes what kind of union?

805 In religion, what is the meaning of the words 'Kyrie Eleison'?

806 A Miss Glover of Norwich invented a system of musical notation, about 1845. What was it called?

807 Brooklyn and Staten Island are connected by the longest and heaviest single span suspension bridge in the world. What is it called?

808 Where was Interpol founded?

809 What is the name of the Roman road which runs between the coast of Devon and Lincoln?

810 The 'Mutiny on the Bounty' is well known, but how many mutinies was Captain Bligh involved in?

811 Arachnida is a word used to describe spiders. What is the origin of this word?

812 Britain has only one woman Professor of Physics, who is she?

813 Tolstoy's *War and Peace* has been adapted as an opera.. Who is the composer?

814 Who was Alexander the Great's general who took over the government of Egypt when Alexander died?

815 Over which kingdom do King Tupou IV and Queen Mata'aho reign?

816 Alessandro di Mariano Filipepi who was born about 1444, the son of a tanner, is remembered by another name. What name?

817 What are the 'Royal Peculiars'?

818 What was the result of the Saar plebiscite in 1935?

819 Born in Paris in 1908, she won the Prix Goncourt with her novel *The Mandarins*. Who is she?

820 What were the followers of John Wycliffe, the regligious reformer, called?

Science Fiction

Set by Tom Shippey

821   In which novel was it the job of the 'fireman' to burn books; as the hero says 'Monday burn Millay, Wednesday Whitman, Friday Faulkner'?

822   What was 'The Seldon Plan' described in the trilogy *Foundation, Foundations and Empire, Second Foundation*?

823   In which novel are 'the Conservationists' an outlawed political party?

824   Who betrayed Duke Leto Atreidea to the Harkonnens?

825   John Carter the Earthman was 'the Warlord of Barsoom', what did he do with a 'thoat'?

826   Of which classic short story are these the first words, 'Put down that wrench'?

827   What have the following novels in common: Brian Aldiss's *Non-Stop*, Harry Harrison's *Captive Universe*, Robert Heinlein's *Orphans of the Sky*, E. C. Tubb's *The Space-born*?

828   Samuel Delany's *Nova* is explicitly presented as the re-handling of an ancient myth. Which one?

829   What is the easiest way of telling a 'slan' from a normal human being?

830   In James Blish's *Earthmen Come ɼome* series, one of the two inventions necessary to permit travel between the stars was the 'anti-agathic' drugs which enormously increase the human life-span. What was the other?

831   Name two weapons or devices used by the Martians in H. G. Wells's *The War of the Worlds*.

832 What was the message that Salo carried from Tralfamadore in the Small Magellanic Cloud to Titan?

833 A famous novel has been written about a society in which most people have the ability to teleport for a 'jaunte'. Name the novel.

834 In what world did Ransom the philologist learn about war? Give its name in English and Old Solar.

835 What is the best-known sign of insanity in the race known to men as 'Pierson's puppeteers'?

836 In which work does the following appear: Hal 9000?

837 Isaac Asimov invented the Three Laws of Robotics in his stories. What was the first law?

838 Who is the author of *The Drowned World*?

839 Who are the players in 'the game of rat and dragon' in the book of that name?

840 In Jack Vance's *Star King* series, Kirth Gersen is committed to vengeance on the five outlaw-leaders known as the Demon Princes. Name two of them.

TOM SHIPPEY: Lecturer at the University of Birmingham.

Spanish and South American Ethnology

Set by Professor J. C. J. Metford

841 Who, after Franco's death, has been nominated to become King and Chief of State?

842 He ranks as an important Spanish painter, but in fact he was not born in Spain. Who was he?

843 What popular dance originated in Argentina?

844 What in history was known as the Spanish Main?

845 A state of war existed between the US and Spain on 21 April 1898, in connection with what?

846 What was the name of the Spanish explorer who discovered the Mississippi River?

847 What, in the ancient world, were the Pillars of Hercules?

848 Between 1808-1821 the Portuguese Royal Family ruled Portugal from where?

849 Which treaty gave Britain official possession of Gibraltar?

850 One Spanish epic poem survives almost in its complete form, what is it called?

851 What is Mestizo Music?

852 Name the main technological achievement prevalent in the Old World which was absent from the New.

853 Which animals were herded by the ancient peoples of the Andes?

854 What was the *Popal Vuh*?

855 What is the oldest dated monument in the New World?

856 Where is Tiahuanaco?

857 What was the Indian name for the plumed ' serpent god?

858 What was the language spoken by the Incas?

859 Who were the Zipa and the Zaque?

860 Who were Xochipilli, Huitzilophoctli and Tlaloc?

Professor J. C. J. METFORD, M.A.: Head of Department of Spanish and Portuguese, Bristol University.

Money, Money, Money

Set by William Keegan

861 It is said that you can buy everything at Harrods. Who paid £40 million for Harrods in 1959?

862 Who delivered the Budget Speech in 1853?

863 Roughly, how much was a 1914 pound worth in 1971?

864 How many countries in 1944 were signatories to the original draft of the Articles of Agreement of the International Monetary Fund?

865 In 1810 which City of London institution's leading members were accused of 'absenting themselves in September, October and November to avoid winter risks'?

866 Who introduced super-tax?

867 Which company started the system of travellers' cheques in 1891?

868 Of which economist was it said that he 'conquered England as completely as the Holy Inquisition conquered Spain'?

869 Which economic law has been summarised as 'supply creates its own demand'?

870 Which famous bank collapsed in London in 1890?

871 When did Britain go off the gold standard?

872 'Our power has brought us into touch with Ambassadors', the chairman said in 1875. Whose Chairman?

873 What was the average rate of interest on UK long term bonds in 1946?

874　From what date were joint stock banks permitted to operate within a radius of 65 miles of London?

875　In 1870-1913, during the heyday of British investment overseas, by far the greater proportion of UK capital exports went into what?

876　During how many years between 1960 and 1970 inclusive did Britain have a visible trade surplus with the rest of the world?

877　Who said: 'Believing that fundamental conditions of the country are sound . . . my son and I have for some days been purchasing sound common stocks'?

878　On the West Coast of America during the Civil War years of 1860-1864 average price levels changed hardly at all. How much did they change in the rest of the Union?

879　Two major powers were not on the gold standard in 1880. Austria-Hungary was one of them; which was the other?

880　The US Government spent between 47 and 50 billion dollars on Lend-Lease aid during and after World War II. What proportion went to the British Empire?

WILLIAM KEEGAN of *The Financial Times.*

General Knowledge 13

881   Which English composer wrote the *Fantasia on a theme of Thomas Tallis*?

882   What shape is the large DNA molecule?

883   The stalk of a plant which originated in China and the far East is used for cooking. What is its name?

884   What poet wrote about 'Flannan Isle'?

885   Giovanni Antonio Canal was born in Venice in 1697. What is he remembered for?

886   They were nicknamed The Bald, The Fat, The Simple, The Fair, The Wise. Who were they?

887   What was the name of Hitler's wife?

888   What is the name of the highest civil decoration that can be awarded in France?

889   The harbour of Rio de Janeiro is dominated by a mountain, what is its name?

890   There is a very famous modern chapel in Ronchamp in France, who was the architect?

891   Which American state has the same name as one of the Russian Soviet Republics?

892   What was the name given to the event that involved a group of anarchists, one of them known as Peter the Painter?

893   What are 'Splendour', 'Mirth', and 'Good Cheer', collectively known as?

894 She was the only female member of the BMA for nearly twenty years. Who was she?

895 *Rule Britannia* was written by James Thomson; who set it to music?

896 Which French King was crowned in the cathedral at Reims with the help of Joan of Arc?

897 It was founded by Robert Tyre Jones on the Augusta Course. What was?

898 Who cut the Gordian Knot?

899 What is the county town of Lanarkshire?

900 When the Conservative Party were known as Tories, what were the chief opposition known as?

ANSWERS
to questions in Book One

General Knowledge 1

1 Sir Barnes Wallis. He also designed the R100 airship, the Wellington bomber, the swing-wing aircraft.

2 Lutine. The bell comes from HMS Lutine, a 32-gun frigate wrecked in 1799 off the Dutch coast. It was carrying money and bullion insured at Lloyd's. It hangs in the Underwriting Room at Lloyd's in London, and is rung to draw attention to the announcement of news items. One stroke means that bad news will follow. Two strokes indicates that the following news is good.

3 1935

4 Roman Catholics, under the Catholic Emancipation Act of 1829. They were allowed to sit in Parliament and hold any public office, except Lord Chancellor or Lord Lieutenant of Ireland, provided they took an oath denying the Pope's right to interfere in British affairs.

5 Dame Ninette de Valois.

6 Daniel Defoe. English novelist and political pamphleteer, 1660–1731. He was born in London, and was also author of *Robinson Crusoe, Moll Flanders* etc.

7 Ceres.

8 Clock Tower and Victoria Tower. The south-western Victoria (or Central) Tower is 336ft high. The Clock Tower (or St Steven's Tower) is 329ft high and contains the clock famous for its 13½-ton bell, Big Ben.

9 Dr Konrad Adenauer (1876–1967). He was founder and Chairman of the Christian Democratic Party (or Union) (1946–1956), and Chancellor of the West German Federal Republic.

10 Arnold Schönberg (1874–1951). The system is illustrated in Schönberg's Suite for Piano, Opus 25, 1923, and was adopted by his pupils Alban Berg and Anton Webern.

11 35 imperial gallons or 42 US gallons.

12 A diamond (the Hope Diamond), which at 44·4
    carats is one of the largest known diamonds, and
    was probably part of a 112½-carat stone found in
    the Killmur mine, Golconda, India.

13 Because they believe that the Dalai Lama is
    re-incarnated in this way.

14 South-east Asia. (Indonesia, includes Bali). The
    Indonesian (and Siamese) orchestra. A full Gamelan
    orchestra is a powerful producer of rich and varied
    tones and depends largely on percussion for its
    effects, using instruments of the marimba, xylophone
    and gong type.

15 Harold Pinter.

16 Swimming. From the Latin *natantem, natare*, to
    swim.

17 Tom Rakewell. The Rake occurs in the well-known
    series of pictures by Hogarth. Stravinsky's last
    opera, *The Rake's Progress*, was based on these
    pictures.

18 Filling the house with invited guests on
    complimentary tickets.

19 Faust, or Doctor Faustus.

20 Katmandu.

Twentieth-century English Literature

21 *Ulysses* (by James Joyce).

22 *To Let.*

23 Borneo. Borneo is part of the Malay Archipelago
    and consists of part of Indonesia and Brunei and
    part of the Federation of Malaysia.

24 Peacock. *The White Peacock*, 1911.

25 *Howards End* (E. M. Forster, 1910).

26 *The Loom of Youth* (1917).

27 They are sister in G. B. Shaw's play *Heartbreak House* (1919).

28 *Brighton Rock* (Graham Greene, 1938).

29 John Masefield.

30 W. B. Yeats.

31 He invented Tono-Bungay, a patent medicine (H. G. Wells *Tono-Bungay* 1909).

32 *Back to Methusalah* (1921).

33 *Under Milk Wood* by Dylan Thomas (1954).

34 *Clea.* By Lawrence Durrell. The titles of the four books in his *The Alexandria Quartet.*

35 David John Moore Cornwell, who wrote under the pseudonym, John Le Carré.

36 *Lord of the Flies* by William Golding (1954).

37 Osbert and Sacheverell.

38 Richard Hillary.

39 A wandering music-hall troupe (Susie Dean, Inigo Jollifant, Jerry Jerningham, Jimmy Nunn and others).

40 Shangri-la.

National Flags Past and Present

41 The flags of the United Nations, of Great Britain, Nepal and India in that order.

42 This was the first emblem of the Confederate States in the American Civil War. It was superseded by the Southern Cross Flag because its resemblance to the Stars and Stripes proved confusing in battle.

43 The Moslem region uses a Red Crescent flag, and Iran uses a variant of its national emblem, a Red Lion grasping a sword. All three emblems are borne on a white field.

44 There are nine horizontal stripes, alternately blue and white, to represent the nine symbols of the Greek slogan *Eleutheria a thanatos*, 'Freedom or death'.

45 'There is no god but God and Mohammed is the Prophet of God' – the Moslem declaration of faith.

46 The legend was that a wandering people might make their home where they saw an eagle alighting on a cactus and bearing a serpent in its beak, and this emblem now appears on the National Flag of Mexico.

47 Miniature Russian flags were scattered on the surface of the Moon by the *Luna 2* in 1959, and the Stars and Stripes was raised above it by Armstrong and Aldrin in 1969.

48 The state flag of Hawaii, the flag also bears eight horizontal stripes, white, red, blue, white, red, blue, white, red.

49 They were at first orange, white and blue, the family colours of the Price of Orange, but the orange stripe was replaced by red to give greater visibility at sea.

50 The reverse of the Standard of the Emperor of Ethiopia.

51 The national emblem of a wreath encircling a hammer and a pair of dividers is placed on the horizontal tricolour of black, red and gold.

52 The relationship between Argentina and Uruguay marked by the use of this emblem, the sudden appearance of this emblem through the clouds when these regions won their independence being regarded as a good omen.

53 Those of Norway and of Great Britain respectively, taken there by Amundsen and Scott.

54 By patterns of horizontal or vertical stripes or by a slight variation of the hammer and sickle emblem.

55 The national flag of Iceland, which also bears a red St George's Cross edged with white on a blue field. However it has no diagonal stripes and the vertical arm of the cross is somewhat nearer the hoist.

56 Malawi and Antigua display the rising sun; British Columbia bears the setting sun, which in that area is seen over the Pacific.

57 A hand emerging from a cloud, mailed in armour and brandishing a sword with the motto *Vince aut Mourir*, 'Victory or death'. A somewhat similar emblem but with a different motto, appeared on a Parliamentary Cavalry Standard in the British Civil War.

58 Edward III (and subsequent monarchs) not only claimed the throne of France but showed that he regarded this as the most important part of his realm by placing the Lilies in the first quarter of his standard. At the Union of England and Scotland, Queen Anne regarded this United Kingdom as the most important part of her realm and placed the emblems of both countries in the first quarter, relegating the French Lilies to the second. George III removed them from the flag in 1802 to show that by the Treaty of Amiens he had relinquished all claim to rule France.

59 That formerly used by New Zealand and now the house flag of the Shaw Savill and Albion Co Ltd. Originally it was the emblem of the United Tribes of New Zealand.

60 It was the Governor's flag of the British North Borneo Company which administered Sabah, formerly a British Protectorate. It displayed a red lion rampant on a small gold disc at the centre of the Union Jack.

General Knowledge 2

61 Sir Alexander Korda.

62 His authorised translation of the Bible. The version of 1611 arose from a recommendation made at Hampton Court Conference 1604 by Dr Reynolds, president of Corpus Christi College, Oxford.

63 Centaur.

64 Ormolu. Derived from the French, *or moulu*, literally ground gold.

65 Orion. A conspicuous and easily recognisable constellation near the equator. Betelgeuse is the brightest star in the constellation.

66 Mrs Bandaranaike, Prime Minister of Ceylon or Shri Lanka.

67 The Sikh religion. It is kept in the Temple of Amritsar.

68 A skull (the Piltdown man). At the time, 1908–12, it was thought that a new genus of man had been found. In fact the skull was made up from ordinary homo sapiens and modern ape bones. This carefully planned hoax which gulled most of the experts was exposed in 1953 by Weimer Oakley and Legros Clerk in the bulletin of the British Museum.

69 A lighthouse – the first pharos. The Pharos, a tower of white marble c. 400ft high built by Ptolemy II Philadelphus at Alexandria about 280 BC. Demolished by an earthquake in the fourteen century, it was usually included among the seven wonders of the world in ancient times.

70 The Republic of Upper Volta.

71 Five. (St Hugh's, St Anne's, St Hilda's, Lady Margaret Hall, and Somerville.) There are 32 for men.

72 President John F. Kennedy, in his inaugural address.

73 The Order of the Garter. Motto is 'Honi soit qui mal y pense'.

74 A massive stalagmite in Wookey Hole caves, Somerset. It is said by legend to be a petrified woman.

75 The Liberal Party.

76 James Abbott McNeil Whistler (1834–1903). The portrait of his mother is also known as *Arrangement in Grey and Black*.

77 Stilton.

78 A sculptor and king of Cyprus who fell in love with his own statue of Aphrodite. He is supposed to have persuaded the goddess Aphrodite through his earnest prayers to give life to the statue – which he married.

79 A kind of glazed and ornamented pottery supposed to have been brought to Europe from Majorca in the fifteenth century.

80 The liver.

Grand Opera

81 *The Bartered Bride* (Smetana).

82 Stravinsky.

83 Works – Latin – opus, the plural being opera.

84 Beaumarchais: *The Barber of Seville*.

85 Alexander Pushkin.

86 Munich, 1869.

87 Dame Nellie Melba.

88 Gounod's *Faust*.

89 Peri's *Dafni* (produced in Florence in 1597).

90 In Venice (Teatro San Cassiano 1637).

91 La Scala Milan. On the site of a church founded by Regine Della Scala in the fourteenth century. Not Covent Garden which stands on the site of a garden.

92 Three.

93 1,003.

94 They stood for 'Viva vittorio Emmanuele re D'Italia' at the time of the Risorgimento, proclaiming Victor Emmanuel King of all Italy.

95 Nine, the eight Walküres plus Brünnhilde.

96 Wagner's name for the covered orchestral pit at Bayreuth.

97 The Fieldmarschallin's Uncle mentioned in act one of *Der Rosenkavalier*.

98 *The Tales of Hoffman* which are related while a performance of *Don Giovanni* takes place at an adjoining theatre.

99 June Bronhill. Her stage name is a contraction of Broken Hill. The residents of this Australian town where she was born helped to pay for her to go to London in 1952.

100 The name by which the Duke of Mantua passed himself off when wooing Gilda in *Rigoletto*.

Astronomy 1

101 Pluto. Pluto was discovered photographically in 1930 and announced in March at Lowell Observatory, Flagstaff, Arizona, USA – although its existence had been suggested many years before.

102 A gap separating two of Saturn's rings. The division is seen as a dark band 2,500 miles wide separating the two other rings of Saturn, ring A and ring B.

103 It would break up into fragments. The Roche limit is a distance equal to 2·44 times the radius of the planet from its centre. If a moon should approach closer than this distance, it is shattered into fragments by the planet's gravitational field. Saturn's rings were probably formed in this way. Our moon is 60 radii away so there is no likelihood of the moon shattering. The limit does not apply to artificial satellites, which are held together by their structural cohesion.

104   Jupiter.

105   Ten. The tenth, Janus, was discovered in 1966.

106   55 to 60 days, or to be exact, 58½ days.

107   A star that produces *regular* pulses of radio waves.
      The pulses are emitted at regular intervals varying
      from 1/30 second up to 3 seconds. Some pulsars
      also produce regular pulses of X-rays and light
      waves.

108   Venus.

109   William Herschel (1738–1822). Discovered 1781.

110   Saturn, which has a density lower than water and
      could float on one of our seas, except that it is 763
      times the volume of the earth.

111   John Flamsteed (1646–1719) made accurate
      observations of the moon that helped Newton to
      formulate the laws of gravitation.

112   The Steady State Theory.

113   On the moon. They are all lunar craters.

114   It will be exactly opposite to the sun in our sky.

115   Tycho Brahe.

116   Mare Humorum.

117   Messier 31 and the Andromeda Spiral.

118   They indicate the official sequence of the spectral
      types of stars.

119   It has an eccentric orbit.

120   R. Coronae Borealis.

General Knowledge 3

121 The Liffey.

122 Lines joining places with the same temperature.

123 The Olympic Games. The Ninth Games, at Amsterdam in 1928, when new attractions were the five track and field events as well as gymnastics, fencing, swimming and diving for women.

124 Tsaritsyn (until 1925), on the Volga, renamed to commemorate its defence by Stalin in 1917 against the White Russians. Stalin died in 1953 and in 1962 the name was changed to Volgograd.

125 Alexandrine.

126 Lanfranc.

127 The Delta Plan. Approved in 1959, it is the largest flood control project in Dutch history.

128 A word formed by the first letter of each line of a poem or other composition. If the final letters also form a word it is a double acrostic. If the middle letters also it is a triple acrostic.

129 Wild cherries.

130 An ancient Herald's Wand carried by a Greek or Roman herald. Also the fabled wand carried by Hermes or Mercury as the messenger of the gods; usually represented with two serpents twined round it.

131 Austerlitz, fought on 2 December 1805. The emperors were Napoleon, Francis II of Austria, and Alexander I of Russia.

132 Nowhere – literally, not place (ou = not, tópos = place).

133 Niccolo Machiavelli (1469–1527), an Italian statesman and author. Machiavellian: 'pertaining to, or characteristic of Machiavelli or his alleged principles – practising duplicity especially in statecraft – astute cunning'.

134 The discovery of the Dead Sea Scrolls in 1947.

135 Westmorland.

136 CD.

137 Attila. The Huns were an Asiatic race that swept over Europe, and were defeated at Chalons-sur-Marne in 451. The death of Attila in 453 terminated the Empire.

138 A *chiton*.

139 Gunwale.

140 Lily of the valley.

Classical Mythology

141 Tending his father's sheep on Mount Ida.

142 Ten years.

143 He was shot in the heel by an arrow sent by either Paris or Apollo.

144 He broke the condition not to look back on the way up.

145 Deucalion and Pyrrha.

146 Alcestis, wife of Admetus.

147 So that Atlas might be free to fetch the apples of the Hesperides.

148 Helen of Troy.

149 Phaedra, wife of Theseus, step-mother of Hippolytus.

150 Lion, goat, and serpent.

151 Hermes was god of both.

152 Persephone (Kore).

153 For giving man fire and/or for cheating the gods of the better parts of sacrificial animals.

154 Man. (The question: What is it that walks on four legs in the morning, on two at noon, on three in the evening?)

155 They had killed them.

156 VIIa.

157 Heinrich Schliemann.

158 To spread the knowledge of corn-growing.

159 The site of an ancient sanctuary of the Muses near Mount Olympus in Thessaly.

160 Cow or Ox-ford since Zeus' love Io swam across in the shape of a cow.

History of Music 1550-1900

161 Largo. But scored 'Larghetto e piano'.

162 Comic Opera. In Italian 'opera buffa'.

163 Bach's two sets of twenty-four preludes and fugues in all twenty-four keys, sometimes known as 'The Well-tempered Clavier' or '*Das wohltemperirte Clavier*'.

164 Purcell's *Dido and Aeneas*.

165 It was a serenade.

166 Galliard.

167 Funeral March Sonata.

168 William Boyce.

169 'Chopsticks'.

170 *Cox and Box*.

171 Leonora.

172 Stephen Collins Foster.

173 Songs without words (Lieder ohne Worte).

174 Because the fourth of the five movements is a set of variations on his song *The Trout* (*Die Forelle*).

175 Dresden.

176 Three string quartets known as the Rasumovsky Quartets (Op. 59 in F, E minor and C).

177   Dublin (at the New Music Hall).

178   Pasticcio.

179   Ceylon (although the characters are Indians).

180   Alphonse Daudet.

General Knowledge 4

181   Aeolus. The personifications of the winds were: Notus was the south or south-west winds, Boreas the north wind, Eurus the south-east wind and Zephyrus the west wind.

182   Presidency of the USA.

183   In law, Assault is threatening to strike, or striking and missing the target, while Battery is actually hitting the target (person).

184   Having a Turkish bath. The original name was hummum.

185   Greta Garbo.

186   The end of the World. He is usually credited with the founding of the Advertists, a Protestant sect.

187   Blaise Pascal (1623–62).

188   John Crome (1768–1821).

189   He was, and is, the youngest recipient of the VC. At the time he was fifteen years old.

190   Ivan the Terrible.

191   The eider duck breeds there. Their down is used to stuff quilts, etc. They also breed in the Hebrides and Donegal.

192   Sergei Pavlovich Diaghilev (1872–1929).

193   The circumnavigation of the world.

194   The Loire. 625 miles long, it flows from the Cévennes Mountains to the Atlantic.

195   Whale Shark. It grows to a length of 40 ft and weighs up to 20 tons.

196 Campanology. The term covers the whole of the knowledge of bells, theoretical, historical, etc.

197 Sir Henry Percy (1364–1403). Son of Earl of Northumberland, helped Henry Bolingbroke to depose Richard II. Popular nickname given to Sir Henry Percy because of his fiery temper and zeal in border warfare. Shakespeare used the pseudonym in the two parts of Henry IV.

198 Lord Annan, Provost of University College, London. Subject was 'What are Universities for Anyway?'

199 A boundary the crossing of which means that one becomes committed. The Rubicon was a stream limiting Caesar's province and crossed by him before war with Pompey.

200 Jean Anouilh, the French dramatist born in 1910.

British Politics Since 1900

201 1931. National Government supporters 554, Labour 52, others 9. Clear National Government majority 493. The position of two or three MP's is arguable but the answer must lie in the 485–501 region.

202 September/October 1903 in protest against Joseph Chamberlain's suggestion of ending free trade.

203 'The House of Lords is not the watchdog of the constitution. It is Mr Balfour's poodle.' Lloyd George said this in 1909, quoted in Roy Jenkins' book *Mr Balfour's Poodle*.

204 Three. In 1910 (13 Feb–28 Nov); 1922–3 (20 Nov–16 Nov), 11 months 27 days with the elections 12½ months apart; and 1924 (8 Jan–9 Oct).

205 Asquith, from 5 April 1908–6 Dec 1916, 8 years 8 months. Others in the list are Macmillan, 10 Jan 1957–Oct 1963, 6 years 9 months; and Lloyd George, 6 Dec 1916–23 Oct 1922, 5 years 10 months. Lord Salisbury was PM for thirteen years in all and his last premiership, 1895–1902, lasted seven years and one month.

206 Prime Minister (May 1940–July 1945). Not
Chancellor of the Exchequer, Oct 1924–May 1929.

207 The Vesting Date under the Iron and Steel Act
1949 was January 1951. The industry was, of
course, de-nationalised by the Iron and Steel Act
1953. The Vesting Date under the Iron and Steel
Act 1967 was 28 July 1967.

208 Under the Ministers of the Crown Act, 1937.

209 Harold Wilson, as President of the Board of Trade
in November 1948.

210 R. A. Butler referring to Sir Anthony Eden in
December 1955.

211 Stanley Baldwin, speaking of the Empire Crusade
Campaign of the Press Lords, Beaverbrook and
Rothermere, during the Westminster by-election of
March 1931.

212 September 1935.

213 Frank Cousins, Oct 1964–July 1966.

214 In 1958 by the Life Peerage Act. There were a few
Law Lords before that.

215 Harold Macmillan as Chancellor of the Exchequer,
in his Budget of 17 April 1956.

216 As a result of protests against the Hoare-Laval
pact over Abyssinia (on 18 December 1935).

217 Anthony Wedgwood Benn, whose efforts not to
become Viscount Stansgate led to the passage of
the Peerage Act 1963 which came into effect on
1 August 1963. Sir Alec Douglas Home and
Quintin Hogg renounced their peerages in October
1963, Wedgwood Benn never used his title.

218 Harold Wilson coined the phrase in Feb 1970 to
refer to what he saw as the Tory attitudes typified
at the meeting of Conservative leaders to discuss
policy at Selsdon Park Hotel, Croydon, on 31
January.

219 Sir Stafford Cripps' devaluation of 18 Sept 1949 when the dollar exchange rate was cut from $4·03 to $2·80.

220 A Government Committee under Lord Fulton which considered the structure and functioning of the Civil Service and reported in July 1968. Among the recommendations that were implemented were the setting up of the Civil Service Department and the abolition of many of the existing barriers between Civil Service grades.

English Costume

221 Lincoln (it was known as Lincoln green).

222 Balls of mixed aromatic substances carried for perfume or as a guard against infection (the term was sometimes used just for the case).

223 Mrs Amelia Jenks Bloomer (she became famous in 1851 for her 'Turkish pantaloons' although she was probably not the first to wear this garment. She advocated their use in her journal 'Lily'. They were especially recommended for cycling).

224 Wooden sandals or overshoes mounted on iron rings to raise the foot above the wet ground (the meaning has changed slightly and come to mean wooden overshoes with a thick wooden sole).

225 Large hat trimmed with flowers or print dress with flower pattern (the first is better and much more frequently used as a 'Dolly Varden'. Dolly Varden was a character who wore these clothes in *Barnaby Rudge*).

226 A Blücher is a low boot and a Wellington is a high boot.

227 A one-piece woman's overdress with a waist and an open skirt.

228 The tail, or streamer from a man's bonnet that hung over his shoulder, or the long tail of a graduate's hood in early academic costume (fifteenth century).

229 As a handkerchief – that is what it was.

230 A hard low-crowned felt hat (Americans call them 'derbies' or 'derby hats').

231 An opera or crush hat.

232 Grey woollen plaids worn in Southern Scotland.

233 Breeches. 'Spanish slops' were loose baggy breeches and 'Venetians' were padded breeches.

234 A large wired stand-up collar. It was worn in Elizabethan times, and it is correct to say 'Queen Elizabeth wore a whisk'. By Pepys' time it had become a neckerchief.

235 Coloured satin that was crimson in the shadows and pink in the highlights.

236 Sugar-loaf.

237 That the traveller had been on a pilgrimage to the Holy Land, which entitled him to be known as a 'palmer'.

238 From the 'sabots' or wooden clogs worn by peasants in the days of the Normans. The French and Dutch peasants wore 'sabots'. Sabotage has derived from the damage done by French peasants to the crops of their lords which they trampled if they thought they were being treated unjustly.

239 A Jewish person.

240 A deep falling collar attached to the top of a low-necked dress.

Words

241 Any word that reads the same backwards as forwards (e.g. Anna).

242 An argument (or form of reasoning) comprising two premises sharing a common term and a conclusion that must be true if the premises are true (first classified by Aristotle).

243 Latin – *lingua*, meaning tongue.

244 According to the value.

245 Simple arrangement of words in a meaningful order.

246 Words that descend from a common ancestor, e.g. chase and catch which come from the Latin *captare*.

247 'Cabriolet' (originally meant leap or caper).

248 The treatment of diseases with small quantities of drugs that produce the symptoms similar to those of the disease (like cures like).

249 It comes from two Latin words *re*, meaning back or backwards, and *calx, calcis*, meaning hoof. The two together in Latin (*recalcitrare*) mean 'to kick back'.

250 A written sign to show changes in sound and pronounciation.

251 Old English after, and mawan, mowing (there is a crop of grass springs up after the first mowing in the summer. When it is cut you reap an aftermath).

252 A newly conceived word that has been generally accepted.

253 From Arabian *hashshashin*, eaters of hashish (original charter-member assassins were a religious sect in Palestine, Moslem fanatics, sworn by their shiekh, 'the old man of the Mountains' to murder all crusaders. When their fervour cooled their leader gave them hashish to drink).

254 The day of the mandate (or commandment) when Christ washed the Disciples' feet (a corruption of the Latin *dies mandati*. First words of an anthem sung on this day in R.C. churches 'Mandatum Novum Do Vobis', 'A New Commandment I give unto you that ye love one another' – Solomon 13, v. 34).

255 Son of the Commandments or one responsible for the Commandments. (Religious ritual and family celebration to commemorate a boy's thirteenth birthday which traditionally is his coming of age and responsibility for fulfilling all the Commandments.)

256 Italian *balla*, ball. Secret voting in early days was done by dropping small balls in an urn or box.

257 'Drink nothing' – an Australian aboriginal word.

258 Latin *candidatus*, white-robed. Romans seeking office had to wear white togas before election day so that voters could recognise them.

259 Latin – *salarium*. Originally salt-money, money given to soldiers for salt or the payment to Roman soldiers given in salt.

260 After John Montagu, fourth Earl of Sandwich (1718–1792). He spent 24 hours on the gaming table without a regular meal and ordered his servant to bring him bread and roast beef. He then put them together and made the first sandwich.

General Knowledge 5

261 Welland Ship Canal.

262 In the Channel Islands. Guernsey and Jersey are Bailiwicks.

263 The seccession of South Carolina which, with ten other Southern States, formed the Confederacy.

264 Archery. The contestants shoot at a small target from a trotting horse.

265 Rudolf Diesel (1858–1913).

266 Irish wolfhound.

267 Henry IV.

268 Forest.

269 Wolfson College, because of a gift of two million pounds from the Wolfson Foundation.

270 Lord Reith.

271 Thomas Cromwell.

272 King Edward VI.

273 Aldous Huxley. *Mortal Coils* a collection of five of Huxley's early short stories which first appeared in 1922.

274 John of Gaunt, in Act 2, Scene 1.

275 During the Boer War. The name was given to centres where Boer civilians were interned by Kitchener from 1900–1902.

276 Jens Otto Krag.

277 John Calvin (1509–64). Founded 'Calvinism', a branch of Protestantism.

278 Gipsy. Hence *Zingaresca*, a gipsy song.

279 A celestial bull was sent to destroy him. The hero was Gilgamesh.

280 Sidney James Webb (1859–1947). He was a founder member of the Fabian Society, and was raised to the Peerage in 1929.

British Moths

281 Silver Y.

282 Elephant Hawk.

283 Because the caterpillar sits in a hunched up attitude similar to that demonstrated in the Egyptian Sphinx.

284 Because it is a good example of industrial melanism and shows natural selection in action. The peppered moth has changed colour to suit conditions. The moths that did not were vulnerable.

285 Burnet moths.

286 Currant moth or Magpie.

287 In a damp cellar in London on the banks of the Thames.

288 Goat moth.

289 The pugs.

290 Emperor moth.

291 Rosy marsh moth.

292 The Burnished Brass.

293 They cannot fly.

294 The moth has no vocal chords but it can produce a squeak by forcing air through its hollow tongue.

295 The caterpillars feed inside the branches or shoots of their food plants.

296 The Footman. For example the *Red-necked Footman*.

297 Moths have an acute sense of smell and males can locate females by scent alone.

298 The Kittens form a separate group; the Sallow, Alder and Poplar Kittens. It is thought that the small caterpillars resemble kittens with their pointed 'ears' and short tails.

299 Completely dark, muggy nights.

300 The wings are covered in white scales which can look ghostlike in the dark.

English Literature

301 Sir Thomas Malory (?–1471) collected and rewrote stories of chivalry for his romance *Le Morte D'Arthur*, published by William Caxton in 1485.

302 Rosalind (*As you like it*).

303 *The Schoolmaster* by Roger Ascham (1515–1568).

304 Earl of Chesterfield (Philip Dormer Stanhope, fourth Earl of Chesterfield). Johnson sent Chesterfield a prospectus of his *Dictionary* and received £10 subscription. Later he claimed he was left waiting in an ante-room when Cibber was admitted. He certainly expected more help from a man who professed to be a patron of literature, and wrote the Earl the famous letter in defence of of men of letters.

305 Joseph Addison (1672–1719).

306 Euphuism. Literary flamboyance demonstrated in *Euphues the Anatomy of Wit* and *Euphues and his England.* John Lyly (1554?–1606) influenced Shakespeare's work.

307 Sir Walter Scott (debts of £130,000 incurred by Ballantyne and Constable).

308 Knutsford in Cheshire. Mrs Elizabeth Gaskell (1810–1865) wrote *Cranford* giving a lively account of village life in the mid-nineteenth century.

309 'Come live with me and be my love' (Marlowe *A Passionate Shepherd to his Love*, Donne *The Bait*).

310 *Joseph Andrews* (it began as a parody but developed its own individuality).

311 *Bleak House* (1853).

312 The name is an anagram of *Nowhere*.

313 United Services College, Westward Ho! In *Stalky & Co* by Rudyard Kipling (1865–1936).

314 Charles Lutwidge Dodgson. The author 'Lewis Carroll' who wrote *Alice in Wonderland.*

315 Sir George Etherege (1633–1693?), author of *The Comical Revenge* etc.

316 Mr W. H. Given in this way in the dedication to Shakespeare's sonnets.

317 Prime Minister of Britain. He was Benjamin Disraeli.

318 *The Life of Samuel Johnson* (by James Boswell, 1740–1795). The meeting took place in 1763.

319 C. Auguste Dupin. He appears in *The Murders in the Rue Morgue* and *The Mystery of Marie Roget*. Edgar Allan Poe (1809–1849) was one of America's greatest writers.

320 Brontë sisters. Charlotte, Emily and Anne.

Tudor History

321 Edward Poynings.

322 Erasmus of Rotterdam.

323 Enclosures (of land especially for pasture, and especially at the expense of the peasantry).

324 Sir Thomas Wyatt.

325 All were burned for their faith, in the time of Mary Tudor.

326 Apprentices rioted against and attacked alien residents. Many were later hanged for taking part.

327 Officially – and probably at least partly – Henry VIII. For his work he was given the title 'Defender of the Faith'.

328 Wednesday was made a Fish Day – though exemptions could be bought.

329 1539, the Act of Six Articles – Henry VIII's Catholic doctrines for his Church of England.

330 Charles Brandon, Duke of Suffolk. (Their descendents were possible claimants to the English throne in later Tudor times.)

331 Printing – he was Caxton's assistant and successor.

332 They were ordered to maintain parish registers of baptisms, marriages and burials – vital evidence for genealogy and the study of local families and population movements.

333 Thomas Howard, fourth Duke of Norfolk, in 1572.

334 A levy on movable property, respectively rural and urban.

335 Sebastian Cabot.

336 A Golden Hind.

337 Consecutive years of deficit to disastrous harvests in a country whose agriculture was still only producing at subsistence level (as a result of bad weather).

338 Nicholas Hilliard.

339 (c) Wolsey the peace-maker; but where he differs from this line it is always in connection with the demands of the King.

340 About 3 million. Russell's estimate is 3·22 million; Cornwall's 2·8 million.

General Knowledge 6

341 The Skylark.

342 Friedrich Wilhelm Nietzsche (1844–1900), the German Philosopher.

343 President Sukarno.

344 Képi.

345 4 p.m. to 6 p.m. (1600–1800). Second dog-watch runs from 6 p.m. to 8 p.m.

346 Yeoman of the Guard.

347 Marlene Dietrich.

348 The first submarine. Robert Fulton (1765–1815), was an American engineer born of Irish parents.

349 Ben Travers.

350 To measure electrical resistance of a conductor.

351 Thomas Hardy (1840–1928).

352 A diamond. (Jonker's Diamond). One of the largest known diamonds, it was found near Pretoria, and later cut into twelve pieces.

353 Harrow School. About 1850.

354 Polyvinyl chloride.

355 Rudolf Friml. Czech-American Composer.

356 Improvised mast used in place of one lost or broken.

357 Washington Irving. American writer who created Rip Van Winkle.

358 The Mystery Cat, in *Macavity; The Mystery Cat*, a poem included in *Old Possum's Book of Practical Cats*.

359 John Buchan (1875–1940). Author of *The Thirty Nine Steps; Greenmantle*, *The Three Hostages*, *Huntingtower*, and much more.

360 Thomas Alva Edison (1847–1931). He constructed the machine, (gramophone or phonograph) with the intention that it should be used as a dictating machine.

Assassinations and Murders

361 Four. Lincoln, Garfield, McKinley, and Kennedy.

362 Spencer Perceval (in 1812).

363 In the lobby of the House of Commons.

364 *Our American Cousin.*

365 Englebert Dollfuss.

366 John Felton.

367 Memphis, Tennessee.

368 Jack Ruby.

369 King Alexander I.

370 Sophie.

371 Sirhan Bishara Sirhan.

372 Mohandas Karamchand Gandhi.

373 Fly papers, which two servants said she soaked in water to extract the arsenic.

374 In the Hammersmith Palace of Varieties.

375 Edith Thompson.

376 John Reginald Halliday Christie. He was hanged in 1953.

377 Ruth Ellis, in 1955.

378 Not proven.

379 That Podola was suffering from hysteria amnesia. He could not remember what had happened.

380 Sir Bernard (or Dr) Spilsbury.

Visual Arts

381 1937.

382 John Piper (1903–).

383 Reg Butler (1913–) *The Unknown Political Prisoner.*

384 Le Corbusier. Professional name of Charles-Edouard Jeanneret (1887–1965). He developed the international style.

385 S. W. Hayter, who in the 1920s established an experimental school of gravure and printmaking.

386 A painting on a wood panel of Christ or the Holy Family, or of the angels and saints.

387 The Virgin.

388 The Cathedral of Montreal near Palermo in Sicily.

389 Fernand Leger (1881–1955), French artist who developed a distinctive style that reflects modern technology.

390 Jack Smith.

391 He was the teacher of the sculptors in a show of that name at the Whitechapel Art Gallery.

392 Robert Rauschenberg (1925–). A founder of the pop art school. He calls his works *combine paintings* or *combions.*

393 Hagia Sophia (The Holy Wisdom).

394 Robert Norris.

395 Joseph Beuys.

396 Torcello Cathedral.

397 Jasper Johns.

398 The Transfiguration.

399 843.

400   A Byzantine manuscript painted about the year AD 700.

History of Aeronautics

401   Louis Blériot. 25 July 1909.

402   The boomerang. Not the arrow which is not airborne aerodynamically and is only aerodynamically stabilised by its feathers.

403   Pilotless hot-air balloons carrying bombs released by time-fuses. Sent over by the Austrians in 1849.

404   Blanchard and Jeffries. The flight was made in a hydrogen balloon on 7 January 1785 from near Dover Castle and ended in the forest of Guines, near Calais. The pilot was the Frenchman Jean Pierre Blanchard and his passenger was the American physician Dr John Jeffries, who paid for the trip.

405   An Antoinette monoplane in July 1909. Hubert Latham took off from Sangatte, near Calais, on 19 July 1909 in the Antoinette IV fitted with ailerons and designed by Leon Levavasseur who also designed the Antoinette engine which powered it. The machine suffered engine failure when seven or eight miles out and had to ditch in the Channel, Latham being rescued and the machine salvaged.

406   The D.H. Moth. Designed by Geoffrey de Havilland.

407   The Heinkel *HE 178*. First flew in 1939 in Germany. The engine was designed by Dr Hans von Chain and the machine made its first flight on 27 August 1939. The engine was a centrifugal flow turbojet.

408   By fitting stub-wings. The first test vehicle to be fitted with such surfaces was the A-7.

409   Supermarine S6 seaplane.

410 Lieutenant T. E. Selfridge (who was killed) or
     Orville Wright (who was injured). Lieutenant
     Thomas E. Selfridge, US Signal Corps, was
     flying with Orville Wright in the military acceptance
     trials at Fort Myer in the Wright Type A. A blade
     of the starboard propeller split and put it out of
     balance, causing it to flatten, lose thrust and
     'wave'; this in turn led to the shaft working the
     outrigger loose until the propeller was waving
     right out of its arc and cut through a bracing wire
     to twin rear rudders; the rudders then collapsed
     and the machine went into a dive and crashed,
     killing Selfridge and injuring Orville Wright.

411 The Antoinette. Designed by Leon Levavasseur.
     First the 50h.p. then the 100h.p. The engine and
     the monoplane Levavasseur also designed were
     both called Antoinette after Antoinette Gastambide
     daughter of the head of the firm.

412 In Germany – between various German cities. Five
     Zeppelins carried over 35,000 passengers, without a
     fatality, between various German cities.

413 Jaques Garnerin, in 1797 in Paris. Garnerin was
     taken up by a balloon and cast off from a height
     of about 3,000 feet. The parachute was ribbed like
     an umbrella and Garnerin went up with it closed.
     It opened as it fell and he came down safely but
     feeling sick from the parachute pendulating badly
     due to lack of porosity of the fabric.

414 To cut the neck-line and let the envelope float up
     into the top of the net and act as a primitive
     parachute. This first happened with Coxwell,
     Gypson and two others in Gypson's balloon in
     1847, Coxwell realising what to do and doing it.

415 Wilbur Wright. Wright flew this first circle on the
     Wright Flyer II at the Huffman Prairie (or Pasture)
     near Dayton, Ohio on 20 September 1904. It was
     witnessed and described by Amos I. Root.

416 Because they remained unpublished until late in the nineteenth century when aeronautical thought was too advanced to be influenced. The first significant publication of da Vinci's work came with an illustrated article by Hureau de Villeneuve in the French aeronautical periodical *L'Aeronaute* in 1874.

417 They were allowed to hinge freely *upwards* but prevented by wires from moving downwards. He adopted this arrangement after he had crashed one of his gliders. He believed that the nose-dive (into which it went) was caused by the pressure of the air on his then rigid tail-plane pushing up the tail-unit and putting the nose down.

418 By warping (twisting) the wings. The device was invented by the Wright brothers.

419 The Wright brothers gliders of 1901 and 1902. Illustrations of these were shown to European pioneers, particularly by Chanute in Paris in 1903.

420 Robert Esnault-Pelterie on his Wright type glider in 1904.

General Knowledge 7

421 The three gorgons.

422 Charlotte Corday, on 13 July 1793.

423 Egypt. The Temple of Amun is surrounded by the modern village of Karnak.

424 Henry Purcell.

425 Like poles repel, unlike poles attract; or, the force between the poles is proportional to their strength, and inversely proportional to the square of the distance between them.

426 When two organisms live together and both derive mutual benefit from the association. An example is the symbiosis of a pea-plant and the bacteria which lives in its roots, or the fungus and alga composing lichens.

427 Between the fore legs of a horse. A leather strap –
one end fastened to the girth of a horse, the other
to the bit.

428 Herefordshire.

429 Mormon, or Church of Jesus Christ of Latter Day
Saints.

430 John Wilkes. (1727–1797). Put in Tower in 1763
for criticising King George III's speech.

431 Cardinal Wolsey in 1525.

432 Holy writings of the Jewish Scriptures.

433 The Hapsburgs. The German is 'Habsburg'.

434 Laurie Lee, in his autobiography *As I Walked Out
One Midsummer Morning*.

435 Field Marshall Paul Von Hindenburg (1925–34).

436 The Potteries. (Arnold Bennett's 'Five Towns'.)
There were actually six (Fenton) but he used
poetic licence in naming five, and gave them
other names.

437 Tempera.

438 Nero. Claudius Caesar Nero (AD 37–68).

439 Scapa Flow. In the Orkney Islands.

440 Franz Peter Schubert.

Old Time Music Hall

441 1921. For many years before his death he was
seriously ill and his act would frequently be
interrupted by fits of coughing.

442 He was a chimney sweep, and his real name was
Charles Vagg. Three years before his death in
1865, he opened a music hall in Islington and his
name survived with it for about a hundred years.

443 James Fawn. Songs about policemen were
particularly popular in the second half of the
nineteenth century and this one was Fawn's most
successful song.

444 1963. An excellent impression of a performance at the Metropolitan can be heard on the Pye record, *Max at the Met* (GGL 0195).

445 Malcolm Scott. Scott began as an actor on the legitimate stage but took to the halls in 1903. He portrayed historical characters – Boadicea, Salomé and the Gibson girl. He was billed as 'The Woman who knows'.

446 1 January 1907. The strike was dramatized in the BBC series, *The Edwardians*, in the programme on Marie Lloyd. The strike lasted about a month.

447 Mrs Ormiston Chant. Mrs Chant was known as one of the 'Prudes on the Prowl', a name coined by the dramatic critic of *The Daily Telegraph*. The LCC decided that the promenade bar and the auditorium should be separated by a partition.

448 Sir Winston Churchill.

449 Harry Fragson. Fragson's father was a Belgian and Harry spoke French and English and performed in both languages, often appearing at the Folies-Bergère. His father shot him in 1903.

450 Nellie Wallace. Nellie Wallace began as a child performer and worked until shortly before her death, aged 78, in 1948. Her recordings – such as that of her song 'Half-past Nine' – evoke, by means of giggles, chuckles, and hiccups, something of her curious figure, with its odd clothes and tatty boa.

451 Belle Elmore, murdered by Dr Crippen. 'Belle Elmore' was Mrs Crippen's stage name. She was not particularly successful and was last seen alive on 31 January 1910. Crippen was hanged on 23 November 1910. His mistress, Ethel Le Neve, was acquitted.

452 Tom Kennedy. Robey was destined for, first the University of Leipzig, and then Cambridge. However his father suffered financial reverses and he had to leave Cambridge and began work as an engineer in Birmingham. A chance visit to Westminster Aquarium led to his volunteering – repeatedly – to be mesmerised by 'Professor' Kennedy.

453 Jack Judge, its part-author, in 1912, Florrie Forde sang it before the War, but revived it in 1914, when it became a hit.

454 Victoria Monks. Two of her songs are especially well-remembered: 'Won't you come home Bill Bailey?' and 'Give my regards to Leicester Square'.

455 Granville Bantock under the name 'Graban'. Bantock succeeded Elgar as Professor of Music, University of Birmingham. The show was called 'The A.B.C. Girl' or 'Flossie the Frivolous'.

456 Alec Hurley. Hurley, a coster comic and singer, was Marie Lloyd's second husband.

457 The New Canterbury (by George Augustus Sala). Charles Morton, known as 'The Father of the Halls' opened the Canterbury Hall in 1851 behind the Canterbury Arms Tavern. Westminster Bridge Road, Lambeth. It was enlarged in 1854 and reopened as the New Canterbury Music Hall.

458 Herbert Campbell. 1878 was the year of the patriotic song, 'By Jingo' which the great Macdermott sang. He referred to the Russo-Turkish war and in its chorus had the words: 'and while we're Britons true, the Russians shall not have Constantinople'. Campbell's parody revived both the senitments.

459 The Wheatsheaf, a public house with a built-on hall. The proprietor was called Balmbra and his name occurs in the song (as does the date, 1862). Three years later the Wheatsheaf became the Oxford Music Hall. The name Balmbra has survived to this day however.

460 Building Societies, Hunting, parody of *Minstrel Boy*. According to the *Daily Telegraph* of 28 November 1901, the choice of songs was left to Leno. He 'first gave his latest one in which he describes his entanglement with a 'building society' and the sort of home he got by going to one'. He followed this with his experiences as a huntsman and then 'as a final effort criticised very freely the *Minstrel Boy*.'

Chemistry

461 The Law of Octaves (an early classification of the elements into groups of eight).

462 Germanium.

463 Prometheum.

464 Lanthanides.

465 They are elements with similar outer electronic structures. They differ in the inner electron shells.

466 Naturally occurring carbon consists of a mixture of isotopes/carbon 12 with (1 %) carbon 13.

467 Yes, a mole is just a number. A mole is the amount that contains the same number of entities as there are atoms of carbon 12 in 0·012 kilograms of carbon 12.

468 6×10^{23} (to be precise $6·022169 \times 10^{23}$).

469 The reaction is exothermic.

470 The enthalpy change for an exothermic reaction is negative.

471 Barium – it is:
   (a) an alkaline earth metal whereas the others are alkali metals
   (b) it is in group 2 of the Periodic Table, the others are in group 1.

472 They are all:
   (a) inorganic complexes
   (b) complex ions
   (c) complexes containing metals linked to non-metal groups.

473 It consists of two interlocked face centred cubes. One face centred cube of sodium ions, one of chloride ions.

474 By electrolysis of molten sodium hydroxide by Sir Humphrey Davey.

475 (a) Delocalization of electrons
(b) Resonance between (valence bond) structures.

476 Two substances, they are:
(a) mirror images
(b) optical isomers.

477 Solutions of the compounds rotate the plane of plane polarized light in opposite directions.

478 (a) Bromine adds to the double bond of hexene
(b) Hexene contains a double bond
(c) Hexene is an olefin.

479 10^{-7} mole per litre. The clue is pH$_7$.

480 In solution in water very few of the molecules dissociate to hydrogen ions and acetate ions. The strength has nothing to do with the concentration. There is an equilibrium between undissociated acetic acid and the hydrogen ions and acetate ions and this equilibrium favours the molecule acetic acid.

History of the English Language

481 Earth.

482 F.

483 From the time of the first Anglo-Saxon settlements in England to about 1100.

484 Water.

485 The plural form of a noun which is made from the singular by changing the main vowel instead of by adding es or s. There are seven: foot, goose, tooth, man, woman, louse and mouse.

486 The word comes from the Anglo-Saxon or Old English word *dun* meaning hill.

487 Erse (originally the Scottish variant for Irish).

488 Italian.

489 Arabic or Turkish (Arabic *gahwah*, in Turkish pronounced *kahveh*).

490 From Captain Charles Boycott, a land agent who in 1880 was so harsh with the tenants of the Irish Estate of Lord Erne that people refused to have anything to do with him.

491 Celtic Irish – *uisque beatha, usque baugh* – water of life. As 'of life' has been dropped, whisky means water.

492 Light green and leaf (Chlos=light green, and phyllon=leaf).

493 And – per se – and (per se=by itself so the phrase is And-by itself-and).

494 Sir Walter Scott.

495 Great Vowel Shift.

496 From the Latin *audire* to hear and then the French *oir oyer* (modern French ouir)=hear ye.

497 Æ made by combining A and E (known as *ash*).

498 English was spoken and read by only a small nation. Latin was used by many nations as it was the international language of that time. Bacon felt that his work 'would live and be a citizen of the the world' as English books could not.

499 The Danes introduced 'by' into English. It stands for 'village' so by-law means village or local law (law also has a Danish derivation).

500 Cowcumber.

General Knowledge 8

501 Berchtesgaden.

502 Sir Francis Beaufort (1774–1857). The Beaufort
Wind Scale. The numbers 0–12 were used as a
scale of wind strength in 1806. Force 12 was
'that which no canvas could withstand'.

503 Ferdinand Magellan. He was trying to find a route
to the Spice Islands.

504 Peter Ustinov.

505 Vedas.

506 Plimsoll Line. Samuel Plimsoll was MP for Derby.

507 River Tay.

508 St Edward's Crown (made for Charles II's
Coronation 1662), The Imperial State Crown
(made for Victoria 1838), and The Imperial Crown
of India (made for the ceremony of crowning King
George V as Emperor of India).

509 The Royal Society. Full title – Royal Society
of London for Improving Natural Knowledge.
First charter passed 15 July 1662, followed by
other charters in 1663 and 1669. Newton was
President and was re-elected annually until his
death in 1727.

510 Edward II. Became first 'English' Prince of Wales.
Murdered in Berkeley Castle.

511 The titles were: The Gnome, The Old Castle,
Tuileries, Bydlo, Ballet of the Unhatched
Chickens, Samuel Goldenburg and Schmuyle,
Market Place at Limoges, Catacombs, Baba-Jaga,
Great Gate of Kiev.

512 William Shakespeare.

513 Henrik Ibsen.

514 El Greco.

515 First walk in space. From Voskhod II on 18
Marsh 1965. His co-pilot was Belyayev.

516 The Three Fates.

517 Charles the Great (742–814) also known as
     Charlemagne.

518 Swans. The birds are identified by notches cut on
     the beak. From the thirteenth to the eighteenth
     century they were regarded as property of the
     Crown. The process of marking is called 'swan
     upping' or 'hopping'.

519 Tycho Brahe.

520 Edward Elgar.

Sea and Ships

521 Five only – the bell, man, foot, bolt and buoy
     ropes. All the others have special names such as
     halliards, clewlines, buntlines, sheets, downhauls
     etc.

522 He was better known as Joseph Conrad. Born in
     Poland, he became a British shipmaster then a
     writer.

523 *Pelican* – renamed the *Golden Hind* later.

524 The cook, because he was expected to do the
     primitive 'doctoring' before this was made a
     responsibility of the master.

525 None. She made several very fast passages but her
     rival *Thermopylae* made two 60-day passages from
     London to Melbourne. The *Cutty Sark*'s best was
     64 days land to land on this run. The
     Thermopylae made a run of 91 days Foochow to
     London in the tea trade which the *Cutty Sark*
     never approached. (The *Lightning* sailed from
     Melbourne to Liverpool in 63 days in 1853 – the
     record.)

526 The *Sirius* in 1838 seems to have been the first
     Atlantic 'liner' as she crossed using engines as
     main power throughout. The *Savannah* of 1819 was
     a sailing-ship which could rig and use briefly a pair
     of power-driven paddles.

527 Since June 1967.

528 *Nautilus*, an American submarine.

529 Challenger Deep in the Mariana's Trench in the Pacific; depth 36,198 ft.

530 Over 70%.

531 She was the first all-iron sailing ship (the first iron steamship, *Aaron Manby*, was also British).

532 *Savannah* – an American vessel.

533 *Great Britain*.

534 The Apollo 15 spaceship was named *Endeavour* in Cook's honour and carried a piece of the original ship.

535 All three are missing ships, which sailed and disappeared. (The *Waratah* with cargo and passengers, the *Admiral Karpfanger*, a German four-masted barque training ship went missing on a grain passage from Australia, the *Sao Paulo* missing without trace in the Atlantic when being towed to Europe to be scrapped.)

536 A compass slung overhead for the Ship's Master to note the course (and steering skill) when below; it was in his saloon.

537 One which carried no permanent royals.

538 Construct the model outside the bottle first, with hinged masts and collapsible rigging. Then set her in carefully and haul up the rigging by means of ends left trailing through the bottle's neck.

539 His surveying in Newfoundland waters and the St Lawrence River brought him to favourable notice. He was used to ships like the Whitby 'Cat' *Endeavour;* most naval officers were not. (Very probably, senior officers did not want the job. It was Cook who made the expedition important. It could have been simply a passage to and from Tahiti.)

540 The Frenchman Louis De Bougainville.

Medical Science

541 Electrocardiogram.

542 5–6 litres. 5–10% of the body weight or approximately 70 ml/kg or 2500–2800 ml/square metre body surface area.

543 Secondary haemorrhage.

544 The Tidal Volume.

545 A hormone released from the stomach which increases the acidity of the gastric juice. Released from the pyloric antrum. A polypeptide made up of amino acids ending with phenylalanine. Two varieties have been discovered.

546 The Clostridia.

547 Shick test.

548 Seeing in the dark (night vision).

549 Micelles.

550 A second graft from the same donor is rejected more rapidly than the first.

551 Serotonin (5-hydroxytryptamine).

552 The presence of lysozyme (antibacterial enzyme), in the saliva.

553 Vitamin B12 (cyano cobalamin). Vitamin K2 synthesised by intestinal bacteria. It is usually isolated from putrid fishmeal.

554 The well-known sounds which are heard with the stethoscope over an artery when taking (measuring) the blood pressure.

555 Giant pyramidal cells situated in the motor cortex of the brain. Betz was a Russian anatomist who lived about 1850.

556 It is the unit of absorbed dose of radioactivity related to the biological effect – in the therapeutic range 1 roentgen=0·97 rads so the dose in roentgens is roughly equal to the number of rads.

557 Any type of immune response – a recall or redevelopment of antibodies in the blood which had previously been present but had disappeared.

558 A period after a muscle contraction in which no stimulus can produce another contraction.

559 Temporary persistence of a reflex muscle contraction after the stimulus has been withdrawn.

560 Kinins (they increase capillary permeability).

Antiques

561 Mahogany.

562 Porcelain is translucent, pottery does not transmit light.

563 St Louis.

564 ·925 (92·5%).

565 Sheffield Plate.

566 Shagreen.

567 Stump work.

568 Liberty.

569 The Barberini vase.

570 Adam and Sheraton who were not practical cabinet makers (or Chippendale and Hepplewhite because they were practical cabinet makers).

571 Holly.

572 Plymouth and Bristol.

573 Kingwood and Tulipwood.

574 The fashion for painting edges of books with heraldic devices and scenes.

575 Lantern.

576 Painted figures on wood (men – women – housemaids etc) standing about Georgian houses.

577 William Pegg *or* William 'Quaker' Pegg.

578 Gouache.

579 A small table with drawer, having a loose movable bookstand with curved handle and drawers on top.

580 Nonsuch (the name of a palace built by Henry VIII at Cheam, Surrey).

General Knowledge 9

581 The Statue of Liberty. Now to be seen in New York harbour. Its full title was originally 'Liberty Enlightening the World'. It is constructed of ⅛″ hammered copper on a steel frame and weighs 225 tons.

582 Poilus. Derived from 'poilu' meaning hairy, because of their beards.

583 Pogroms. A Russian word, meaning 'destruction' or 'riot'. The Russian central Government did not organise pograms, as was widely believed, but the anti-Semite policy that it carried out from 1881–1917 made them possible. Pogrom has come to mean an attack against a minority (religious, racial, or class) which is either approved or condoned by the authorities.

584 Scapula.

585 Captain Nemo in *Twenty Thousand Leagues Under the Sea* by Jules Verne.

586 Pilgrim Fathers of *The Mayflower*, in December 1620.

587 General Grivas.

588 The Royal Scots. A name given in 1633 by one of the senior French regiments.

589 Jerome K. Jerome (1859–1927).

590 Soldiers of Destiny

591 Luther's 95 Theses against the Papal Legate.

592 Figures of horses carved on slopes of chalk hills, at Westbury, Wiltshire, and Uffington, Berkshire.

593 John Keats. Sonnet to Fanny Brawne.

594 Arnold Wesker.

595 Lourdes, in France, at the Grotto of Massabielle. Miraculous healings have been claimed from a spring which arose near the site of Bernadette's vision of Mary.

596 Judy Garland.

597 The Duke of Wellington (1796–1852).

598 Galileo.

599 Japanese suicide-pilots. Means literally 'Divine Wind'.

600 Bathsheba.

Gardening

601 The art of training and cutting plants into ornamental shapes.

602 Anther (anther and filament make up the stamen).

603 Soilless gardening.

604 The tip of an unflowered shoot of pink or carnation which can be pulled out and rooted like a cutting.

605 Club root.

606 Cut it hard back to the third or fourth outwardly-pointing bud from the base.

607 Not below $\frac{1}{2}$ inch.

608 A numerical scale on which is measured the degree of acidity or alkalinity of the soil. (Neutral is ph 7 and in scientific terms it is the negative of the number of hydroxyl ions per unit volume of soil).

609 The degree of fineness of the soil particles or crumbs. Thus a good tilth means there are no big lumps in the soil.

610 In spring or early summer.

611 Capability Lancelot Brown (1715–1783).

612 Dwarfing trees, perfected by Japanese gardeners.

613 Cuckoo spit.

614 Shortening the stem of a variety of orange by taking a piece out of the centre and grafting the top back on the base.

615 Erica cinerea.

616 Saintpaulia.

617 That it is not attacked by or susceptible to wart disease (Black Scab) caused by synchytrium endobioticum.

618 An apple stock. Malling Merton 106 is a semi-dwarfing stock immune to woolly aphis.

619 Crown bud.

620 34 chromosomes. Pitmaston is a triploid pear
(3 × 17) while Louise is a diploid (2 × 17 = 34).

Mammals

621 The reindeer – called caribou in America.

622 Bats, hedgehogs, dormouse (not squirrel or
badger).

623 The mother licks a wet strip in her fur and the
baby crawls along it to her pouch.

624 Because it curls the end of its prehensile tail into a
ring (not because it is marked with rings).

625 The hippopotamus, which exudes a reddish sticky
sweat that turns brownish on drying and protects
the skin from sun-burn.

626 Either (a) Sea otter, which uses a stone held on
chest as an anvil for cracking sea-urchins; or
(b) Chimpanzee, which uses twigs to fish white
ants out of their nests.

627 The soft palate, blown out with air.

628 The South American rabbit (Sylvilagus), in which
it produces only a mild disease.

629 The American shrew (Blairna), (also European
water-shrew (Neomys), the Solenodon of Cuba and
Hispaniola).

630 The ratel or honey-badger (Mellivora). The bird
calls and flies ahead leading it to a bees' nest.

631 The polar-bear, which stores excess vitamin A
from its vitamin-rich diet in its liver.

632 By resonance in the throat-pouches under the skin
of the neck and chest.

633 Hedgehogs (the prickly Hedgehog-Tenrecs of
Madagascar).

634 Eel grass (Zostera) and similar flowing plants (not
seaweeds or algae).

635 The female gelada baboon – a line of swellings like
beads from neck onto chest.

636 Fisherman bats (Noctilio) of Caribbean; Pizonyx
of Lower California.

637 They trawl for small fish near the surface with their large hind feet with long toes and claws.

638 The eland (in south Africa and at Askania Nova in the Crimea).

639 It is thought to be a sort of acoustic lens to focus sonar ultrasonic sounds in echo-location.

640 The sloths of South America – sometimes as low as 24°C.

General Knowledge 10

641 Cohort.

642 Charles Mason and Jeremiah Dixon. The line is called the Mason Dixon Line.

643 Fruit flies.

644 At Berkeley Castle, Gloucestershire. He was murdered there in 1327.

645 When Charles I attempted to arrest five MP's in the Commons in 1642.

646 Parnassus. Also sacred to Dionysus.

647 Nadir. The pole vertically below the observer's feet.

648 Sir Rowland Hill (in 1840).

649 *Hôtel Des Invalides.*

650 George Washington.

651 Octavian and Antony.

652 The seven kingdoms into which Anglo-Saxon England was divided before AD 900. They were, East Anglia, Essex, Kent, Mercia, Northumbria, Wessex, and Sussex. From the Greek 'rule of seven'.

653 Karlheinz Stockhausen. Born 1928.

654 Slieve Donard. 2,796 ft high, in the Mountains of Mourne. Carrantuohill in the Republic of Ireland is higher.

655 *Iolanthe* by Gilbert and Sullivan.

656 He was drowned – lost in the cruiser *Hampshire* off the Orkneys in 1916. The cruiser was struck by a mine on the passage to North Russia.

657 Pavlov. (Ivan Petrovich).

658 Baseball. The 'bull-pen': an area off the field where substitutes can warm up. 'Strike-out': is three strikes and counts as an out.

659 Chromosomes.

660 Einstein's Theory of Relativity.

Scandinavian Mythology

661 Skirnismal.

662 Freyja.

663 A star.

664 Heimdall.

665 Gold.

666 Thor.

667 Sjaelland (Zealand) and Malaren (old name: Logurinn).

668 Vanir.

669 Edda (Snorri Sturluson c. 1220).

670 A ship.

671 Austri is one of the four dwarves supposed each to support a corner of the heavens.

672 Nerthus in Tacitus: Njord (Njorthur) in Norse sources.

673 Fishing for the Midgard Serpent. (World Serpent, *Mithgarthsorm* [ur] or *Jormungand* [ur]).

674 Ragnarok 'doom of the gods'.

675 The drowning of all the giants save one in Ymir's blood.

676 The fetter, Gleipnir.

677 They said he had choked in his wisdom because nobody there was wise enough to be able to ask him questions.

678 He governed thunder and thunderbolts, winds and rainstorms, fair weather and the fruits of the earth, they invoked him in times of famine and disease.

679 Odin's (Othin's) self-immolation; Odin (Othinn) as all-father Bald(u)r as innocent victim; ideas of punishment and reward in after life; doomsday conceptions.

680 Gods of fertility and prosperity; Njord (Njorthur), Frey (Freyr).

Scottish History

681 Chevy Chase (1388).

682 Catherine Douglas (Barlass) (in an attempt to save King James the first).

683 Devorgilla, daughter of Lord of Galloway, wife of John de Baliol (1250–1313), completed both in memory of her husband.

684 The slaying of the guest involved.

685 1719, at the Battle of Glensheil.

686 Mary MacGregor of Comar (not Helen, as Scott called her).

687 Robert and Edward Bruce in the thirteenth century (Edward was King of Ireland).

688 Simon, Lord Lovat (in 1746, the island was in Loch Morat).

689 *L'Heureux.*

690 They were hereditary custodians of specially precious Celtic saints' relics.

691 Blank papers signed by the Catholic Earls of Huntley, Erroll and Angus for the King of Spain to fill in his own terms for the invasion of Scotland, 1592–93.

692 An offer to return the Stone of Destiny (or scone) – probably because it was not the genuine article.

693 The Gowrie Conspiracy (in 1660).

694 A farcical engagement between the Covenanters and Gordons (in 1639).

695 A shoulder-brooch torn from Bruce with his plaid at Battle of Dal Righ. (Torn off by a MacDougall clansman and retained as a precious trophy by that Clan.)

696 Alexander, Earl of Mar.

697 Bernard De Linton, Abbot of Arbroath.

698 At Garmouth, Moray (on his abortive landing in Scotland, 1650).

699 A game of medieval Scotland, enjoyed particularly by King James V and his Court, consisting of tobogganing on an ox skull.

700 Robert Bruce and John Comyn the Red.

First World War

701 1915 (chlorine gas on 22 April).

702 The Hindenburg Line.

703 They were members of the BEF, and the name comes from an Imperial Order issued by the Germans: 'to walk over General French's contemptible little army'.

704 Austria–Hungary declared war on Serbia. (Britain did not enter the war until 4 August when she declared war on Germany.)

705 Heligoland.

706 At the Battle of Tannenberg and the Mazurian Lakes.

707 King Constantine of Greece.

708 RFC aircraft. Single-seater biplane scouts.

709 Yarmouth and King's Lynn (L3 and L4 on 19 January 1915).

710 Russian and Austro-Hungarian (Russians won the battle, September and October 1914).

711 The Schlieffen Plan, prepared by Count Alfred von Schlieffen, former chief of general staff. German armies would first crush France in a great fan-like drive through neutral Belgium, then crush Russia, Great Britain, the Balkans and Asia.

712 Enver Pasha.

713 The Kaiser, through his Chancellor.

714 To save Salonika from the enemy, and from the Bulgarians in particular, and to impose an obstacle to Germany's efforts to effect a junction by the most direct route with Turkey.

715 Off the Falkland Islands.

716 Gallipoli Peninsula (Dardanelles). These were the chosen landing sites.

717 The Canadians.

718 Battle of Cambrai, 1917.

719 Marshall Ferdinand Foch, appointed at Doullen 1918.

720 China. Kiau-Chan (Harbour Tsing-Tau).

General Knowledge 11

721 A giant hero of immense drinking and eating capacity.

722 The Tolpuddle Martyrs. Sentenced in 1834 for administering unlawful oaths for seditious purposes at Tolpuddle in Dorset.

723 A Viking Boat. This takes place on the island of Shetland. Held on the last Tuesday in January to welcome the return of the sun. It is a survival of pagan sun worship in which a Viking ship is carried in procession by torchbearers.

724 Californian Gold Rush.

725 *Elements* by Euclid. Said to have a greater circulation than any book in history except the Bible.

726 Hector Hugh Munro (1870–1916). Writer of satirical short stories and novels.

727 Edict of Nantes.

728 Cats eyes. Invented in 1934.

729 Titus Oates. In 1678 Oates revealed an alleged 'popish plot' to kill the King (Charles II) and put his brother James on the throne in order to restore Catholicism.

730 Zero Energy Thermonuclear Assembly. Devised in 1957 by British physicists at Harwell in an attempt to create electrical energy directly from nuclear fusion.

731 Pandora.

732 Jupiter, in Holst's *Planet Suite*.

733 To impress (recruit) men into naval service.

734 Access to the Baltic. The corridor was ten miles wide and 100 miles long, it contained the Port of Danzig.

735 *Pilgrim's Progress*. Written by John Bunyan in 1675.

736 Catherine of Aragon. First wife of Henry VIII, previously the wife of Arthur his elder brother.

737 The Bayeux Tapestry. The tapestry of Queen Matilda – wife of William the Conqueror. Believed to have been made by her.

738 Retiarius.

739 She was the first woman to swim the English Channel, on 6 August 1926.

740 Lorenzo De'Medici (the Magnificent). He ruled with Giuliano De'Medici until 1478, and then alone until 1492.

Poetry

741 A 'Dirty British coaster' (John Masefield's *Cargoes*).

742 *Lyrical Ballads*. Compiled by William Wordsworth and Samuel Taylor Coleridge and published in 1798.

743 My bonnie Mary (the title of the poem; 'Go fetch to me a pint o' wine').

744 The Ettrick Shepherd.

745 The cuckoo (in *To the Cuckoo*).

746 Dylan Thomas (in *Fern Hill*).

747 Father and son (Rustum the father, and Sohrab the son in *Sohrab and Rustum*).

748 Hugh McDiarmid.

749 The mountain lion. (The title of the poem. The animal is sometimes called a puma.)

750 The Franklin.

751 *Epithalamion*. Published at the same time were the *Amoretti*, a cycle of sonnets commemorative of his moods in courtship. They did not celebrate his wedding. *Prothalamion* describes himself as a disappointed suitor at court.

752 'Here he lies where he longed to be; Home is the sailor, Home from the sea; and the Hunter, home from the hill'.

753 East Coker.

754 *Marmion*

755 'Earth has not anything to show more fair'.

756 In the Claypit. (Title: *Christ in the Claypit*.)

757 Auburn.

758 'My three and twentieth year.' (Title: *How soon hath time, the subtle thief of youth*.)

759 'On first looking into Chapman's Homer' (title of the sonnet).

760 Henry Reed.

Astronomy 2

761 Carbon dioxide.

762 Astronomer Royal (of England – Scotland has her own).

763 The fall of the Tunguska Meteorite.

764 Aristarchus.

765 Vulcan.

766 Arcturus. (Sirius, Canopus and Alpha Centauri are all brighter, but lie south of the equator. Arcturus is very slightly brighter than Capella and Vega.)

767   Sir Richard Woolley.

768   Halley's Comet.

769   Sigma Octantis.

770   Auriga, The Charioteer or Wagoner.

771   Oberon.

772   Jack Bennett.

773   In the Pleiades (in Taurus).

774   Ceres.

775   Gregorian.

776   George Alcock.

777   Wilhelm Beer.

778   Mare Imbrium.

779   O-type.

780   John G. Bolton and Gordon J. Stanley.

French Literature

781   Harpagon.

782   Lamartine. (In 1816, at the age of 26, he met a young married woman, Julie Charles, at Aix-les-Bains, on the Lac du Bourget; they planned to meet again the following year, but Mme Charles was then too ill to travel and died shortly afterwards of tuberculosis. In 1820 Lamartine published a short book of poems, *Méditations poétiques*, in memory of their idyll. It was the first book of Romantic poetry to be published in France.)

783   *Les Plaideurs* – 1668 (the play is very freely based on Aristophanes, and is a satire on the French law courts and on the mania of private persons for going to law).

784 Julien Sorel, a passionately ambitious young man who chose the black robe of the priest rather than the red uniform of the soldier to make his way up the ladder.

785 Ferney – now Ferney-Voltaire. He chose to live near the border between Geneva and France so that he could cross the frontier whenever persecution by either the Genevan or the French authorities seemed likely.

786 *L'invitation au Château* (1947).

787 Prosper Mérimée, 1803–70. His story was written in 1845. Mérimée was a civil servant who for some time held the post of Inspector of Ancient Monuments.

788 Etienne Martin. A young student who lives with his mother in a small Paris apartment.

789 *Les Iambes*. (Chénier was executed in 1794, during the Terror, at the age of 32. *Les Iambes*, however, were not published until 1819, when they immediately aroused great interest among the young Romantic poets. The theme of these poems was politcal satire, coupled with lamentations on his own fate.)

790 Angoulême, some 300 miles south-west of Paris, (From Angoulême, Lucien Chardon – later known as Lucien de Rubempre – set out to seek fame and fortune in Paris.)

791 Jean-Paul Sartre, the leader of the Existentialist Movement.

792 *Les Thibault* (eleven volumes were written between 1922 and 1940).

793 Pléiade.

794 *Thérèse Desqueyroux*, 1927 (by François Mauriac, one of his best and possibly most characteristic novels).

795 *L'Espoir*, 1937. (Malraux was an organiser and pilot of the Republican Air Force. Politician, man of letters and art historian, André Malraux was for several years Minister for Cultural Affairs under General de Gaulle.)

796 The Cévennes, which form the eastern part of the massif central.

797 Clément Marot. His poem *L'Enfer* was written after this experience, and is topically interesting in these days of political persecution.

798 *Perceval* by Chrétien de Troyes. (This verse romance, written in the 1180s and left incomplete on the poet's death, introduces the myth of the Grail into the Arthurian legend.)

799 Roger Caillois, who was elected to the Académie Française in 1971. (His work, *Pierres*, was published in 1966. Roger Caillois combines literature with a career in administration – he holds an important post at UNESCO in Paris.)

800 Jean de Meung, who added some 18,000 lines to the 4,000 written by his predecessor. (This long poem was the most popular single work of the thirteenth century.)

General Knowledge 12

801 Lord Nelson. Destroyed 8 March 1966.

802 Daedalus.

803 Tobias Smollett.

804 A marriage union between one of royal or noble rank and one of lower rank in which the wife does not acquire the husband's rank and the offspring do not inherit the titles or possessions of the father.

805 Lord Have Mercy.

806 Tonic Sol-fa. Established and perfected by John Curwen (d. 1863).

807 The Verrazano-narrows bridge. Opened in 1964.

808 Vienna, in 1923. The Central Radio Station for this organisation is centred near Paris.

809 The Fosse Way. One of the principal Roman roads of Britain. It runs on the line: Axmouth-Ilchester-Bath-Cirencester-Leicester-Lincoln. The name derives from the Latin for ditch (*fosse*) which ran on each side of the road.

810 Three. *Bounty*, 1789; *Nore*, 1797; *Australia*, 1808.

811 From the Greek legend of the mortal Arachne who challenged the gods to surpass her at weaving. She failed and was turned into a spider by Minerva.

812 Daphne Jackson, Surrey University.

813 Prokofiev.

814 Ptolemy I.

815 The Friendly Islands. The king's full name is King Taufa'ahau Tupou IV of Tonga.

816 Botticelli (Sandro di) (1444/5–1510). Properly Alessandro Di Marian or Di Vanni Filipepi.

817 A district, parish, church, or deanery of the Church of England which lies under the jurisdiction of the Crown and not of the Bishop of the Diocese in which it is situated. Included are the Chapel Royal, St James' Palace, London, and St George's Chapel in Windsor Castle.

818 The area was returned to Germany. It had been ceded to France after the First World War under the supervision of the League of Nations.

819 Simone de Beauvoir. She won the Goncourt Prize in 1954.

820 Lollards. Lollardy, a Medieval English movement for ecclesiastical reform. Led by John Wycliffe whose 'poor priests' spread his ideas throughout the countryside in the late fourteenth century.

Science Fiction

821 Ray Bradbury's *Fahrenheit 451* (the hero's name is Guy Montag).

822 The Plan was to establish two centres of learning at opposite ends of the galaxy, to promote Civilisation after the fall of the galactic empire as predicted by the psycho-historian Hari Seldon (by Isaac Asimov).

823 *The Space Machine* by Frederick Pohl and C. M. Kornbluth (earlier title in the USA was *Gravy Planet*).

824 Dr Wellington Yueh (in Frank Herbert's *Dune*).

825 Ride it. It is an eight-legged beast of burden. (Character created by Edgar Rice Burroughs.)

826 Robert A. Heinlein's *Blow Ups Happen*.

827 They are all set in 'Generation Starships', Spaceships designed to travel for centuries while supporting an entirely self-sufficient population.

828 The Quest for the Holy Grail (much is made of the Tarot pack, but this is of course subsidiary).

829 Make him take his hat off, or possibly pull his hair. The mind-reading powers of true Slans are governed by golden tendrils growing among the hair (*Slan* by A. E. van Vogt).

830 The 'Spindizzy' drive, enabling ships and worlds to travel faster than light.

831 The Heat Ray, the poisonous black smoke, the three-legged fighting machines, the multi-legged crab-like handling machines. (Also mentioned are three cylindrical spaceships and the Red Weed.)

832 It was a dot, a single dot, which means in Tralfamadorian: 'Greetings' (in Kurt Vonnegut's *The Sirens of Titan*).

833 *Tiger! Tiger!* by Alfred Bester. (Earlier title, *The Stars My Destination*. Its hero is Gulliver or Gully Foyle alias Fonrmile of Ceres.)

834   Venus, or Perelandra, where Ransom fought the Un-Man (C. S. Lewis's *Out of the Silent Planet* trilogy).

835   Courage. All sane puppeteers are cowards (Larry Niven's *Neutron Star* and *Ringworld*).

836   Arthur C. Clarke's *2001*.

837   A robot may not injure a human being, or, through inaction, allow a human being to come to harm. (The second law was: A robot must obey the orders given it by human beings except where such orders would conflict with the first law; the third law was: A robot must protect its own existence as long as such protection does not conflict with the First or Second laws.)

838   J. G. Ballard.

839   The 'Players' are, on the one side, hostile amorphous entities who prey on planoforming spaceships; and on the other, telepathically linked pairs of cats and human sensitives (*The Game of Rat and Dragon* by Cordwainer Smith a pen-name for Paul T. Linebarger).

840   Attel Malagate (the Woe), Viole Falushe, Kokor Hekkus (the killing machine), Howard Alan Treesong, Lens Larque. (Vance has already produced novels about the first three, respectively, *Star King*, *The Temple of Love* and *The Killing Machine*.)

Spanish and South American Ethnology

841   Prince Juan Carlos Bourbon.

842   El Greco.

843   Tango.

844   The northern coast of South America.

845   Over the issue of the liberation of Cuba.

846   Hermando de Soto.

847   Gibraltar was one of them, and the other, Ceuta stood across the Straits of Gibraltar on the African coast.

848   Rio de Janeiro, Brazil.

849   Treaty of Utrecht, 1713.

850   Poem of the Cid. *El Cid* written about 1140. Real name of El Cid, a Spanish national hero, Rodrigo Diaz.

851   A mixture of sorrowful Indian and joyous Spanish music (native American).

852   The wheel.

853   Llamas and Alpacas. Guanacos and vicunas run wild and were hunted by them.

854   The Sacred Book of the Quiche Maya Indians who lived in Central America. The original is now lost, but it survived in oral tradition and was rewritten in Latin characters in the middle of the sixteenth century.

855   A stone column (or stele) found at Tres Zapotes (one of the centres of Olmec culture) bearing a hieroglyphic date corresponding to the year 31 BC.

856   Tiahuanaco is in the south Bolivian highlands near Lake Titicaca. Around AD 500 it was the ceremonial centre of unknown Indians with an advanced culture, as is attested by the imposing stonework ruins which were left after their conquest by the Incas.

857   Quetzalcoatl.

858   Quechua.

859   The names given to the two co-rulers of the chibcha Indians (Colombia). The Zipa controlled the lands around modern Bogota, and the Zaque the district around Tunja.

860 They were the Gods of Ancient Mexico. (Xochipilli, depicted as a young god of maize, was the god of vegetation, games, singing and dancing; Huitzilopochtli, who appeared as a humming bird, was the chief tribal god who demanded to be fed on human hearts; and Tlaloc, a serpent, was the rain god and guardian of water.)

Money, Money, Money

861 The House of Fraser.

862 Gladstone.

863 About fourteen pence.

864 Fourty-four countries.

865 Lloyd's of London.

866 Lloyd George, in 1909.

867 American Express.

868 Ricardo (described by Keynes).

869 Say's Law.

870 Barings.

871 1932.

872 The London Stock Exchange.

873 2·60%.

874 1833.

875 Overseas Government Bonds and Railway Securities.

876 One, 1970.

877 John D. Rockefeller, 1929.

878 They doubled.

879 Czarist Russia.

880 65%.

General Knowledge 13

881 Ralph Vaughan Williams.

882 Double Helix (Deoxyribonucleic acid).

883 Rhubarb. The stalk used in cooking and the root in medicine, notably as a purgative.

884 Wilfred Wilson Gibson (1878–1962). A member of the 'Georgian Group', published: *Daily Bread* 1910, *Thoroughfares* 1914, and many other titles.

885 His paintings – he is better known as Canaletto (1697–1768).

886 French Kings. Charles I to V, although Louis VI was also called 'The Fat' and Philip IV was called 'The Fair'.

887 Eva Braun. They married on 29 April 1945 and committed suicide 30 April.

888 Legion of Honour.

889 Sugar Loaf.

890 Le Corbusier (1887–1965). Professional name of Charles Edouard Jeanneret.

891 Georgia.

892 The Siege of Sidney Street. Churchill was Home Secretary at that time.

893 The Three Graces. Their Greek names are Aglaia, Eruprosyme and Thalia. The Three Graces or three charities. Also known as the personification of Beauty, Charm, and Grace; and Brightness, Joyfulness and Bloom.

894 Elizabeth Garrett Anderson.

895 Dr Thomas Augustine Arne, about 1740.

896 Charles VII (1403–1461). Crowned 1429.

897 Golf US Masters Tournament or Golf Augusta Tournament.

898 Alexander the Great. The Oracle foretold that who-ever did this would rule over Asia.

899 Hamilton.

900 Whigs.

MASTERMIND
BOOK TWO

General Knowledge 1

1 On what day of the Creation did God make the Sun, Moon and stars?

2 Lollius Urbicus was responsible for building a defensive wall against Scottish tribes. What was it called?

3 Edda is the name given to two important collections of literature, of which country?

4 Who commanded the Indian forces at Little Big Horn?

5 In Greek mythology anemones sprang from his blood after he had been gored by a wild boar. Who was he?

6 Where was the first World Cup held?

7 Timbuktu was founded in 1807. Whereabouts is it?

8 What are blue brindles, headers, flettons, and common reds?

9 Which war was brought to an end by the surrender of forces under the command of General Cornwallis?

10 Mr Russell Means led a group of people in revolt against Government. Who were they?

11 He negotiated the Louisiana Purchase in 1803, and in 1816 was elected fifth President of the USA. Who was he?

12 Dicentra Spectabilis is a plant. By what other name is it known?

13 Which modern author would you associate with Glencoe, Culloden and the Highland Clearances?

14 Who is supposed to have established the measurement of a yard?

15 Who was immortalised in George Borrow's novels *Lavengro* and *Romany Rye*?

16 In medieval times what was the Mangonel used for?

17 Who are designated by the term Scotists?

18 How many records are castaways allowed to take to their imaginary island in 'Desert Island Discs'?

19 Tisiphone, Magaera and Alecto pursued earthly sinners. Who were they?

20 Who described assassination as 'the extreme form of censorship'?

Astronomy

Set by Patrick Moore

21 Which planet has a Great Red Spot?

22 What is remarkable about the direction of a comet's tail?

23 What kind of variable star is Algol?

24 In which lunar sea did the Apollo 11 astronauts land in 1969?

25 Who first suggested the principle of the reflecting telescope?

26 Which two planets in the Solar System show lunar-type phases as seen from Earth?

27 Which is the more distant – a pulsar or a quasar?

28 Which spacecraft sent back the first close-range pictures of Venus?

29 Which is the brightest of the asteroids?

30 Which bright periodical comet will return to perihelion in 1986?

31 What is meant by saying that the Moon is at syzygy?

32 What is the name of the bright meteor shower seen every August?

33 What is the colour of an F-type star?

34 Which is the only satellite in the Solar System known to have a reasonably dense atmosphere?

35 In which lunar 'sea' would you find the crater Bessel?

36 Where would you find the Nix Olympica and the Syrtis Major?

37 What famous celestial object is known officially as Messier 31?

38 Who was the Danish astronomer who measured the velocity of light in 1675?

39 Which major planet was discovered in 1846?

40 Where, today, would you find the crater named after Dr Gerard P. Kuiper?

PATRICK MOORE: Well-known television personality, author, and expert on astronomy.

Legends of Britain

Set by T. A. Shippey

41 First in the line of kings that includes Cymbeline, old King Cole and King Arthur, who was this legendary founder of Britain?

42 From which city did Brutus originate?

43 Whose is the 'Isle of Gramarye' quoted by T. H. White in the opening verse to *The Once and Future King*?

44 Which Welsh king is said to have invited Hengest and Horsa into Britain?

45 In Burns's *Tam o' Shanter*, the hero used a legendary method of escaping from witches. What was this?

46 Who is said to have rescued England from the Danes by killing their giant Colbrand?

47 In his legendary exploits, what abbey was sacked by Hereward the Wake?

48 What is a silkie?

49 Which saint nipped the Devil's nose with red-hot tongs?

50 Who was the legendary foster-son of Grim of Grimsby?

51 According to the Tudor dramatists, and William Stukeley's pedigree, of which county was Robin Hood the rightful earl?

52 Who made the 'brazen head' at Oxford?

53 What is a kelpie?

170   Answers on pages 262-3

54 Peg Powler appears in Teesside legends and Jenny Greenteeth in Lancashire legends. What were they?

55 In the Welsh *Mabinogi*, who was 'Prince of Dyfed', called 'Pen Annwn', the 'Head of Hades', and who reigned at Narberth?

56 According to Briggs' *Dictionary of Folk Lore*, which race knew the secret of the 'heather ale'?

57 In which British county is Pontius Pilate said to be born, with a yew to mark his birthplace?

58 What did young Lambton catch when fishing in the Wear?

59 At what time of year is the Glastonbury thorn said to flower?

60 Who brought the Holy Grail from Palestine to England?

T. A. SHIPPEY, M.A.: St John's College, Oxford.

General Knowledge 2

61 Who was the goddess who mooned about Endymion?

62 What substance was responsible for the phrase 'mad as a Hatter'?

63 Which famous English novelist collaborated on the libretto of *Billy Budd* (Benjamin Britten's opera)?

64 What solo instrument is featured in the Largo of Dvořák's *New World* Symphony?

65 What was the official residence of British sovereigns from 1698 until 1837?

66 What is the name of the earliest known Chinese Dynasty?

67 Who was Britain's second-in-command at the Battle of Copenhagen in 1801?

68 'Court' cards on British packs are costumed as of the time of which monarch?

69 Who was the French artist who painted *The Progress of Love* for Madame du Barry?

70 What does the abbreviation O.L.A.S. stand for?

71 What Victorian novelist adopted the pseudonym Michael Angelo Titmarsh?

72 What should you be brought in a restaurant if you order Bigorneaux?

73 What was the name popularly given to women who sat knitting by the guillotine?

74 Who is the Peruvian who once won the Wimbledon Singles Lawn Tennis Championships?

75 What is myosotis better known as?

76 How many hoops are used in a game of croquet?

77 Noël Coward's play *Still Life* was adapted as a film. What was it then called?

78 Where in London exactly is the Mermaid Theatre sited?

79 Who directed the classic Russian film *Battleship Potemkin*?

80 In 1958 the French established the Fifth Republic, which was approved by all French territories except one. Which one?

20th-Century British Politics

Set by Dr David Butler

81 What was the shortest premiership in this century?

82 What was the Liberal Party's first post-war by-election win?

83 How long was David Lloyd George a Minister?

84 When did women get the vote at 21?

85 Who was the first Secretary of State for Wales?

86 Who was the first Scottish National Party MP?

87 Give the years for the two Nationalisations of steel.

88 Who finally took Britain off the gold standard?

89 Which was the first general election in which public opinion polls were published?

90 How many times did Winston Churchill stand for Parliament unsuccessfully?

91 Who established the Cabinet Secretariat?

92 Who announced the first 'Wage Freeze'?

93 What was the dramatic affair at Invergordon in 1931?

94 What was the official position of Sir Warren Fisher from 1919 to 1939?

95 Who was the first Minister of Munitions?

96 Under whose premiership were Life Peerages introduced?

97 What have Bewdley, Warwick and Leamington, and Bexley in common?

98 When were MPs first paid?

99 What was the Taff Vale decision?

100 Who were the hedgers and who were the ditchers?

DR DAVID E. BUTLER, M.A., D.Phil.: Fellow of Nuffield College, Oxford. Author of: *The British General Election of 1951*, *The Electoral System in Britain 1918–1951*, *The British General Election of 1955*, *British Political Facts 1900–1966*, etc.

Science Fiction
Set by T. A. Shippey

101 What did Winston Smith find in room 101?

102 In Gordon Dickson's stories, what does the world of 'the Dorsai' export?

103 Complete this sentence: 'Space is a province of —'

104 What letter should precede the name Daneel Olivaw?

105 Teela Brown was selected to explore the Ringworld for one quality. What was it?

106 In which book are these creatures to be found: crocksocks, traversers, burnurns, killerwillows?

107 In which story are these creatures implements of war: Termagants, Juggers, Fiends, Blue Horrors?

108 Which author created the concept of 'slow glass'?

109 In which book would you find Captain Washington working with Sir Isambard Brunel?

110 In which book would you find a Mickey Mouse watch regarded as an *objet d'art*?

111 For what was Delos D. Harriman famous?

112 What was the name of E. E. Smith's 'Gray Lensman'?

113 For what was the Blessed Leibowitz martyred?

114 Of which classic short story are these the last few words: 'Robot atom bombs do not make up their own minds'?

115 Which author created doctor Calhoun and his *tormal* Murgatroyd?

116 Which planet is defended by 'Mother Hitton's Littul Kittons'?

117 The first Earthman to visit the stars travelled inside a sperm whale: in which book?

118 The philosopher Bokonon informs us that a *granfalloon* is a false *karass*: in which book?

119 In Kipling's story 'As Easy as A.B.C.', what does A.B.C. stand for?

120 Why was Barlennan the Mesklinite afraid of heights?

T. A. SHIPPEY, M.A.: St John's College, Oxford.

General Knowledge 3

121 Mohorovičić Discontinuity describes what?

122 What was the special happening at Massabielle, on the banks of the River Gave, 115 years ago?

123 Who was the first Negro to be awarded the Nobel Peace Prize?

124 Which German pocket battleship in 1939 was out-manoeuvred to such an extent by three British cruisers that her Commander was forced to scuttle her?

125 On what story is the musical *Chu Chin Chow* based?

126 In what sort of building is a working area called the 'prompt side'?

127 Who is the English novelist who has made a speciality of one word titles, such as *Loving*, *Living*, *Caught* and *Nothing*?

128 How long is an American Presidential term?

129 Of what nationality was the physicist Ohm?

130 Who was responsible for giving us 'Bank Holidays'?

131 The standard language of China is based on the Chinese of Peking. What is its name?

132 What is the modern Turkish name for the mound where the city of Troy stood?

133 What was surrendered to Lieutenant-General Tomoyuki Yamashita on 15 February 1942?

178 Answers on pages 267-8

134 Where would you find the piece of ordnance known as 'Mons Meg'?

135 In 1572 who observed a nova in the constellation of Cassiopeia?

136 Which highly developed civilisation preceded the Aztecs in Mexico?

137 Why was Julian called the Apostate?

138 What term is used to express 1/10th of a nautical mile?

139 Who was the ancient Egyptian God of the Sun?

140 What is the correct name for the upper body shell of tortoises and crustaceans?

Gilbert and Sullivan

Set by Albert Truelove

141 What was the name of the girl whom the Judge
married in *Trial by Jury*?

142 Name four of the items of food the villagers had for
tea in *The Sorcerer*.

143 Which portrait comes alive in *Ruddigore* and marries
an old flame who has survived him? And what is
the name of the old flame?

144 What movements does Gilbert satirise in
(a) *Trial by Jury*, (b) *Patience*, (c) *Princess Ida*?

145 What is the first line of the song first used in *Thespis*
and then repeated in *The Pirates of Penzance*?

146 Which are the two places in London where hearts
may beat as pure and fair?

147 Whom did Elsie marry in *The Yeomen of the Guard*,
and how much was she paid?

148 If Colonel Fairfax had not married, what was the
name of the character who would have succeeded
to his estate?

149 In *The Gondoliers* there are two gondoliers, Marco
and Giuseppe. What are the names of their
respective brides?

150 Although the Savoy Theatre is associated with
Gilbert and Sullivan operas, what was the name of
the other London theatre opened by Richard D'Oyly
Carte, and what was the name of the grand opera
written by Sullivan that opened it?

151 What was the name of the first Gilbert and Sullivan
opera?

152 When Katisha denies that she is beautiful, what is it that she has that she says is a miracle of loveliness?

153 Name three of the crimes committed by Sir Ruthven Murgatroyd.

154 Why didn't Sir Ruthven Murgatroyd commit a crime on Monday?

155 Name King Gama's three sons in *Princess Ida.*

156 What relations did Sir Joseph Porter bring on board 'H.M.S. Pinafore' with him?

157 What advice does Sir Joseph Porter give in order to become the ruler of the Queen's Navy?

158 At which theatre was *The Pirates of Penzance* performed in order to obtain the British copyright?

159 Where did the London première of *The Pirates of Penzance* take place and when?

160 Who was in the audience at the first night of *Iolanthe* who suddenly found himself being sung to by name?

ALBERT TRUELOVE: Secretary, Bridget D'Oyly Carte Ltd.

Greek Mythology

Set by Dr Wolfgang Liebeschuetz

161 What bird was associated with the goddess Athena?

162 How did Achilles die?

163 When Odysseus returned home he was recognised by
his old dog. Name the dog.

164 A divine husband caught his wife in bed with the god
of war and entangled both in a net as a laughing
stock for the gods. Who was the husband?

165 How did Apollo punish Cassandra for refusing
his love?

166 On returning home from Troy Agamemnon was
killed by his wife, Clytemnestra, and her lover.
Name the lover.

167 A King tried to stop the worship of Dionysus and was
torn to pieces by his mother. Who was he?

168 A Greek god with horns, beard, tail and goat's feet
lived in wild places and enjoyed frightening
travellers. Name him.

169 With what princess did Zeus unite in the shape of a
rain of gold?

170 The British Museum has famous carvings of Centaurs
fighting Lapiths. Why did they fight?

171 Who was the mother of Hercules?

172 How many sons did Priam have by Hecuba?

173 Which Athenian princess was saved from the wrath
of her brother-in-law by being transformed into a
nightingale?

182 Answers on page 270

174   Why did the *curetes* clash their weapons around the infant Zeus?

175   Homer contains a single reference to a message in writing. Who carried it?

176   What god roared like a bull after being wounded by a Greek hero at Troy?

177   Who were the parents of the Minotaur?

178   'O for a beaker full of the warm south,
      Full of the true, the blushful Hippocrene.'
      (Keats, 'Ode to a Nightingale') What was the original 'Hippocrene'?

179   A Mycenean settlement has been preserved by a thick layer of volcanic ashes. Where?

180   The goddess Demeter acted as nurse to an infant prince. The locality became the scene of a famous initiation festival. What was its name?

DR WOLFGANG LIEBESCHUETZ: Department of Classics, Leicester University.

General Knowledge 4

181 Who, in politics, were the Adullamites?

182 In the canine sense, what is the etymology of the word 'terrier'?

183 The hero of a Babylonian epic offended the goddess Ishtar and was punished. How was he punished?

184 Who was the sculptor of Lord Nelson's statue in Trafalgar Square?

185 The site of one of the seven wonders of the ancient world was discovered in the nineteenth century. Which one?

186 In which book would you expect to find Piscator – a fisherman, Auceps – a fowler, Venator – a hunter?

187 Which country declared itself an independent republic on 17 June 1944?

188 What is the Japanese word for 'Good-bye'?

189 In which famous book would you find the characters Denisov and Dolokhov?

190 In what year did Marx and Engels issue the Communist Manifesto?

191 In classical legend, who were the Moirae?

192 Name the four breeds of draught horses used in the United Kingdom.

193 Of which country did Sir Seretse Khama become President?

194 Alice Liddell received a Christmas gift in memory of a summer's day. What was it?

195   From what fruit was marmalade originally made?

196   What substance is processed in a Ginnery?

197   In which novel would you find reference to the 'Black Riders' and 'Cracks of Doom'?

198   What is the name of the vestment worn by deacons over their left shoulders?

199   What part of a horse-drawn carriage is a Felloe or Felly?

200   Who wrote *The Cabinet-Maker and Upholsterer's Guide*?

British Ornithology

Set by Bruce Campbell

201 What are the popular names for the bony structure called the furcula?

202 Where is the alula?

203 What is an eclipse plumage?

204 Which British bird has most feathers?

205 What is the gonys and what is its purpose?

206 What is a nidifugous species?

207 How would you distinguish an adult female great spotted woodpecker *Dendrocopos major* from an adult male in the field?

208 What is the most favoured winter food of the bullfinch *Pyrrhula pyrrhula*?

209 Why is a male falcon called a tiercel?

210 *Caprimulgus:* to what bird does this name refer and why?

211 Two Kentish place names occur in the common names of British birds (not counting the Kentish plover *Charadruis alexandrinus*); what are they?

212 What, ornithologically, have Sula Sgeir, North Rona, St Kilda and Flannan Isles in common?

213 Three-quarters of the world breeding population of a sea bird is concentrated round the British Isles: which species?

214 To what is the remarkable spread of the fulmar petrel *Fulmarus glacialis* round the British Isles usually attributed?

215 With what rare breeding bird do you particularly associate Minsmere and Havergate Island in Suffolk?

216 What notable event in British ornithology took place on the island of Fetlar (Shetland)?

217 When did the golden eagle *Aquila chrysaetos* last nest in England?

218 What bird is recorded as nesting on a Scottish Cathedral in 1416?

219 What flightless bird was found in Britain in historic times?

220 Which is the smallest British bird?

DR BRUCE CAMPBELL: Joint Honorary Secretary, Council for Nature; Council Member, the Wildfowl Trust; Member, Scientific Advisory Committee, Royal Society for the Protection of Birds.

United States Presidents

Set by Professor D. K. Adams

221 How many times was Franklin D. Roosevelt elected president?

222 What is the address of the White House?

223 Who assassinated President Garfield and where did it happen?

224 Whose ambition was said to be 'a little engine that knew no rest'?

225 Which President was known as 'the little Magician'?

226 Name the university of which Dwight D. Eisenhower was president in the late 1940s.

227 Who said, and on what occasion: 'Against the insidious wiles of foreign influence . . . the jealousy of a free people ought to be *constantly* awake'?

228 To which political party did Rutherford B. Hayes belong?

229 What was the family relationship of Presidents William Henry Harrison and Benjamin Harrison?

230 Who was the first US president to be awarded the Nobel Peace Prize and for what was it awarded?

231 Whose portrait is on the $5 bill?

232 Who was the only bachelor president?

233 According to Article II(2) of the Constitution, who, after the vice-president, is next in line for the presidency?

234 Who lived at 'The Hermitage'?

235 Which former president later became Chief Justice of the US Supreme Court?

236 In which city did the inauguration of John Adams take place?

237 Who was the author of *The Winning of the West*?

238 Who succeeded President Tyler?

239 According to the Constitution, what is the minimum age that a president has to be?

240 Who first planted poplars along Pennsylvania Avenue to beautify the city of Washington?

PROFESSOR D. K. ADAMS, M.A., D.Phil: Department of American Studies, Keele University.

General Knowledge 5

241 For what are the Caves of Lascaux famous?

242 Who was Escoffier?

243 What is the mathematical term that means without end or limit?

244 Chequers is the official country residence of the Prime Minister. Where is it?

245 Which country has borders with Austria, Czechoslavakia, Russia, Romania, and Yugoslavia?

246 Which game originated in Persia, but takes its name from the Tibetan for ball? It was introduced into England in 1869.

247 Who said: 'The philosophers have only interpreted the world, in various ways; the point, however, is to change it'?

248 Jaroslav Hasek wrote a novel about a soldier. What was it called?

249 Of which islands is Hugh Town the capital?

250 According to Greek mythology whom did Apollo's lyre come from?

251 The General Strike in 1926 was called in support of which union?

252 The term 'Impressionism' was first used abusively to describe which artist's painting of a sunrise?

253 In 1519 the *Trinidad, San Antonio, Concepcion, Vittoria* and *Santiago* made up the fleet of a famous explorer. Who was he?

254 Indonesia was declared a Republic in 1945. Who was its first President?

255 From which of Burns's poems are these lines taken:
'I am truly sorry man's dominion
Has broken nature's social union'?

256 The Germans call this World War I battle the Battle of the Skagerrak. By what other name is it know?

257 Japanese have two popular forms of wrestling. Judo is one, what is the other?

258 Who was the Swedish Nightingale?

259 In a Parliamentary Election, what percentage of votes does a candidate need to avoid losing his deposit?

260 What is the supreme policy-making body of the Soviet Union?

The Works of J. R. R. Tolkien

Set by T. A. Shippey

261 How many rings 'for the dwarf-lords in their halls of stone'?

262 What was the nickname of Thorin son of Thráin son of Thror?

263 What was the nickname of Gríma (pronounced Greema) son of Gálmód (Garl-mode)?

264 What was the name given to Saruman in the Shire?

265 Who killed the dragon Smaug?

266 For what was Tobold Hornblower of Longbottom in the Southfarthing famous?

267 What shape could Beorn the skin-changer take besides the human one?

268 What was the name of Gandalf's sword?

269 What was Gollum's original name?

270 What was the name of the inn kept by Barliman Butterbur?

271 Which river ran through the Old Forest?

272 Who was the master of the Last Homely House east of the Sea?

273 In the Shire Calendar, what is the month between Winterfilth and Foreyule?

274 Who was given the advice 'Seek for the Sword that was broken'?

275 What did Galadriel (pronounced Ga*lad*riel) give to Sam Gamgee (Gam-jee)?

276 Of which race were trolls made in mockery?

277 What is the common or rustic term for the herb 'athelas'?

278 Whose epitaph begins 'Faithful servant yet master's bane'?

279 What was the device on the King of Rohan's flag? (pronounced Roe-han)

280 What is the supposed etymology of the word 'hobbit'?

T. A. SHIPPEY, M.A.: St John's College, Oxford.

Grand Opera since Verdi

Set by Harold Rosenthal

295 On what dramas is Berg's *Lulu* based?

296 What opera tells of the martyrdom of members of a religious order during the French Revolution?

297 Why was Strauss's *Schweigsame Frau* banned by the Nazis after only three performances?

298 Which was the first opera that made use of the quarter-tone scale?

299 On what quotation is Strauss's *Capriccio* based?

300 What opera lead to the formulation of 'socialist realism' as an artistic principle in the USSR?

HAROLD ROSENTHAL: Editor of *Opera.*

General Knowledge 6

301 The Chiltern Hundreds consist of three stewardships. Stoke and Burnham are two, what is the third?

302 A bathroom scale is a simple type of computer. What type?

303 Which philosopher coined the phrase, 'Cogito ergo sum'?

304 Who was the last king of Israel – he ruled from 732 to 724 BC?

305 Which Saint translated the Vulgate?

306 Doctor George MacLeod founded a religious community. What is it called?

307 In which city did Harold Macmillan make his 'wind of change' speech?

308 What is the name of the famous whirlpool between the islands of Moskenesøya and Vaerøy?

309 Can you say what vodka really means?

310 What is the name of the special straw used to drink maté or Paraguay Tea?

311 What sort of person is a benedick?

312 Who wrote the mid-Victorian novels of 'Barsetshire'?

313 What American state is nicknamed 'Show Me State'?

314 What is Caper-spurge?

315 Which European prince was called 'The Navigator'?

316 What befell Arachne when she challenged Athena at weaving?

317 Who wrote under the occasional pen-name of 'Peter Porcupine'?

318 Who designed the Welsh town of Portmeirion?

319 To what islands was Archbishop Makarios exiled (in 1956)?

320 Upon whose work was the Julian calendar based?

The Old Testament

Set by Professor A. R. C. Leaney

321   In the Garden of Eden story, what were Adam and Eve forbidden to eat?

322   What plague brought upon Egypt moved the magicians to say: 'This is the finger of God'?

323   In what place did the Lord first appear to Moses?

324   What was the name of the army officer with whose wife David committed adultery?

325   When David died who contended with Solomon for the throne?

326   In the book of Esther who was the queen whose place was taken by Esther?

327   Which king consulted the witch (or 'woman that hath a familiar spirit') at Endor?

328   From what village did the prophet Jeremiah come?

329   What decorative material is associated with the house built by Ahab for himself?

330   Naaman the Syrian came to Elisha to be cured of leprosy; what did Elisha prescribe?

331   What was the name of the last king of Judah in the Old Testament?

332   Name the three friends who came to talk to Job in his misery.

333   Where can be found the prophecy that men would turn their spears into pruning-hooks?

334 With what subject is the book of Nahum occupied?

335 What name did the prophet Hosea give to the daughter born to him by his wife Gomer?

336 What was the historical occasion of Isaiah's prophecy which begins with the words: 'A young woman is with child, and she will bear a son, and will call him Immanuel' (Isaiah 7.14)?

337 When did the prophet Haggai prophesy?

338 What was the disaster which moved the prophet Joel to call for a national fast?

339 Job chapter 28 is a poem on the search for Wisdom. How does it end?

340 'The Lord' is a substitute for the name of God as revealed to Moses. What consonants represent the actual Hebrew name?

PROFESSOR A. R. C. LEANEY, MA, DD: formerly Department of Theology, University of Nottingham.

The New Testament

Set by Professor A. R. C. Leaney

341 In the Gospel of Mark what are the first few words
uttered by Jesus?

342 In the Gospel of John, who were the first two disciples
to join Jesus?

343 In the story of the Temptations of Jesus, from what
book of the Old Testament does he answer the devil?

344 Name the parents of John the Baptist.

345 Give the two different names of the disciple called
from the 'receipt of custom'.

346 At what point in the story did Mary say the
Magnificat?

347 Name the co-author with Paul of I Corinthians.

348 Where did the visions recorded in the book of
Revelation take place?

349 What was the name of the scribe to whom Paul
dictated his letter to the Romans?

350 Which was the first town in Europe evangelised by
Paul?

351 In what books of the New Testament does the word
Antichrist occur?

352 What are the two Aramaic words recorded in the
Gospel of Mark as spoken by Jesus to a twelve-year-
old girl, and what do they mean?

353 To whom is the Letter of James addressed?

354 When Paul and Barnabas split up, where did Barnabas go?

355 What festival was it when 'On the last . . . day of the Festival Jesus . . . cried "If anyone is thirsty, let him come to me" '?

356 To whom was the letter addressed from the Council at Jerusalem described in Acts 15?

357 What passage in the New Testament appears to support the tradition that Mark was a follower of Peter?

358 What clues are given in Acts as to the date when Paul was first in Corinth?

359 What action of Paul's at Lystra apparently contradicts his teaching that the authority of the Law had been destroyed by Christ?

360 How many visits did Paul pay to Corinth (a) according to Acts (b) according to the evidence of his letters?

PROFESSOR A. R. C. LEANEY, MA, DD: formerly Department of Theology, University of Nottingham.

General Knowledge 7

361 In what type of space capsule did John Glen first circle the earth?

362 It was owned by the Barberini family until 1780, smashed by a maniac in 1845, repaired and is now owned by the nation. What is it?

363 In which city would you find the Jacques Cartier Bridge?

364 *Pulex irritans* is a parasitic insect. What is it more commonly known as?

365 Osborne Henry Mavor was a Scottish author. Under what pseudonym did he write?

366 At the time of Edward VIII's abdication, who was Prime Minister?

367 As an expert in excavating and tunnelling, this Australian animal stands supreme. What is it called?

368 What did the Polish corridor give to Poland after the first World War?

369 'The better part of valour is discretion.' Who said this?

370 If you lapidated someone, what would you be doing to them?

371 What 20th-century war did the Treaty of Portsmouth end?

372 In astronomy, what is an Occultation?

373 What is the name of the Moorish palace in Granada which is named after the Arabic word for *the red*?

374 Of whom was it said: 'He will be looked upon by posterity as a brave, bad man'?

375 Across which city does the statue of Christ on the Corcovado look?

376 Which battle in 1882 marked the beginning of British occupation in Egypt?

377 The Royal Standard is divided into quarters. The first and fourth contain three lions passant, the second the lion rampant, what is the third?

378 She became famous with her writings on proper behaviour and good manners. One of her books was entitled *Etiquette*. Who was she?

379 Describe the European flag.

380 What was the original name for the Royal Albert Hall?

The Works of Dorothy L. Sayers

Set by Julian Symons

381 What is the motto of the Wimsey family?

382 Give the full name of the man who wrote a short biography of Lord Peter Wimsey.

383 What were Lord Peter's clubs, as mentioned in his *Who's Who* entry?

384 In one book Dorothy Sayers had a collaborator. What was his name?

385 What was the name of Harriet Vane's chief defence counsel?

386 What was Sir Impey's hobby?

387 Who gave away Harriet Vane at her marriage?

388 What happened to the Warden immediately after the marriage?

389 According to Bunter's letter to his wife, how long had he been in Lord Peter's service at the time of the marriage?

390 At the marriage, what was the bride's gift to the groom?

391 Who capped a Wordsworth quotation of Lord Peter's by another from the same poet?

392 'Tell Bunter to give you a bottle of the . . . , it's rather decent,' Lord Peter says to Parker. What was the wine?

393 Where did Lord Peter and Miss Tarrant go to dinner?

394 What was the address of Lord Peter's bachelor flat?

395 Lord Peter called it 'The case of cases, the murder without discernible means, or motive, or clue'. What book gives an account of it?

396 To what murderer does Lord Peter say that he's a decent fellow, and that 'in your place I know what I should do'?

397 What was the subject of Miss Lydgate's forthcoming work?

398 What happened to the manuscript introduction to the work, which she lent to Harriet Vane?

399 Who is written to as 'Darling Old Bungie, old thing', in what book?

400 How did Dr Waters describe the cause of a case of muscarine poisoning?

JULIAN SYMONS: Well-known critic and detective novelist; author of *The Detective Novel*.

Norse Mythology
Set by Professor Peter G. Foote

401 What is the name of Thor's hammer?

402 Which god was born of nine mothers?

403 Who was the blind god, and for what is he chiefly famous?

404 Which goddess owned the necklace called Brisinga-men?

405 What weapon did Freyr use against the giant Beli (Bell-i)?

406 Which tree is called the 'salvation of Thor'?

407 What was Draupnir and what its peculiar virtue?

408 Why does one associate the number eight with Sleipnir (Slaypneer) and Starkath (or Starkather)?

409 For what benefits did people invoke the god Njorth(ur) (Nyorth(er))?

410 What was made of the blood of Kvasir mixed with honey?

411 What was Naglfar (Naggle-far) supposed to be made of, and who steers it at the Doom of the Gods?

412 What did Thor do to the dwarf Lit(ur) (Litt(er)) after Baldur's death?

413 Who was called the 'god of hanged men' and why?

414 How did Loki (Lokki) rescue Ithunn and her apples from the giants?

415   Thokk (or perhaps Loki in disguise) said: 'Let Hel
      keep what she has' – what did Hel have?

416   Why could a poet call a shield 'the seat of the soles of
      Hrungnir's feet'?

417   What did Othin first gain from his self-immolation?

418   In early poetry Hlin (Hleen) appears as a name of
      Frigg. Who does Snorri say Hlin was?

419   What is the main difference between Baldur in
      Snorri's Edda and Balderus in Saxo's Gesta
      Danorum?

420   We are told a heathen oath was: 'So help me
      Njorth(ur) (Nyorth(er)) and Freyr and the almighty
      one of the AEsir (Ayseer)'. Why do some scholars
      think this contains evidence of Christian influence?

PROFESSOR PETER FOOTE: Professor of Old Scandinavian
and Director of Scandinavian Studies, University College
London. Secretary, Viking Society, Chevalier, Icelandic
Order of the Falcon. Author: *The Viking Achievement*, etc.

General Knowledge 8

421 Whom did Jenny von Westphalen marry?

422 Which French town housed the British Army Headquarters between 1914 and 1916?

423 Kipling wrote: 'Let us admit it fairly, as a business people should, we have had no end of a lesson'. What was the lesson?

424 In Greek legend King Minos of Crete demanded yearly payment. What was this payment?

425 What are the Latin words often used to express the meanings: (a) word for word (b) letter for letter?

426 How many operas comprise the Ring Cycle?

427 He was a French astrologer, consulted among others by Catherine de'Medici. Who was he?

428 In Roman myth, who opened the gates of heaven every morning for the Sun God Apollo?

429 Who was the designer of the airship R 100?

430 In the history of New Orleans in America three flags have flown over the city on different occasions. Of what nationalities were they?

431 Who, according to legend, was the second wife of Priam and mother of Hector, Paris and Cassandra, among others?

432 Who led the Chetniks in their war-time Resistance movement?

433 The Egyptian god Anubis had the head of an animal. Which animal?

434 He developed his own theory of analytical psychology, and wrote *Modern Man in Search of a Soul*. Who was he?

435 By whom was Erithacus rubecula murdered?

436 A horse's height is measured from the ground – to what point?

437 For what kind of art is Roy Lichtenstein famous?

438 Who was the only British king of the House of Saxe-Coburg?

439 'The eternal mystery of the world is its comprehensibility.' Who said this?

440 Cesare Borgia was the favourite son of his father. Who was his father?

Railways of Great Britain

Set by Ian Allan

441 What is the wheel arrangement of a 'Mikado'-type locomotive?

442 Until recently there were four terminal stations in Glasgow. What were they?

443 Which was the *number* of the last steam locomotive to be built by BR?

444 The locomotive 'King George' is still operating. What was its BR running number?

445 Another GWR locomotive named 'Lloyds' had an unusual number. What was it?

446 What is the longest station platform in Great Britain?

447 What is the function of a short-armed signal with horizontal red, white and red stripes surmounted by the letter 'C'?

448 On what voltage does the London Midland Southport electric service operate?

449 What does the term 'Syphon G' mean to you?

450 Two lines which might be termed 'Underground' railways are operated by BR. What are they?

451 The former 'Southern Electric' system was developed under a famous General Manager. Who?

452 There was once a regular through service from Windsor to Victoria. What route did it take?

453 BR operate several shipping services but only one is inland. Where does it operate from?

454 What is the horse power of a Class AL5 electric locomotive?

455 Pontypridd used to be an important junction on the former GWR but what was the original owning Company?

456 What is an 'RKB'?

457 A specific locomotive was allocated to haul Southern Railway's royal trains. What was its number and class?

458 Midland Railway operated a mineral line from Whatstandwell, trains being hauled for part of their journey by cable. What was it called?

459 At which station in Birmingham do express trains from Paddington arrive?

460 What is the most northerly station on BR?

IAN ALLAN: Publisher of magazines and books on railways and other transport subjects.

British Chemical Industry

Set by Dr T. F. West

461 Which party leader has worked as a research chemist in industry?

462 Which class of compounds are polymers (e.g. polyethylene) made from?

463 What is the main use of an alkyl benzene sulphonate?

464 Which two companies, besides BP and Esso, produce ethylene in the UK?

465 At which stage in oil refining is paraffin wax produced?

466 Which chemical name is abbreviated in the letters DDT?

467 Which valuable chemical is produced with phenol by the cumene route?

468 What significance have the letters ASP?

469 What is a 'sniff gas' or 'tail gas'?

470 Who discovered the polyester fibre given the trade-name 'Terylene'?

471 One of the main uses of ethylene glycol is antifreeze. What is another?

472 Which are the principal elements present in most chemical fertilisers?

473 Which class of organic chemicals may be added to give odour to natural gas?

474 Why has Tobias acid replaced 2-naphthylamine in making dyes?

475 What is 'ullage'?

476 From which naturally occurring mixture is argon derived?

477 Which has the higher boiling point, ethyl alcohol or methyl ethyl ketone?

478 What are 'bottoms' or 'heel'?

479 Which chemicals are the raw materials for the production of urea?

480 Which is the principal chemical that can be made by the Wulff Process?

DR T. F. WEST: Editor-in-Chief, Society of Chemical Industry.

General Knowledge 9

481 Who said: 'Some books are to be tasted, others to be swallowed, and some few to be chewed and digested'?

482 Which race of people is considered to be the tallest in the world?

483 The Queen's Awards to Industry are announced each year – when?

484 On what type of camera would you expect to find Parallax Compensation?

485 The object of Snoopy's fantasies, who was the Red Baron?

486 Who, in legend, was the father of the Nine Muses?

487 Who was the first of the Lancastrian Kings?

488 A Phoenician goddess, she was the legendary founder of Carthage. Who was she?

489 What famous porcelain is marked with crossed swords?

490 Who, according to Greek myth, created Pandora, the first mortal woman?

491 Who was the husband of Corretta Scott?

492 What are the 'White Horses' of Westbury and Uffington?

493 What fish would you be eating if you were given Brochet au Beurre Blanc?

494 The Spanish Government moves from Madrid to which city during the summer months?

495 In the Morse Code, what combination comprises the letter 'O'?

496 In Greek mythology, which king outwitted death?

497 Captain Cook discovered the Hawaiian Islands. What were they originally called?

498 According to Lord Byron, 'who kill'd John Keats'?

499 'Arnolfini and his Wife' is a famous painting by whom?

500 Which of the Gorgons in Greek mythology was the only mortal?

Famous Russians

Set by Professor R. E. F. Smith

501 Who organised the 'Oprichnina'?

502 Who is said to have opened a window on to Europe?

503 What Russian anarchist prince spent much of his life in England?

504 Who propounded a theory of realistic acting?

505 Who said 'I know nothing more beautiful than the "Appassionata", I could hear it every day'?

506 Who was the first Soviet Commissar of Education?

507 What famous composer was a relative of Molotov?

508 Who proposed a 'new model for the universe'?

509 Name the first Romanov on the throne of Russia.

510 What polymath developed new techniques for making glass and challenged the 'Norman' theory of Russia's origins?

511 Who is the Russian author of stories about the Don Cossacks who was awarded the Nobel Prize for Literature in 1965?

512 Who almost toppled Catherine the Great from the throne?

513 Who was director (and principal playwright) of the first permanent Russian theatre?

514 What lawyer became a leader of modern abstract painting?

515 What icon painter has given his name to a recent film?

516 Who wrote *From the other shore*?

517 What Russian poet married Isadora Duncan?

518 What Russian poet married the daughter of Mendeléyev?

519 What Russian general committed suicide early in World War I?

520 Who invented 'pan-geometry'?

PROFESSOR R. E. F. SMITH: Department of Russian Language and Literature, University of Birmingham.

Geography of Great Britain
Set by Trevor Marchington

521 What are clints?

522 What is the highest peak in England and Wales?

523 Where is the Fylde?

524 What is a sarsen stone?

525 Which city is located at Latitude 53° 58″ North, Longitude 1° 5′ West?

526 What is a bourne?

527 What is Ordnance Datum?

528 Which National Park was Britain's first?

529 Name five of the crofting counties.

530 What significance had the Whin Sill for the Romans?

531 What have these places in common – Wylfa, Trawsfynyd, Hunterston?

532 What do the letters C.B.D. stand for?

533 What is the Helm wind?

534 What is the most westerly point of the mainland of Great Britain?

535 What is the Caledonian trend?

536 What is Kentish Rag?

537 What would you drive along the Parallel Roads of Glen Roy?

538   Which British landowner owns the largest acreage?

539   What does I.B.G. stand for?

540   On what map projection does the Ordnance Survey
       base the National Grid?

TREVOR MARCHINGTON, MA: Senior Lecturer in Geography,
Shoreditch College.

General Knowledge 10

541   Mass suicide is said to have ended the defence by the zealots of which fortress?

542   What is the largest extant rodent in the world?

543   It was double-headed for Russia and Austria, single-headed for Germany. What is it?

544   To what did the Reverend Sydney Smith refer when he said, 'It is as though St Paul's had gone down to the sea, and pupped'?

545   Which English queen bore her husband fifteen children?

546   Who was the Archbishop of Canterbury at the time of King Edward VIII's abdication?

547   On what day is the October Revolution celebrated?

548   Which is the city that Lord Byron, having spent 23 days there, described as, 'my country! city of the soul!'?

549   What is the unit of currency used in Israel?

550   Eton College was founded by which monarch?

551   Alberto Santos-Dumont in 1901 won 100,000 francs for a flying achievement. What was it?

552   Its headquarters are now at Aubagne but used to be at Sidi-bel-Abbes. What is it?

553   What did the Bishop of Ely establish in 1284?

554   Where would you find the Gatun Lake, the Gaillard Cut and the Miraflores Locks?

555 Which British University was the first to admit women to degrees?

556 'How many divisions has the Pope?' is a saying that has been attributed to whom?

557 Winston Churchill and Franklin Roosevelt met on board ship in August 1941. What was the result of their meeting?

558 What did the Redcliffe-Maud Commission inquire into?

559 $MgSO_47H_2O$ is the chemical formula of something you can drink or bathe in. It was named after a town in England. What is this substance?

560 What is the noun of assembly for goldfinches?

English Literature

Set by Boswell Taylor

561 Who was the poet laureate who once declared:
'I must go down to the seas again, to the lonely sea
and the sky'?

562 Who was the early English scholar who composed
'The Ecclesiastical History of the English Race'?

563 What name is Dr Johnson said to have given to the
school of poets among whom are George Herbert,
Henry Vaughan and John Donne?

564 Who wrote:
'No longer mourn for me when I am dead
Than you shall hear the surly sullen bell'?

565 Who was the Professor of Latin at Cambridge who
called himself 'The Shropshire Lad'?

566 What was the work of George Chapman that inspired
one of our greatest sonnets?

567 Where did J. M. Synge find his setting for *Playboy
of the Western World*?

568 What was the title of John Bunyan's spiritual
autobiography?

569 Who is the Jesuit poet who was not 'discovered' until
nearly thirty years after his death in 1889?

570 Who dedicated a number of poems to Lucasta . . .
going beyond the Seas, going to the Wars?

571 Who was the poet who dedicated love poems to
'Jean', 'Mary' and also 'Bonnie Lesley'?

572 What is the 'scene' referred to in these famous lines
by Marvell:
                    'He nothing common did or mean
                    Upon that memorable scene'?

573 Who is the king who plays a big part in Scott's
Quentin Durward?

574 Who is the seventeenth-century philosopher who
wrote the classic 'An Essay Concerning Human
Understanding'?

575 What was the 'domestic horror', to quote Walter
Pater, that affected the life and work of
Charles Lamb?

576 Who was the poetess sister of Dante Gabriel Rossetti?

577 Who was the mathematics tutor who wrote *Leviathan*,
a book concerned with political theory?

578 What is the name of Prospero's island in
The Tempest?

579 Who is the author whose formula for the novel was
'Make 'em laugh, make 'em cry, make 'em wait'?

580 What was the Gothic novel written by Shelley's wife?

History of Music
Set by Professor Ivor Keys

581 Which Beethoven symphony was originally dedicated to Napoleon?

582 How many instruments are needed to perform Bach's Italian Concerto?

583 Who was the 'London' Bach?

584 What was the profession of Mozart's father?

585 Who was Bach's Musical Offering offered to?

586 What is the name of the sequel to the Fantastic symphony?

587 Who was Figaro's mother?

588 What composer wrote piano pieces called 'Chopin' and 'Paganini'?

589 What Weber opera has an original English libretto?

590 What orchestra was called 'an army of generals'?

591 In what other opera does Mozart quote Figaro?

592 What was Schubert's second Christian name?

593 Who wrote the music *Rule Britannia*?

594 What is the 'hateful colour' in Schubert's *Fair Maid of the Mill*?

595 Whose victory is celebrated in Beethoven's so-called Battle Symphony?

596 What is the connection between Handel and Gibraltar?

597 What work of Berlioz employs gunpowder?

598 What composer was nicknamed the Red Priest?

599 What work is inscribed thus: 'It comes from the heart: may it go to the heart'?

600 What Mozart air has piano variations by Chopin?

PROFESSOR IVOR KEYS: Department of Music, The Barber Institute of Fine Arts, Birmingham University.

General Knowledge 11

601 Which Abbey became the main meeting place for the Hell Fire Club?

602 Who wrote the brilliant pamphlet (in 1835) entitled *Vindication of the English Constitution*?

603 After what battle did Brutus commit suicide?

604 The Acropolis in Athens literally means what?

605 If you were at a meeting of SALT, what would you be discussing?

606 What are the three stanzas on which the Pindaric Ode is built?

607 What city besides Pompeii was overwhelmed in the earthquake of AD 79?

608 Whose daughter was 'The Fair Rosamund'?

609 What was the name of the flying island in *Gulliver's Travels*?

610 What is the inscription on the reverse of the Military Medal?

611 How many dimes would you get in exchange for an American dollar?

612 The name 'Irene' comes from the Greek. What does it mean?

613 What are pelagic animals?

614 What island is separated from the mainland by the Swale?

615 Why was 46 BC known as 'The year of confusion'?

616 What is the Binney Award?

617 Gainsborough painted the 'Blue Boy'. Who painted the 'Red Boy'?

618 Who collaborated with Alfred Binet in devising the first scales for measuring intelligence?

619 In the Greek alphabet A is alpha, what is E?

620 For what crimes did Oedipus blind himself?

Personalities in Russian History and the Arts

Set by Professor F. M. Borras

621 Ivan the Terrible co-operated with a group of clergy and boyars. Give its name.

622 What was the fate of the Zemsky Sobor?

623 Define the Time of Troubles.

624 Where did Peter the Great lay the foundations of the Russian capital, St Petersburg?

625 What decisive law did Peter the Great promulgate in the year 1722?

626 Who was Alexander Danilovich Menshikov?

627 What was Catherine the Great's most powerful ambition concerned with the British Empire?

628 Who was the leader of the so-called Russian parody of the Protestant reformation?

629 What were the principal aims of the Decembrist Revolution?

630 What was especially significant about the day upon which Alexander II was assassinated?

631 Who inspired the reactionary policies of Alexander III and what was his title?

632 Who suggested the name for the Revolutionary Party, the Socialist Revolutionaries?

633 Which of Pushkin's works of fiction were used as the basis for operas by Tchaikovsky?

634 What reply did Gogol's *Selected Passages from Correspondence with my Friends* evoke from a Russian critic?

635 With whom does Bazarov, Turgenev's Nihilist hero, fight a duel in *Fathers and Sons*?

636 Which Russian writer wrote a Memoir of two others whom he knew well in the Crimea?

637 In which novel does Dostoevsky describe the pretence that he was to be executed?

638 Who resigned from the Academy of Sciences upon the Tsar's rejection of Gorky's election to it?

639 Who was awarded the Nobel Prize for Literature while in exile?

640 Which Russian writer's obituary appeared twice in *The Times*?

PROFESSOR F. M. BORRAS: Head of the Department of Russian Studies, Leeds University.

English Cathedrals

Set by Professor J. G. Davies

641 Who was responsible for the foundation of Salisbury cathedral?

642 What was Paul's Walk?

643 In which cathedral is there a tablet commemorating Nurse Cavell?

644 On the west façade of one cathedral there are statues of eleven kings from William the Conqueror to Edward III. Which cathedral is it?

645 In which cathedral is there a font of Tournai marble depicting three scenes from the life of St Nicholas of Myra?

646 Who was the architect of the Anglican cathedral in Liverpool?

647 In which cathedral is the tomb of King John (d. 1216)?

648 On the tomb on King John there is a carving of a lion biting the end of a sword. To what is this said to refer?

649 Legend has it that after the murder of St Ethelbert by Offa of Mercia (c. 794), his ghost demanded burial in a certain place which is now the site of a cathedral. Which cathedral is it?

650 Which English cathedral is also a college chapel?

651 For what order of monks was Rochester cathedral originally built?

652 In St Alban's cathedral there is a watching loft. What was it used for?

653 Which cathedral of medieval origin has neither triforium nor clerestory?

654 Which cathedral is dedicated to St Saviour?

655 In which part of Canterbury cathedral was Thomas à Becket murdered?

656 High up on the wall of the nave is carved a grotesque face to scare away demons from spying on the monks. In which cathedral is it to be found?

657 In which cathedral is there a chantry chapel decorated with owls?

658 What is the position of the bishop's chair in Norwich cathedral?

659 Who designed the stained-glass window by the font in the new Coventry cathedral?

660 Where is the earliest example of fan-vaulting?

PROFESSOR J. G. DAVIES, MA, DD: Institute for the Study of Worship and Religious Architecture, University of Birmingham.

General Knowledge 12

661 Tallinn is its largest city and capital. What is the name of this state?

662 Who succeeded Vic Feather as General Secretary of the Trades Union Council?

663 He was a Scholastic Theologian born in 1225, known as Doctor Angelicus. Who was he?

664 Which family holds the hereditary right to the Office of Earl Marshal of England?

665 Which Italian premier signed the armistice with the Allies in 1943?

666 From which century are the Paston Letters?

667 Sir Winston Churchill was a war correspondent during the South African war. For which paper did he write?

668 Where was King Arthur taken after he was mortally wounded?

669 Lord Frederick Cavendish and Thomas Henry Burke were assassinated. What has this tragedy become known as?

670 Who was the sculptor responsible for the lions at the base of Nelson's Column in Trafalgar Square?

671 Des Moines is the capital of which American State?

672 What sea does the Volga empty into?

673 Thomas Moore's poem 'Meeting of the Waters' immortalised which village?

674 Who was the Greek philosopher who believed that only atoms and empty space exist?

675 Which is the largest of the Trucial States?

676 What was the name of Shylock's wife?

677 He was British Commandant of the Arab Legion's Desert Patrol between 1939 and 1956. Who is he?

678 In which of Shakespeare's plays would you find Costard, a clown?

679 Who created the gardens at Versailles?

680 Bernard Shaw wrote the part of Eliza Doolittle especially for which actress?

British Church Architecture
Set by Bruce Allsopp

681 Of what period is a lancet window typical?

682 What is Boston Stump?

683 What is a porticus?

684 Who was the architect of St Martin-in-the-Fields, Trafalgar Square, London?

685 Where are the earliest existing ribbed high vaults in England?

686 What Anglo-Saxon church tower has a helm roof?

687 Which cathedral has a free-standing tower on the north side?

688 What is the literal meaning of 'basilica'?

689 Who was the designer of the nave of Canterbury Cathedral?

690 What is the chapter house of Southwell Minster specially famous for?

691 Which cathedral has an octagonal timber lantern over the crossing?

692 Who designed the stained-glass windows behind the high altar of St Paul's Cathedral, London?

693 Who was the architect of Westminster Cathedral?

694 What church imitated in its structural form an up-turned Viking ship?

695 What is a mason's mitre?

696 St Wilfred was said to have built the largest church
   north of the Alps. Where?

697 What are 'commissioners' churches'?

698 What connection is there between St Mary's
   Cathedral, Newcastle-upon-Tyne, and a hansom cab?

699 Who was the architect of St Giles-in-the-Fields,
   Holborn, London?

700 What is an arch-lintel?

BRUCE ALLSOPP: Reader in the History of Architecture,
University of Newcastle-upon-Tyne.

Grand Opera

Set by Harold Rosenthal

701 How did Covent Garden Opera House get its name?

702 What was the Shakespearian opera Verdi wanted to write all his life, but never actually got round to doing?

703 Who completed Puccini's *Turandot* after the composer had died?

704 What was the 'Grand Boutique'?

705 On whom did Wagner base the character of Beckmesser in *The Mastersingers*?

706 What is verismo?

707 When the *Ring* had its first performance at Covent Garden in 1892, conducted by Mahler, it was not given in the correct order. Why was this?

708 In what opera do we meet the stage manager of the Comédie Française?

709 The characters Manrico, Florestan and Don Alvaro share three things in common – what are they?

710 Name a famous singer who collapsed and died on stage during a performance.

711 What is the difference between opéra comique (without a hyphen) and opéra-comique with a hyphen?

712 During the première of which famous opera did a cat walk across the stage?

713 Who wrote the libretto for Verdi's *Otello*?

714 Which opera is based on Ben Jonson's *Epicoene*?

715 Which was the first opera of Verdi?

716 What do the Puccini Mimi, Tosca and Butterfly all have in common – besides, of course, being sopranos and the heroines of their respective operas?

717 The title of one of Verdi's familiar operas is mentioned by one of the characters in a very well-known opera by Mozart. What are the two operas?

718 Who are known as La Stupenda and La Superba?

719 In Tchaikovsky's *The Queen of Spades* the old Countess sings a little song by another composer – who?

720 Who taught Walther von Stolzing how to sing?

HAROLD ROSENTHAL: Editor of *Opera*.

General Knowledge 13

721 What was Operation Dynamo in the Second World War?

722 Name one of the Angevin Kings of England.

723 In which calendar would the year 1974 be numbered 1394?

724 Which country was the first to open a scheduled passenger air service?

725 Which one-act ballet is set in a toy-shop?

726 This British Prime Minister entered the House of Commons as MP for Limehouse in 1922. Who was he?

727 What Bishop (in 1654) placed the date of the Creation in 4004 BC?

728 When offered his freedom his answer was always the same: 'If you set me free today, I will preach again tomorrow'. Who was he?

729 Which Greek philosopher is said to be the founder of the atomic theory?

730 Ships are warned of rocks to the west of Alderney in the Channel Islands by a lighthouse. Which one?

731 In 1866 William Steinitz became a world champion. Of what?

732 From what kind of animal is rennet obtained?

733 Who was the American actor who turned film director and was responsible for the two three-hour silent epics – *The Birth of a Nation* and *Intolerance*?

734 Name the smallest of Switzerland's Cantons.

735 What was the title of the opera Berlioz based on Shakespeare's *Much Ado About Nothing*?

736 The old halfpenny coin had a ship on the reverse side. Which famous ship inspired this design?

737 What do the initials B.M.E.W.S. stand for?

738 In what year in the 19th century did Europe see widespread revolutions?

739 On which island is Fingal's Cave?

740 By what is the Great Ape Pongo Pygmaeus commonly known?

History of World Theatre

Set by Simon Trussler

741 Who is the odd-man-out among these four famous
Greek dramatists: Aeschylus, Aristophanes,
Euripides, Sophocles?

742 Name the *two* dramatists who have written the best-
known plays concerning the Faust Legend.

743 Who wrote *An Enemy of the People*?

744 Name the two Elizabethan actors who were
responsible for the collection of Shakespeare's plays
into the First Folio of 1723.

745 Name the dramatist whose political satires prompted
the passing of the Licensing Act of 1737, which
imposed the Lord Chamberlain's censorship over
stage plays.

746 Name the play by J. M. Synge which provoked a riot
at its first performance at Dublin's Abbey Theatre
in 1907.

747 Whose theoretical writings *originated* the recently-
revived concept of a 'theatre of cruelty'.

748 Who wrote the music for Bertolt Brecht's *The
Threepenny Opera*?

749 To which equally famous actor is the French actress
Madeleine Renaud married?

750 Which play 'made Gay rich and Rich gay'?

751 Who wrote *Waiting for Lefty*?

752· Which recently-opened London theatre is named
after a famous Irish playwright?

753 Which member of a famous theatrical family made his first appearance in 1921 as the Herald in *Henry V*, and was knighted in 1953?

754 What is the name of the American experimental theatre group directed since its formation in 1947 by Julian Beck and Judith Malina?

755 Name two of the four English towns whose cycles of medieval mystery plays have survived more or less intact.

756 Which were the two London theatres whose 'letters patent' theoretically entitled them to a monopoly of 'straight plays' until 1843?

757 Which pop singer appeared at the Old Vic in 1960 as Tony Lumpkin in Goldsmith's *She Stoops to Conquer*?

758 Who was the first Artistic Director of the English Stage Company at the Royal Court Theatre after its formation in 1956?

759 What are the *christian names* of the Italian actor and playwright brothers, De Filippo?

760 The memoirs of probably the best-known of English pantomime clowns were edited by Charles Dickens. Who was he?

SIMON TRUSSLER: editor, *Oxford Companion of the Theatre*.

19th-Century English History

Set by John D. Bareham

761 Which Act made the Secret Ballot effective and prevented electoral corruption?

762 Which Prime Minister died in office at the age of almost 81?

763 Which British subject, born a Portuguese Jew, made claims against the Greek Government in 1849-50?

764 Approximately how much money did the Whig Education Grant of 1833 make available to Church School Societies?

765 Who was Gladstone's Secretary for War who carried through a series of Army Reforms?

766 What were the three 'Fs' of the Irish?

767 At what rate did Peel levy his reintroduced income tax?

768 What clause in 1870 gave parents the right to withdraw children from prayers and scripture lessons in schools?

769 Explain the initials G.O.M. and M.O.G. used for Gladstone.

770 Which Minister was largely responsible for the detail of the many basic social reform acts of 1875-6?

771 What were the contents of the 'Extraordinary Black Book' of 1831?

772 Which writer spread the idea from 1859 that by thrift and hard work any moral person could rise to eminence?

773 Who remained Commander-in-Chief of the British Army for 40 years?

774 Which corporation remained unreformed throughout the 19th century?

775 Whom did Disraeli describe as 'an old, painted pantaloon, very deaf, very blind . . . '?

776 What was the main function of local party organisations down to 1914?

777 What important census was held in 1851 in addition to the normal ten-yearly one?

778 Which English novelist held official positions in South Africa in 1875–9, and hoisted the Union Jack over Pretoria in 1879?

779 Which historian claimed that the English had colonised half the world 'in a fit of absence of mind'?

780 Which Company sent the Government a bill for over £500 after the 1848 Chartist disturbances?

JOHN D. BAREHAM, BA: Head of History and Economic History Sections, Exeter College.

The Iliad and the Odyssey

Set by Dr Wolfgang Liebeschuetz

781 Who was the first man to shelter the returned Odysseus in Ithaca?

782 Why is the Iliad so named?

783 Who was the Gerenian horseman?

784 Who was forced to kiss the hands that had slain his sons?

785 By what sign did Eurycleia recognise Odysseus?

786 What topic is announced at the beginning of the Iliad?

787 What was the effect of the Cyclops Polyphemus' cursing of Odysseus?

788 What way of life did Achilles consider the most miserable on earth?

789 What was the shape adopted by Athene and Apollo to watch Hector challenging the Greeks?

790 Which hero compared the generations of men to the leaves of trees?

791 The son of a hero was frightened by his father wearing a helmet. Name the boy.

792 The Trojan war might have been stopped as a result of a duel between Menelaus and Paris. Which Trojan prevented this?

793 Two extremely happy men wailed like vultures whose young have been taken from the nest. Who were they?

794 Which god was most hateful to Zeus?

795   What was the name of the horse which foretold Achilles' death?

796   What was a hippocampus?

797   Name the American scholar who proved that the *Iliad* and *Odyssey* are oral compositions.

798   Ajax's shield 'like a tower' could shelter an archer behind it. When were such shields used in Greece?

799   A line of battle is described as 'a hedge of spears and shields, buckler to buckler, helmet to helmet ...' (*Iliad, XIII*, 130–5). When were these tactics introduced in Greece?

800   Who is the divine messenger in the *Iliad*?

DR WOLFGANG LIEBESCHUETZ: Department of Classics, Leicester University.

General Knowledge 14

801 What was the non-military role of Admiral Horthy?

802 Darwin was a scientist on board the *Beagle*. Who was the famous biologist who served as a medical officer on *HMS Rattlesnake*?

803 According to legend where were the Kings of Ireland crowned?

804 Electrical resistance is measured by the ohm. What unit measures the reciprocal of resistance, which is conductance?

805 Born in Paris in 1908, she won the Prix Goncourt with her novel *The Mandarins*. Who is she?

806 Voltaire's character Candide witnessed the execution of an Admiral. Upon which real event was this based?

807 In the play *Who's Afraid of Virginia Woolf* George was the husband. Who was the wife?

808 Who were 'the great Twin Brothers to whom all Dorians pray'?

809 Who was responsible for the building of the Pantheon in Rome?

810 Of what nationality was Malthus, the theorist on population?

811 What is marzipan made of?

812 Where is the GPO communications satellite/earth station which relayed the first television pictures by satellite?

813 Who was the poet who perfected 'Sprung' and 'Counterpoint' rhythms?

814 A famous allegory was written in Bedford gaol. What was the title?

815 Why was the awarding of the Scottish Cup withheld in 1908–9?

816 A useless piece of labour is sometimes called a 'Sisyphean task'. Why?

817 Her name is the title of an opera by Richard Strauss, a Jean Giraudoux play and a Michael Cacoyannis film. Who is she?

818 Which country administers the territory known as the Ross Dependency?

819 Who is the author of *King Solomon's Ring*?

820 Who was Freud's notable disciple who developed the concept of the birth trauma?

Classical Mythology

Set by Dr Wolfgang Liebeschuetz

821 Which day of the week includes the name of a Roman god?

822 Which god was described as the 'earth shaker'?

823 What was the name of the Cyclops blinded by Odysseus?

824 Where was Dido born?

825 What is a Dryad?

826 What mythological people lived on the island of Corfu?

827 Who was the hero who went mad outside Troy, slaughtering first a herd of sheep then himself?

828 Who was the muse of epic poetry?

829 He founded Thebes and was turned into a serpent. Give his name.

830 What was the origin of the Titans?

831 What is the title of a poem of Hesiod which describes the origin of the gods?

832 Apollo threw a discus and killed the boy he loved. Who was the boy?

833 An uncle fed his nephews' flesh to their father. Who was the father?

834 One of the seven heroes fleeing from Thebes was swallowed by the earth. What was his name?

835 Justice once lived among men. Later she fled and became a constellation. What is the name of this constellation?

836 Who was required to bring back from Hades a casket full of the beauty of Persephone?

837 A weaver wove the love-life of the gods. Who was this weaver who was turned into a spider?

838 What god had an oracle at Dodona?

839 Why was the mother of Dionysus reduced to ashes?

840 During a sacrifice girls wore saffron robes and pretended to be bears. Who was the goddess who was worshipped at this ceremony?

DR WOLFGANG LIEBESCHUETZ: Department of Classics, Leicester University.

Arthurian Literature

Set by T. A. Shippey

841 Which knight, in English sources, throws away Excalibur?

842 Which three knights of Arthur achieved the Holy Grail?

843 What name does Malory give to Arthur's mother?

844 At which battle did Arthur kill 960 of the enemy single-handed?

845 Who was Lucius Hiberius?

846 In which century did Geoffrey of Monmouth write the *History of the Kings of Britain*?

847 In which century did Saint Gildas write of the battle of Mount Badon?

848 Which knight struck the dolorous stroke that laid waste three Kingdoms?

849 What was the real name of the Green Knight who played at beheading with Sir Gawain?

850 What did Sir Erec or Sir Geraint forbid his wife to do?

851 Why did Sir Gawain swear revenge on Sir Lancelot to the death?

852 What animal caused by accident the last battle between Arthur and Mordred?

853 What was the relationship between Arthur and Mordred?

854 Which knight did Sir Lancelot fight without helmet or shield, and with his left hand behind his back?

855 If Arthur's sword was Calibeorn, and his shield Pridwen, what was the name of his spear?

856 In which poem are we told of a warrior: 'he glutted black ravens on the rampart of the fort, though he was not Arthur'?

857 Whose task was it to pursue the Questing Beast, or Beast Glatisant?

858 In a modern work King Arthur has to undergo an ordeal in the shape of a hawk. What is the ordeal?

859 In a tournament at Winchester Sir Lancelot wore a red sleeve embroidered with pearls. Whose was it?

860 In Tennyson's *Gareth and Lynette*, what is the secret of the Black Knight, Death?

T. A. SHIPPEY, MA: St John's College, Oxford.

General Knowledge 15

861 What is the famous work that followed the researches of a scientist on the Galapagos Islands?

862 His name was Joel Chandler Harris. What was the nom-de-plume he adopted when he told his stories about Brer Rabbit and Brer Fox?

863 Who was the reluctant American vice-presidential candidate who was described as 'the contrariest Missouri mule I've ever dealt with'?

864 What is the chemical element found in all proteins?

865 Who was the Swiss psychiatrist who gave his name to a personality test which directs the subject's attention to ink blots?

866 What is the bird that aroused Wordsworth to question whether it could be called a bird 'or but a wandering voice'?

867 There are some strange subjects for dictionaries. What was the subject of a dictionary compiled by Ambrose Bierce?

868 In British folk-lore, who was the monster slain by Beowulf?

869 An element has an atomic number of 26 and it has 30 neutrons. What is its atomic weight?

870 Two men shared the power in Russia for a time after Khrushchev fell. Who were they?

871 What is the name that housewives give to the substance that chemists call sodium hydroxide?

872 Who changed the misogynist Sultan Shahriyar and turned him into a happily married man, and by what means?

873 What is the acronym for light amplification by stimulated emission of radiation?

874 A symbol of atomic power stands on the place at the University of Chicago where man experimented with the control of atomic energy. Who sculpted this monument?

875 'Defenestration' was the old Bohemian custom that sparked off the Thirty Years War. What happened to the victim?

876 What are getting old when they are worn down to monadnocks and peneplanes?

877 What is the republic that was first a settlement following the landing of Jan van Riebeeck at Table Bay in 1652?

878 Who described Russia as 'a riddle, wrapped in a mystery, inside an enigma'?

879 Who is recorded as having said that 'no man but a blockhead ever wrote except for money'?

880 What is the disease that was sometimes known as St Anthony's fire?

Kings and Queens of England

Set by John D. Bareham

881   Which exiled English king was lent the Palace of
      St Germain-en-Laye by Louis XIV?

882   Which king suppressed Oldcastle and the Lollards?

883   What nickname is given to Queen Elizabeth I's last
      speech to a deputation from the House of Commons?

884   Name the two husbands of the Empress Matilda.

885   Which English king was buried under a cathedral
      tower which collapsed the next year?

886   What was the other nickname of Richard Coeur
      de Lion?

887   Where were Henry II and his queen buried?

888   What did Charles II offer the English Parliament in
      1649 in a vain attempt to save his father's life?

889   Which English king was said by his son to have
      'a gruff blue-water approach to all human problems'?

890   What 'wrestler' defeated Henry VIII in France
      in 1520?

891   Who was the mother of Charles II's illegitimate son,
      the Duke of Monmouth?

892   What is now considered most likely to have caused
      George III's so-called madness?

893   On what subject did Edward VII as Prince of Wales
      make his only full speech in the House of Lords?

894   What was Jane Grey's 'claim' to the English throne
      in 1553?

895 Who was Elizabeth I's 'little-black husband'?

896 On what first occasion after the death of Prince Albert did Victoria again dance the Valse?

897 Which English monarch attended more Cabinet meetings than any other?

898 What did William IV offer when the Houses of Parliament were destroyed by fire in 1833?

899 What is the meaning of 'porphyrogeniture'?

900 Which Plantagenet, according to Maurice Ashley, established the 'nucleus of a royal navy' by having galleys specially built?

JOHN D. BAREHAM, BA: Head of History and Economic History Sections, Exeter College.

Shakespeare's Plays

Set by Boswell Taylor

901   Who was the Shakespearian heroine who disguised herself as Ganymede, after 'Jove's own page'?

902   Who described the Earl of Gloucester as 'the foul fiend Flibbertigibbet'?

903   Which play has 'Cupid and Amazons in the Masque' among its dramatis personae?

904   Whose servants are Nathaniel, Joseph, Nicholas, Philip, Walter and Sugarsop?

905   Of whom is Hamlet thinking when he says: 'Frailty, thy name is woman'?

906   Which play begins: 'In delivering my son from me, I bury a second husband'?

907   Who, at his life's end, played with flowers and smiled upon his fingers' ends?

908   In *Cymbeline*, what future is prophesied for Britain by the Soothsayer?

909   In *The Merchant of Venice*, of what was the casket made that bore the words: *Who chooseth me must give and hazard all he hath*?

910   Who was the father of Katharina and Bianca?

911   In which city is 'the moated Grange at St Luke's' a scene setting?

912˙   Who, when asked by royalty what he would eat, requested a peck of provender . . . good dry oats . . . and good hay, sweet hay?

913 In which play do we get the song 'Who is Sylvia?'

914 Who was 'a fellow of infinite jest, of most excellent fancy'?

915 Who declared that he was as 'pretty a piece of flesh as any in Messina' but wished that he 'had been writ down an ass!'?

916 What was the basket said to contain besides the asp that killed Cleopatra?

917 Who dies saying 'the rest is silence'?

918 Who was 'the fantastical Spaniard'?

919 What did Prince Hal call a 'polish'd perturbation! golden care!'?

920 What is Elbow in *Measure for Measure*?

ANSWERS
to questions in Book Two

General Knowledge 1

1 On the fourth day.

2 Antonine Wall.

3 Iceland. (The older of the two is the Elder (or Poetic) Edda written about 1270 and the other is Sronri Sturhuson's Younger (or Prose) Edda.)

4 Chief Sitting Bull of the Sioux, or Crazy Horse (they were joint leaders, but Sitting Bull was the medicine man and Crazy Horse the field leader. In 1876, better known as Custer's Last Stand).

5 Adonis.

6 Montevideo, Uruguay, 1930.

7 Mali, at the southern boundary of the Sahara.

8 Varieties of bricks.

9 American War of Independence (surrendered to the Americans at Yorktown in 1781).

10 Members of the Sioux Indian Tribe (Siege of Wounded Knee).

11 James Monroe (1758–1831).

12 Bleeding Heart.

13 John Prebble.

14 King Henry I (by the measurement from his nose to his thumb).

15 Jasper Petulengro.

16 Launching missiles (rocks). It was a siege engine.

17 Followers of (The Schoolman) Dune Scotus (*c.* 1265/1308). (The word 'Dunce' is derived from his birthplace, Dunse.)

18 Eight. (The programme has run for over 30 years and must be known to every listener in the land.)

19   The Furies (Erinyes or Eumenides).

20   George Bernard Shaw (*The Rejected Statement*, Part One).

Astronomy

21   Jupiter.

22   It always points more or less away from the Sun – so that when a comet is receding from the Sun it travels tail-first.

23   An eclipsing variable – sometimes, more properly, called an eclipsing binary. (Its apparent fluctuations of light are due to the fact that it is made up of two stars, revolving round their common centre of gravity; when the fainter star passes in front of the brighter, as happens every 2½ days, Algol seems to give a long, slow 'wink'.)

24   The *Mare Tranquillitatis*, or Sea of Tranquillity.

25   James Gregory. (*Not* Newton, who did however build the first reflector some years later. Gregory's pattern was rather different from Newton's, and Gregory never actually attempted the construction.)

26   Mercury and Venus (which are closer to the Sun than we are).

27   A quasar, which is beyond our Galaxy, whereas a pulsar is contained in our own Galaxy.

28   Mariner 10, in 1974.

29   Vesta. (Not the largest, which is Ceres. Only Vesta among the asteroids is ever visible with the naked eye.)

30   Halley's Comet.

31   It is either new or full.

32   The Perseids.

33   An F-type star is *yellowish*; a K-star, orange.

34 Titan, the largest satellite of Saturn. (The ground
    atmospheric pressure is probably about 100 mb., or
    ten times greater than that on the surface of Mars.)

35 The *Mare Serenitatis* (Sea of Serenity).

36 On Mars.

37 The Great Spiral in Andromeda – an external galaxy
    at a distance of 2.2 million light-years from us.

38 Ole Romer.

39 Neptune.

40 On Mercury. (This is a bright ray-crater, identified
    from the Mariner 10 pictures in March 1974.
    Dr Kuiper died in 1974.)

Legends of Britain

41 Brut or Brute or Brutus.

42 Troy. (Said to be the grandson of Aeneas of Troy.)

43 Merlin's.
    'She is not any common earth
    Water or wood or air,
    But Merlin's Isle of Gramarye
    Where you and I will fare.'
    (Gramarye meaning occult, magic (OED). From
    Sir Walter Scott, revived by him in 1740.)

44 Vortigern or Guorthigirnus or Wyrtgeorn (the first
    is the common pronunciation and spelling). (More
    legend than historical fact, but certainly well
    established as a legend. Vortigern was a Celtic king.
    Possibly invited Germans under Hengest to assist him
    against attacks. Said to have married Rowena,
    daughter of Hengest.)

45 He crossed running water.
    'So Maggie (the mare) runs, the witches follow . . .
    A runnin' stream they dare na cross . . . '

46 Guy of Warwick. (In *Guy of Warwick*, an English verse romance of the 14th century, Guy rescued King Athelstan from the Danes under Anlaf, defeating the Danish champion near Winchester.)

47 Peterborough.

48 A creature part seal, part man.

49 St Dunstan.

50 Havelock the Dane. (Hero of stories which appeared about 1290. After the death of his father, King Birkabeyn, the Earl of Godard ordered that Havelock should be drowned. A fisherman named Grim fled with the boy to England.)

51 Huntingdon.

52 Friar Bacon (and Friar Bungay). (In Robert Green's *Friar Bacon and Friar Bungay*. The friars are magicians. The 'brazen head' is destroyed by a mysterious power as soon as it attained to speech.)

53 A water-demon, usually in the shape of a horse.

54 Female cannibalistic hags and/or river spirits.

55 Pwyll. (The *Four Branches of Mabinogi* is a recognised source of Welsh legends. The first of the Four Branches tells the story of Pwyll.)

56 The Picts or Pechs.

57 Perthshire (at Fortingall). (Quoted in county histories, AA information sheets, etc. Fortingall yew cited in *Guinness Book of Records* as oldest tree in Britain.)

58 The Lambton Worm. (From a well-known north-east ballad. Lambton catches the Worm, the Worm escapes from the well, and in a final combat between the two, the Worm loses out.)

59 At Christmas.

60 Joseph of Arimathea. (Referred to by Malory and T. H. White. First introduced into medieval romances about 1200 by Robert de Borron.)

General Knowledge 2

61 Selene, the Greek moon-goddess who fell in love with the sleeping Endymion.

62 A compound of mercury (mercurous nitrate), which was used in the manufacture of felt hats; its effects could produce St Vitus's Dance and other symptoms. (Lewis Carroll only popularised the phrase; it is found earlier in Thackeray's *Pendennis* (in 1848) and earlier still in American literature.)

63 E. M. Forster (collaborated with Eric Crozier).

64 The Cor Anglais.

65 St James's Palace. (It became the official residence of the sovereign from 1698, when Whitehall Palace was destroyed by fire, until 1837 when Queen Victoria made Buckingham Palace the official residence.)

66 Shang (or Yin), *c.* 1766–*c.* 1123 BC. (Two royal houses earlier than the Shang have been mentioned – Yu and Hsia – but their historicity has not been determined.)

67 Nelson. (Then a Vice-Admiral, under the command of Sir Hyde Parker.)

68 Henry VII and Henry VIII. (This is also true of American packs.)

69 Jean Honoré Fragonard.

70 The Organisation of Latin American Solidarity (*Organizacion Latinoamericana de Solidaridad*). (Inspired by Castro, the movement aims to model the whole of South America on the Cuban pattern by revolution.)

71 William Makepeace Thackeray.

72 Winkles (periwinkles).

73 Tricoteuses. (Also, but less commonly, known as the Furies of the Guillotine.)

74 Alex Olmedo in 1959.

75 Forget-me-not (blue, pink or white flowers).

76 Six.

77 *Brief Encounter*.

78 Puddle Dock.

79 Sergei Eisenstein (made in the USSR in 1925).

80 French Guinea, which therefore became independent.

20th-Century British Politics

81 Andrew Bonar Law (23 October 1922 to 20 May 1923).

82 Mark Bonham Carter's win at Torrington
(27 March 1958).

83 17 years. (From the formation of the Campbell
Bannerman Liberal Government in December 1905
to the fall of his own government on 19 October 1922).

84 In May 1929, under the terms of the Representation
of the People Act of 1928.

85 Jim Griffiths (appointed by the new Labour
Government in October 1964).

86 Dr Robert McIntyre (elected in a by-election on
12 April 1945 and defeated in the general election
three months later).

87 Under a 1949 Act the industry was first nationalised
on 1 January 1951. It was denationalised in 1953 and
renationalised on 28 July 1967.

88 Philip Snowden, Chancellor of the Exchequer in the
newly formed National Government (on
21 September 1931).

89 1945. (When all obervers were assuming a Churchill
victory, the Gallup poll in the *News Chronicle* got
the Labour landslide in votes almost exactly right.)

90   Five. (Oldham 1899, Manchester 1908, Dundee 1922, Leicester 1923, Westminster (Abbey Division) 1924.)

91   David Lloyd George (in December 1916).

92   Sir Stafford Cripps on 4 February 1948.

93   It was the scene of a naval 'mutiny' in September 1931 in protest against pay reductions.

94   Permanent head of the treasury.

95   David Lloyd George (May 1915 to July 1916).

96   Harold Macmillan in 1958.

97   They were all represented by Conservative Prime Ministers (Baldwin, Eden, Heath).

98   1912 (£400 a year).

99   A judgement in 1901 that Trade Unions could be sued for damages caused by strikes. It was revenged by the Trades Disputes Act of 1906 but it gave impetus to the launching of the Labour party.

100 In 1910–11 the ditchers were those Conservative Peers who were prepared to die in the last ditch in the fight against cuts in the House of Lords powers. Those who were willing to compromise became known as the hedgers.

Science Fiction

101 The worst thing in the world: in this case, rats (George Orwell, *1984*).

102 Mercenary soldiers (Dickson, *Dorsai!*, etc.).

103 Brazil (John Wyndham & Lucas Parkes, *The Outward Urge*).

104 R – for Robot (Isaac Asimov, *The Caves of Steel*).

105 Luck: she was born lucky (Larry Niven, *Ringworld*).

106 Brian Aldiss's *Hothouse*.

107 Jack Vance's *The Dragon Masters*.

108 Bob Shaw (*Other Days, Other Eyes*).

109 Harry Harrison's *A Transatlantic Tunnel, Hurrah!*

110 Philip K. Dick's *The Man in the High Castle*.

111 He was 'the man who sold the moon' (Robert Heinlein, *The Man who Sold the Moon*).

112 Kimball Kinnison (Smith, *Gray Lensman*, etc.).

113 He was caught 'booklegging', i.e. smuggling books (Walter Miller, *A Canticle for Leibowitz*).

114 A. E. van Vogt's *Dormant*.

115 Murray Leinster (*S.O.S. from Three Worlds*, etc.).

116 Old North Australia, or Norstrilia (Cordwainer Smith, *Mother Hitton's Littul Kittons*).

117 A. C. Clarke's *Childhood's End*.

118 Kurt Vonnegut's *Cat's Cradle*.

119 The Aerial Board of Control.

120 Being used to living under 700 gravities, he assumed that all falls were fatal (Hal Clement, *Mission of Gravity*).

General Knowledge 3

121 The boundary between the Earth's crustal and mantle rocks. (The Earth's interior is divided into 3 chief layers: a liquid core, a surrounding mantle and a thin crust. The upper boundary of the mantle is thought to be the Mohorovičić Discontinuity, sometimes called the Moho, or M. Discovered in 1909 by Yugoslav seismologist A. Mohorovičić.)

122 Bernadette's vision of Our Lady.

123 Ralph Johnson Bunche in 1950.

124 *Graf Spee* (also called the *Admiral Graf Spee*. Scuttled off Montevideo on 17 December).

125 Ali Baba and the Forty Thieves. (First performed 1916.)

126 In a theatre (the side from which an artist receives a prompt – generally but not always on the right-hand side facing the audience).

127 Henry Green.

128 Four years.

129 German. (Georg Simon Ohm, who gave his name to the unit of electrical resistance.)

130 Sir John Lubbock (later Baron Avebury). He promoted the Bank Holidays Act, 1871.

131 Mandarin (Potonghua).

132 Hissarlik.

133 Singapore, by Lt-Gen. Percival.

134 Edinburgh Castle (made at Mons in Flanders).

135 Tycho Brahe.

136 Toltecs. (The Toltec civilisation was very much in decline at the beginning of the 12th century AD whilst the Aztecs were searching for a place to settle.)

137 Julian, a Roman Emperor, renounced his Christianity and adopted pagan beliefs.

138 A cable (or cable length). (The nautical mile is 6080 feet.)

139 Ra (sometimes Re or Phra). (Curiously there is another Sun God Ra, in Raiatea in Polynesia.)

140 Carapace. (Carapace is sometimes extended to the hard case investing the body in some other animals, e.g. certain Infusoria, a class of Protozoa.)

Gilbert and Sullivan

141 Angelina.

142 From: eggs, ham, mustard and cress, strawberry jam, (rollicking) bun, muffin, toast, Sally Lunn.

143 Sir Roderic Murgatroyd, who marries Dame Hannah.

144 (a) Legal, (b) aesthetic, (c) feminist.

145 Climbing over rocky mountains.

146 Belgrave Square and Seven Dials. (Sung by the Peers pleading their suit to Phyllis in *Iolanthe*.)

147 She married Colonel Fairfax, and was paid 100 crowns.

148 Sir Clarence Poltwhistle.

149 Marco marries Gianetta and Giuseppe marries Tessa.

150 The Royal English Opera House, later known as the Palace Theatre; the opera was *Ivanhoe*.

151 *Thespis*.

152 Left shoulder blade.

153 He falsified an income tax return, forged a will, shot a fox, forged a cheque and disinherited his unborn son.

154 It was a bank holiday.

155 Arac, Guron, Scynthius.

156 His sisters and his cousins and his aunts.

157 Stick close to your desks and never go to sea And you all may be Rulers of the Queen's Navy.

158 The Royal Bijou Theatre, Paignton.

159 The Opera Comique, 3 April 1880.

160 Captain Shaw of the London Fire Brigade.

Greek Mythology

161 Owl.

162 He was shot by Paris with Apollo guiding the arrow.

163 Argos.

164 Hephaestus.

165 She would prophesy truth but no one would believe it.

166 Aegisthus.

167 Pentheus.

168 Pan.

169 Danae.

170 The Centaurs had tried to rape the Lapiths' women.

171 Alcmena.

172 19 out of 50.

173 Philomela. (This is the usual version, but in one ancient author Philomela's sister Procne is transformed into a nightingale.)

174 So that his father, Cronos, should not hear his cries.

175 Bellerophon.

176 Ares.

177 Passiphae and a bull.

178 Water from a spring on Mount Helicon.

179 The island of Thera.

180 Eleusis.

General Knowledge 4

181 Whigs who rebelled against the Liberal Government's proposals for further Parliamentary reform in 1866.

182 A dog that pursues its quarry into the *earth* or *unearths* its prey. (From the Latin 'terra' = earth, via medieval Latin 'terrarius'.)

183 A celestial bull was sent to destroy him. (He was Gilgamesh.)

184 Edward H. Bailey.

185 Temple of Diana. (Excavations at Ephesus, between 1863 and 1874.)

186 In Izaak Walton's *The Compleat Angler*.

187 Iceland. (Ruled by Denmark until then.)

188 Sayonara. (Not to be confused with cyanide, which is good-bye in any language!)

189 Tolstoy's *War and Peace*.

190 1848.

191 'The Fates.' (Their names were Lachesis, Clotho, Atropos. Moirae was the Greek original, Parcae the Latin equivalent.)

192 Clydesdale, Shire, Suffolk, Percheron.

193 Botswana Republic.

194 Lewis Carroll's manuscript of *Alice's Adventures Underground*. (Later published with added material to make it twice the length as *Alice's Adventures in Wonderland*.)

195 Quinces. (Word derives from Portuguese 'marmelo' = quince.)

196 Cotton. (A Gin is a machine for separating cotton from its seeds.)

197 *Lord of the Rings* by J. R. R. Tolkien.

198 A stole (a narrow strip of silk or linen).

199 The rim of the wheel (the curved piece of wood which, joined with others, forms the rim).

200 George Hepplewhite.

British Ornithology

201 Wishbone or Merrythought.

202 Also called *ala spuria* or bastard wing. It is a tuft of small quill feathers attached to the first digit of the wing; used in flight, especially by birds of prey, to prevent stalling, and by some ducks when swimming.

203 A plumage resembling that of the female adopted for a short period in late summer by many male ducks (drakes) and often accompanied by temporary loss of flight feathers.

204 The mute swan *Cygnus olor* has about 20,000.

205 The projection on the lower mandible of certain birds, especially in Britain the large gulls, in which it is coloured red, in contrast to the yellow bill. Its purpose is to attract the chick to take food from the parent's bill.

206 The young of a nidifugous bird leave the nest within a few hours or less of hatching; examples are ducks, waders, game birds. Also called 'precocial' in America.

207 The female lacks the small red patch at nape of neck.

208 The fruit or 'keys' of the ash *Fraxinus excelsior*.

209 Because he is considered to be a third less in size than the female, often called the 'falcon'. From Latin tertius = third.

210 Scientific name of genus of nightjars, including the British *Caprimulgus europaeus*; an allusion to their supposed sucking the udders of goats; hence also old English name 'goatsucker'.

211 Dartford warbler *Sylvia undata*; Sandwich tern *Sterna sandvicensis*.

212 They are the four known British breeding stations of the fork-tailed or Leach's petrel *Oceanodroma leucorrhoa*.

213 The (North Atlantic) gannet *Sula bassana*, so called from the Bass Rock, its oldest known colony.

214 To the increase in offal thrown overboard from fishing vessels of all kinds. But the possibility of a genetic mutation has also been suggested.

215 The two biggest colonies of avocets *Recurvirostra avosetta* in Britain.

216 First recorded breeding of snowy owl *Nyctaea scandiaca* in 1967.

217 In 1974; a pair had bred or attempted to breed since 1970 in the Lake District.

218 The white stork *Ciconia alba* on St Giles's, Edinburgh; the only known British breeding occurrence.

219 The great auk *Pinguinus impennis*. Last bird killed on St Kilda as a witch about 1840. (Last in world was killed at Eldey, Iceland, 1844.)

220 The goldcrest *Regulus regulus* or firecrest *Regulus ignicapillus*, now nesting in several English counties, are both about $3\frac{1}{2}''$ long and weigh $4\frac{1}{2}$ gms or about 0.16 oz.

United States Presidents

221 Four (1932, 1936, 1940, 1944).

222 1600 Pennsylvania Avenue, Washington, D.C.

223 Charles J. Guiteau, on 2 July 1881, at a railway station.

224 Abraham Lincoln.

225 Martin Van Buren.

226 Columbia University (New York City).

227 George Washington in his Farewell Address, 1796.

228 The Republican Party.

229 Grandfather and grandson.

230 Theodore Roosevelt, 1906, for negotiating peace in Russo-Japanese war. (Woodrow Wilson was awarded it in 1919.)

231 Abraham Lincoln.

232 James Buchanan.

233 The Speaker of the House of Representatives.

234 Andrew Jackson. (He lived at 'The Hermitage', a plantation near Nashville, in 1796. He returned there after his presidency and died there in 1845.)

235 William Howard Taft.

236 Philadelphia. (He was president 1797–1801. The government moved from Philadelphia to Washington during his administration. His son John *Quincy* Adams also became president.)

237 Theodore Roosevelt.

238 James K. Polk.

239 At least 35.

240 Thomas Jefferson.

General Knowledge 5

241 Well-preserved prehistoric cave paintings. (In the Dordogne Department of France, they have attracted millions of tourists and scientists from all over the world.)

242 A famous chef.

243 Infinity.

244 Two miles south of Wendover, Buckinghamshire.

245 Hungary.

246 Polo.

247 Karl Marx. (From the *German Ideology, XIth Thesis of Feuerbach*, written 1845, published by Engels in 1888.)

248 *The Good Soldier Svejk* (or Schweik).

249 Isles of Scilly. (On St Mary's Island.)

250 Hermes (a gift from him). (Hermes had stolen Apollo's cattle and it was a making-up gift; Hermes had invented it.)

251 Mine Workers union.

252 Claude Monet. ('Impression, Sunrise'.)

253 Ferdinand Magellan. (He was trying to find a route to the Spice Islands.)

254 President Sukarno.

255 'To a Mouse.'

256 The Battle of Jutland (31 May to 1 June 1916).

257 Sumo.

258 Jenny Lind.

259 $12\frac{1}{2}\%$ (one eighth).

260 Politbureau. (Its full name is Political Bureau of the Central Committee of the Communist Party. Called the Praesidium from 1952–66.)

The Works of J. R. R. Tolkien

261 Seven. (These are the rings of power listed in the verse epigraph to the *Lord of the Rings*.)

262 Oakenshield. (Thráin pronounced as dissyllable, Thra-in.)

263 Wormtongue.

264 Sharkey (also the Boss, but this is a title not a name and so not an acceptable answer). (The Shire is the country of the hobbits, laid waste by the wizard Saruman near the end of *Lord of the Rings*.)

265 Bard (Bard the Bowman, Bard of Dale, or of Esgaroth – but the name on its own is an acceptable answer).

266 He was the first hobbit to grow pipe-weed in the Shire. (Pipe-weed might be tobacco, though the term is not used by Tolkien: the phrase pipe-weed is a necessary part of the answer.)

267 That of a bear. (He is a were-bear, in *The Hobbit*.)

268 Glamdring (this is Foe-hammer elsewhere, which is just about acceptable: Beater, though, its goblin nickname, is not acceptable).

269 Sméagol (this is the name used throughout the book, but in the appendix Sméagol is said to be a translation of Trahald: Trahald is therefore also correct).

270 The Prancing Pony.

271 The Withywindle.

272 Elrond (he is sometimes called the Half-Elf, but that is not his name, and not an acceptable answer).

273 Blotmath, pronounced Blodmath or Blommath.

274 Boromir (his brother Faramir received the same advice, and is therefore acceptable as an answer, but only Boromir acted on it).

275 A box of earth from her orchard, and the seed or nut of a mallorn-tree.

276 The Ents. (These are also creatures of enormous size, but benevolent and tree-like. Sauron the sorcerer is said to have made the trolls during the Great Darkness, as he made orcs in mockery of elves.)

277 Kingsfoil.

278 Snowmane, the horse of Theoden King of Rohan (the second line of the epitaph is 'Lightfoot's foal, swift Snowmane': but the name alone is sufficient answer).

279 White horse on green field.

280 It is a worn-down form of 'hol-bytla', which means hole-dweller (both the word and the translation should be in the answer).

Grand Opera since Verdi

281 George Crabbe's *The Borough*.

282 It stopped at the point where Puccini had ceased composing and Alfano had taken over – Toscanini, who was conducting, laid down his baton and turned to the audience saying, 'At this point the Maestro laid down his pen'.

283 Strauss's *Intermezzo*, which describes an episode in his early life and puts himself and his wife on the stage.

284 Prophetically, Wagner's *Götterdämmerung*.

285 An ape dressed in human clothing – Henze's opera entitled *The Young Lord*.

286 Vrenchen and Sali, the lovers in Delius's opera, *A Village Romeo and Juliet*.

287 Puccini's *La Rondine*.

288 W. H. Auden and Chester Kalman.

289 Krenek's *Jonny Spielt Auf* (the hero is a jazz-band leader), produced at Leipzig in 1927.

290 The Viennese Waltz which had not been 'invented' as a musical form at the time of Maria Theresa's Vienna.

291 Cardillac in Hindemith's opera of that name.

292 Arkel in Debussy's *Pelléas et Mélisande*.

293 Emily Marty (or just E.M.) in Janácek's *The Makropoulos Case*.

294 *Julien.*

295 Wedekind's *Erdgeist* and *Pandora's Box.*

296 Poulenc's *Dialogue des Carmélites* which tells of the Carmelite Nuns going to the scaffold rather than renounce their beliefs.

297 Because the libretto was by Stephan Zweig who was Jewish.

298 *The Mother* by the Czech composer Alois Haba.

299 'Prima le parole; dopo la musica?' - what is more important in opera - words or music?

300 Shostakovich's *The Nose* in 1932.

General Knowledge 6

301 Desborough. (Now a nominal office, under the Chancellor of the Exchequer. Allows MPs to resign their seat.)

302 Analogue. (Transforms one quantity into another; the spring transforms weight into movement on a dial. Other types are digital or hybrid.)

303 René Descartes (1596–1650) in *Le Discours de la Méthode.*

304 Hoshea.

305 St Jerome (331–420). (The Vulgate is the Latin version of the Bible, and is still the authorised Latin version of the Roman Catholic Church.)

306 The Iona Community.

307 In Cape Town, to both Houses of the South African Parliament, on 3 February 1960.

308 The Maelstrom.

309 Little water.

310 Bombilla.

311 A newly married man – especially one who has long disdained marriage. (From the character Benedick in *Much Ado About Nothing* by Shakespeare. Benedick is also spelt Benedict.)

312 Anthony Trollope (1815–82).

313 Missouri.

314 A family of herbs, shrubs and trees. (Caper-spurge is one of the Euphoribiaceae; they have usually milky, often poisonous juice. Sometimes called the Mole Plant, as it is reputed to repel moles.)

315 Prince Henry of Portugal (1394–1460).

316 Athena tore up her work, Arachne then hanged herself and Athene turned her into a spider.

317 William Cobbett (1763–1835).

318 Clough Williams-Ellis. (A distinguished Welsh architect, his idea was to create a living museum of architecture based on Italianate styles.)

319 The Seychelles.

320 Sosigenes, an Egyptian astronomer.

The Old Testament

(References are drawn from the *New English Bible*, but other versions support.)

321 The fruit of the tree of knowledge of good and evil (Genesis 2.17).

322 Lice *or* Flies *or* Fleas *or* Maggots *or* Gnats (any of these will do) (Exodus 8.16–19).

323 Horeb, the mountain of God (Exodus 3.1).

324 Uriah (the Hittite) (II Samuel 11.1–21).

325 Adonijah (I Kings 1.5 ff).

326 Vashti (Esther 1.11 etc.).

327 Saul (I Samuel 28.7 ff.).

328 Anathoth (Jeremiah 1.1).

329 Ivory (I Kings 22.39).

330 Wash in the River Jordan seven times (II Kings 5.10).

331 Zedekiah (II Kings 25.1–7).

332 Eliphaz, Bildad, Zophar (Job 2.11).

333 *Either* Isaiah (2.4) *or* Micah (4.3).

334 The destruction of Nineveh (Nahum 1.1).

335 Lo-ruhamah (Hosea 1.6).

336 The threat of attack on Judah by the two kingdoms to the north, Ephraim (i.e. Israel) and Syria (or Aram, or the Aramaeans) (Isaiah 7.1–17).

337 In the second year of Darius, or 521 BC (Haggai 1.1 etc.).

338 A plague of locusts (Joel 1.1–7 etc.).

339 The fear of the Lord is wisdom and to turn from evil is understanding (Job 28.28).

340 YHWH or JHVH (Exodus 3.15).

The New Testament

341 'The time has come; the Kingdom of God is upon you; repent and believe the Gospel.' (Mark 1.15.)

342 Andrew and an unnamed disciple (John 1.35–40).

343 Deuteronomy (Matthew 4.4, 7, 10).

344 Zacharias and Elisabeth (Luke 1.5).

345 *Levi* in Mark 2.14 and Luke 5.27; *Matthew* in Matthew 9.9.

346 On her visit to Elisabeth, when the two women met and greeted one another (Luke 1.39–55).

347 Sosthenes (I Cor. 1.1).

348 Island of Patmos (Revelation 1.9).

349 Tertius (Rom. 16.22).

350 Philippi (Acts 16.12 ff.).

351 First and Second Letters of John ('One and Two John' is a correct answer) (I John 2.18, 2.22, 4.3, II John 7).

352 Talitha cumi, meaning 'Get up, little girl' or similar (Mark 5.41).

353 The Twelve Tribes (James 1.1).

354 Cyprus (Acts 15.36–39).

355 Tabernacles (John 7.2, 37).

356 Gentile Christians in Antioch, Syria and Cilicia. (Gentile Christians in Asia Minor is not a correct answer.) (Acts 15.23.)

357 A reference to 'Mark, my son' at the end of the First Letter of Peter (I Peter 5.13).

358 The edict of Claudius (Acts 18.2), the proconsulship of Gallio (Acts 18.12).

359 He circumcised Timothy (Acts 16.1–3).

360 (a) 2 (Acts 18.1 ff.; 20.2); (b) 3 (cf. II Cor. 12.14; 13.1).

General Knowledge 7

361 Mercury.

362 The Portland Vase.

363 Montreal.

364 Flea (human flea).

365 James Bridie (1888–1951).

366 Stanley Baldwin. (Abdication in 1936.)

367 Wombat.

368 Access to the Baltic. (The corridor was 10 miles wide and 100 miles long, and contained the port of Danzig.)

369 King Henry IV. (In *King Henry IV Part I* by Shakespeare.)

370 Stoning them to death.

371 The Russo-Japanese War of 1904–5. (The Portsmouth here is that in New Hampshire, USA. President Theodore Roosevelt mediated.)

372 Generally the concealment of one heavenly body by another passing between it and the observer. (Also the disappearance of a star in the sun's rays when in apparent position near that of the sun. The concealment of a heavenly body behind the earth's body.)

373 Alhambra.

374 Oliver Cromwell.

375 Rio de Janeiro.

376 Battle of Tel-el-Kebir (13 September 1882).

377 The Harp of Ireland.

378 Emily Post (née Price).

379 Twelve gold stars on an azure blue background.

380 The Hall of Arts and Sciences. (Opened under this name by Queen Victoria on 29 March 1871.)

The Works of Dorothy L. Sayers

381 'As my Whimsy takes me.'

382 Paul Austin Delagardie, his uncle.

383 The Marlborough and the Egotists.

384 Robert Eustace (*The Documents in the Case*).

385 Sir Impey Biggs (*Strong Poison*).

386 He kept canaries (*Strong Poison*).

387 The Warden of her College (*Busman's Honeymoon*).

388 She got a £250 cheque for the Latymer scholarship (*Busman's Honeymoon*).

389 Twenty years (*Busman's Honeymoon*).

390 A manuscript letter of John Donne (*Busman's Honeymoon*).

391 Detective Inspector Parker (*Clouds of Witness*).

392 Château Yquem (*Clouds of Witness*).

393 The Soviet Club (*Clouds of Witness*).

394 110a Piccadilly (*Clouds of Witness*).

395 *Unnatural Death.*

396 Dr Penberthy. He shoots himself. (*Unpleasantness at the Bellona Club.*)

397 A new prosodic theory of verse (*Gaudy Night*).

398 It was burnt (*Gaudy Night* – not scrawled on or defaced).

399 Elizabeth Drake, in *The Documents in the Case.*

400 As 'a synthetic preparation in racemic form' (*The Documents in the Case*).

Norse Mythology

401 Mjollnir (Myol-neer).

402 Heimdall(ur) (Haym-dall(er)).

403 Hoth(ur); he threw the mistletoe twig that killed Baldur.

404 Freyja (Fray-ya).

405 The antler of a hart.

406 The rowan (mountain ash).

407 Othin's gold bracelet from which eight bracelets of equal weight dripped every ninth night.

408 Sleipnir (Slaypneer) had eight legs and Starkath(ur) was born with eight arms.

409 Prosperous voyaging; good fishing; wealth in lands and goods.

410 The mead of poetry.

411 The nails of dead people; Loki (Lokk-i) in one source, Hrym(ur) in another.

412 He kicked him into the fire at Baldur's cremation.

413 Othin, who is said to have learnt secrets of the dead by communing with victims on gallows.

414 He changed himself into a hawk and Ithunn into a nut and flew off with her in his talons.

415 Hel had Baldur.

416 The giant Hrungnir in combat with Thor stood on his shield because he had been falsely warned that Thor would attack him from underground.

417 Runes (probably representing occult secrets in general).

418 A separate goddess whom Frigg set to protect people she wished to keep from danger.

419 Baldur appears as a just and innocent victim; Balderus appears as lustful and pugnacious.

420 The use of the verb 'help'; a trinity of divine figures; the idea of an omnipotent god.

General Knowledge 8

421 Karl Heinrich Marx (in 1843).

422 St Omer.

423 The Boer War.

424 Seven young men and seven maidens for the diet of the Minotaur.

425 (a) Verbatim, (b) Literatim.

426 Four (*Das Rheingold; Die Walküre; Siegfried; Götterdämmerung*).

427 Nostradamus (1503–66), the Latinised name of Michel de Notre Dame.

428 Aurora.

429 Barnes Wallis.

430 Spanish, French, American.

431 Hecuba.

432 Colonel (Draga) Mihailovic. (Chetniks were the Serbian Resistance movement. Britain eventually backed the other, more effective Resistance movement – the Partisans – led by Tito.)

433 Jackal.

434 Carl Jung (1875–1961).

435 By the sparrow. Erithacus rubecula is the zoological name for the robin. (The zoological name for the sparrow is Passer. Passer domesticus — house sparrow: Passer montanus = tree sparrow.)

436 The highest part of the withers (which start at the base of the crestline of the neck).

437 Pop art cartoons.

438 Edward VII (1901–10).

439 Albert Einstein.

440 Pope Alexander VI (Rodrigo Borgia).

Railways of Great Britain

441 2–8–2.

442 Central, St Enoch, Buchanan, Queen Street.

443 No. 92220 ('Evening Star').

444 6000.

445 100A1.

446 Colchester, 1981 ft. (Formerly Manchester Victoria/ Exchange, not now extant.)

447 Calling-on arm permitting a train to pass a stop signal at danger.

448 630V DC.

449 A GWR bogie ventilated van.

450 Waterloo and City (SR); Mersey Railway (LMR).

451 Sir Herbert Walker.

452 GWR route via Slough, Addison Road and the West London Extension Railway.

453 Bowness (Lake Windermere).

454 3200 hp.

455 Taff Vale.

456 Restaurant/Kitchen/Buffet Car.

457 119, Class T9.

458 Cromford and High Peak line.

459 New Street (Snow Hill being now closed).

460 Thurso.

British Chemical Industry

461 Mrs Margaret Thatcher.

462 Monomers. (Single molecules is an alternative answer.)

463 As a detergent (products such as washing-up liquids).

464 Shell and ICI.

465 In lubricating oil purification.

466 Dichloro-Diphenyl-Trichloroethane.

467 Acetone.

468 They stand for 'American Selling Price' (a method of assessing for duty imports of chemicals into the USA).

469 Terms applied to residual gases after liquefaction in the process of manufacturing liquid chlorine.

470 J. R. Whinfield (a research chemist working at Calico Printers Association Ltd).

471 Manufacturing polyester fibres. ('Terylene', although a trade-name, would be acceptable.)

472 Nitrogen, phosphorus and potassium.

473 Organic sulphur compounds (the word mercaptans is also acceptable).

474 2-naphthylamine can cause papilloma of the bladder (cancer) or (alternatively) 2-naphthylamine is a carcinogen.

475 The air- or gas-filled space above a liquid in a closed container.

476 Air.

477 Methyl ethyl ketone (79.6° C.). Ethyl alcohol has boiling point 78.5° C.

478 The name for the residue after a batch distillation.

479 Ammonia and carbon dioxide.

480 Acetylene.

General Knowledge 9

481 Francis Bacon (of studies).

482 Tutsi (also known as Watutsi, Batutsi or Watussi, herdsmen of Rwanda and Burundi, Central Africa).

483 On the Queen's birthday (21 April).

484 On a twin-lens camera. (This has two lenses, one above the other, one being a viewing and the other a taking lens. They have widely different views of a subject, necessitating parallax compensation.)

485 Baron Manfred von Richthofen, German airman of World War I.

486 Zeus. (Mnemosyne was their mother.)

487 Henry IV.

488 Dido. (Virgil makes her fall in love with Aeneas.)

489 Meissen.

490 Hephaestus, god of fire and metal-working. (Hephaestus made her, the other gods gave her a variety of wicked traits.)

491 Martin Luther King.

492 Figures of horses carved on slopes of chalk hills (Westbury, Wiltshire; Uffington, Berkshire).

493 Pike.

494 San Sebastian.

495 Dash-dash-dash.

496 Sisyphus.

497 Sandwich Islands. (Discovered in 1778 and named after the 4th Earl of Sandwich.)

498 'I', says the Quarterly,
So savage and Tartarly;
'Twas one of my feats.'

499 Jan van Eyck.

500 Medusa.

Famous Russians

501 Ivan IV (the Terrible).

502 Peter I.

503 Kropótkin.

504 Stanislávsky.

505 Lénin.

506 A. Lunachársky.

507 Scriábin.

508 P. D. Uspensky.

509 Mikhail Fédorovich.

510 Lomonósov.

511 Mikhail Shólokhov.

512 Pugachev.

513 Sumarókov.

514 Vassily Kandínsky.

515 Rublev.

516 Hérzen.

517 Yesénin.

518 Blok.

519 A. V. Samsónov.

520 ' Nikoláy Lobachévsky.

Geography of Great Britain

521 Bare, flat limestone surfaces between furrows or
     fissures.

522 Snowdon (more strictly Y Wyddfa, at 3560 feet the
     highest of Snowdon's five peaks).

523 West Lancashire, between the estuaries of the Ribble
     and the Wyre (or the area of which Blackpool is the
     chief town).

524 A mass of hard sandstone found particularly in
     southern England on the chalk downs.

525 York.

526 A seasonal or intermittent stream which flows in chalk country after heavy rain.

527 Mean sea level measured at Newlyn, Cornwall.

528 Peak District.

529 From: Shetland, Orkney, Caithness, Sutherland, Ross & Cromarty, Inverness, Argyll.

530 It formed a natural defensive line for Hadrian's Wall.

531 All are nuclear power-stations.

532 Central Business District.

533 A strong north or north-east wind blowing downhill from Cross Fell (or any strong wind blowing downhill in the northern Pennines).

534 Ardnamurchan (point or peninsula).

535 NE to SW alignment of mountains and faults (or the grain of the country).

536 A hard rock sometimes used for building, from the Lower Greensand in Kent (or the Hythe Beds of the Lower Greensand).

537 Nothing, or a flock of sheep or a Land Rover, etc. (the 'Roads' are former shorelines of a lake which fluctuated in level because of damming by ice at different heights).

538 The Forestry Commission.

539 Institute of British Geographers.

540 Transverse Mercator.

General Knowledge 10

541 Masada. (Masada was a great rock on the edge of the Judaean desert where the Zealots made their last stand against the Romans. When defeat was certain their leader persuaded them to draw lots to select 10 men to kill the remaining 960 defenders. One of these finally slew his nine fellows and then slew himself.)

542 The capybara of South America.

543 Eagle (as a heraldic symbol).

544 The Royal Pavilion, Brighton. (Designed for the Prince Regent by John Nash in the style of an Indian Emperor's palace complete with onion-domes and minarets.)

545 Queen Charlotte, wife of George III.

546 Cosmo Gordon Lang. (Lang, a Scotsman, was born in 1864 and died in 1945. He was Archbishop of Canterbury from 1928 until his retirement in 1942, when he was created Baron Lang of Lambeth.)

547 7 November. (This is, of course, the Russian October Revolution, 1917.)

548 Rome.

549 Pound. (In divisions of 100 Agorot.)

550 Henry VI (1440).

551 His flight around the Eiffel Tower in an airship.

552 French Foreign Legion.

553 The first Cambridge College (Peterhouse). (Hugh de Balsham was the Bishop.)

554 On the Panama Canal.

555 London University in 1878.

556 Joseph Stalin.

557 The Atlantic Charter. (A statement of principles.)

558 Local Government.

559 Epsom salts.

560 A charm (or chirm).

English Literature

561 John Masefield (in 'Sea Fever').

562 The Venerable Bede.

563 Metaphysical Poets.

564 William Shakespeare (Sonnet LXXI).

565 A. E. Housman.

566 Translation of Homer (Keats's 'On First Looking into Chapman's Homer').

567 Aran Islands, Ireland.

568 *Grace Abounding*.

569 Gerard Manley Hopkins (first published in 1918).

570 Richard Lovelace.

571 Robert Burns.

572 The execution of King Charles I.

573 The French King Louis XI.

574 John Locke.

575 His sister Mary, in a fit of insanity, stabbed her mother to death and wounded her father.

576 Christina Rossetti.

577 Thomas Hobbes (*Leviathan, the Matter, Form and Power of a Commonwealth, Ecclesiastical and Civil*).

578 It has no name.

579 Wilkie Collins.

580 *Frankenstein*.

History of Music

581   *Third* or *Eroica*.

582   One (harpsichord).

583   Johann Christian (youngest son of Johann Sebastian).

584   Musician or violinist.

585   Frederick the Great.

586   Lélio (by Hector Berlioz).

587   Marcellina.

588   Schumann.

589   *Oberon*.

590   Mannheim (by Charles Burney, in 1772).

591   *Don Giovanni* (supper scene).

592   Peter.

593   Dr Thomas Arne.

594   Green (in *Die böse Farbe*).

595   Wellington's (at Vittoria) entitled *Wellington's Victory*.

596   Handel composed the *Utrecht Te Deum* and *Jubilate* for the celebration of the Peace of Utrecht in 1713, by which England kept Gibraltar.

597   'Hamlet' Funeral March (volley-firing behind the scenes).

598   Vivaldi.

599   Beethoven's *Mass in D* or *Missa Solemnis*.

600   La ci darem (from *Don Giovanni*).

General Knowledge 11

601 Medmenham (near Marlow on the River Thames).
(The Hell Fire Club was a notorious 18th-century
côterie founded about 1755 by Sir Francis Dashwood,
afterwards Baron Le Despencer. Its 13 members
conducted their profanities and revelries at
Medmenham Abbey, which formed part of the
Dashwood property.)

602 Benjamin Disraeli, Earl of Beaconsfield.

603 After the second Battle of Philippi. (Marcus Junius
Brutus (*c.* 86–42 BC) was successful against Antony
and Octavian in the first Battle of Philippi, though
Cassius was defeated.)

604 (The) highest town (or city at the top). (From the
Greek akros = highest, polis = city.)

605 Arms limitation (Strategic Arms Limitation Talks).

606 Strophe, antistrophe and epode.

607 Herculaneum.

608 Lord Clifford's (Walter de Clifford). (Mistress of
Henry II and poisoned by Queen Eleanor in 1177.)

609 Laputa.

610 For bravery in the field. (The MM was instituted by
George V in 1916.)

611 Ten.

612 Peace. (Eirene was the Greek goddess of peace.)

613 Animals of the open sea, far from any shore, such as
the jelly-fish, the whale sharks, whales, young
herring and a great variety of small crustaceans.
(Living or growing at or near the surface of
the oceans.)

614 Isle of Sheppey.

615 The Julian Calendar was then introduced. (46 BC had
455 days. The Julian Calendar was based on a solar
cycle of 365¼ days, but this was superseded by the
Gregorian calendar which rectified the overplus of a
few minutes each year, and was adopted in England
in 1752.)

616 Award for bravery in support of law and order.
(Awarded by the Goldsmiths Company in memory of
Capt. Ralph Binney who stopped a robbery in 1944.
Applies only to the City of London and cannot be
awarded to a policeman.)

617 Sir Thomas Lawrence. (The correct title is 'Master
Anesby'.)

618 Théodore Simon.

619 Epsilon.

620 Patricide and incest. (He murdered his father, Laius,
and married his mother Jocasta.)

Personalities in Russian History and the Arts

621 The Selected Council.

622 It was abolished by Peter the Great.

623 It lasted from 1598 to 1613. During these years there
were five Tsars in Moscow, all of whose claims
were doubtful. The period ended with the
establishment of the House of Romanov.

624 Ingria in Sweden.

625 A law whereby each monarch was to nominate his
own successor.

626 A statesman who rose from a poor Moscow family
to be Peter the Great's most powerful collaborator
in his reforms.

627 To dislodge the British from India.

628 Archpriest Avvakum.

629 The abolition of serfdom and the establishment of a liberal constitution.

630 On that very day he had signed a decree approving a plan for a representative assembly.

631 Konstantin Petrovich Pobedonostsev, Procurator of the Holy Synod.

632 Yekaterina Breshko-Breshkovskaya, the 'grandmother of the Russian Revolution'.

633 *Eugene Onegin* and *The Queen of Spades*.

634 *Letter to Gogol* (from Belinsky).

635 Pavel Petrovich Kirsanov.

636 Gorky (the other two were Tolstoy and Chekhov).

637 *The Idiot*.

638 Chekhov. (Tolstoy refused to resign because he did not recognise the existence of the Academy.)

639 Ivan Bunin.

640 Tolstoy's. (Rumour spread in the West that the writer was dead some days before he actually died.)

English Cathedrals

641 Bishop Robert Poole (he instituted the work in 1220 and it took 45 years to complete).

642 The nave and aisles of St Paul's cathedral which, from the fifteenth to the nineteenth century, were used for the sale of goods and as a promenade for the citizens of London.

643 Peterborough.

644 Lincoln.

645 Winchester.

646 Gilbert Scott.

647 Worcester Cathedral.

648 To the signing of Magna Carta (1215) when the royal power was curbed by the barons.

649 Gloucester.

650 The cathedral of Christ Church, Oxford.

651 The Benedictine order.

652 It was used by the monks to watch over the treasures in the shrine of the patron saint.

653 Bristol.

654 Southwark.

655 The north-west transept.

656 Chester (half-way along the north side of the nave).

657 Exeter (Bishop Oldham's Chantry, 1519 – the owls being a punning reference to the founder's name).

658 Behind the high (or main) altar (thus preserving the plan of the sanctuary normal till *c*. 1000).

659 John Piper.

660 In the cloisters of Gloucester Cathedral.

General Knowledge 12

661 Estonia (now a Russian Republic).

662 Len Murray (at the Annual Congress in September 1973).

663 Thomas Aquinas.

664 Howard family (Dukes of Norfolk).

665 Pietro Badoglio.

666 15th Century. (This collection of letters, preserved by the Pastons of Norfolk, was written between *c*. 1420 and 1503. They give a unique picture of domestic and political life.)

667   *Morning Post.*

668   Isle of Avalon.

669   The Phoenix Park murders.

670   Sir Edwin Henry Landseer.

671   Iowa.

672   Caspian Sea.

673   Avoca (County Wicklow).

674   Democritus.

675   Abu Dhabi.

676   Leah.

677   Glubb Pasha (Sir John Bagot Glubb).

678   *Love's Labour's Lost.*

679   André le Nôtre.

680   Mrs Patrick Campbell.

British Church Architecture

681   13th Century (early English).

682   The tower of St Botolph's Church, Boston,
Lincolnshire (built 1409–50).

683   A compartment off a main room, especially off the
nave of a Saxon Church; also called an *exedra* or
oriel, in some cases.

684   James Gibbs.

685   Durham Cathedral, sanctuary and chancel aisles
(built 1093–1104).

686   Sompting, Sussex.

687   Chichester.

688   Royal hall.

689 Henry Yevele (pronounced Yeaveley).

690 The carved leaves of its decorated capitals.

691 Ely.

692 Brian Thomas.

693 John F. Bentley (1839–1902).

694 St Andrew, Roker by E. S. Prior (built 1906–7).

695 A junction of mouldings at right angles in which the joint is horizontal instead of at 45°.

696 Hexham. (Its 1300th anniversary was in 1974.)

697 Churches built for the commissioners appointed to administer the Act of 1818 providing a million pounds for building new churches. (There was also a commission of 1715 but the term is usually applied to churches under the 1818 Act. There were about 230 of them.)

698 The spire of St Mary's R.C. Cathedral was designed by J. A. Hansom who invented the 'Patent Safety Cab' named after him.

699 Henry Flitcroft (built 1731–3).

700 A stone lintel with an arch-shape cut out of it, as in the Saxon part of St Peter's, Bywell.

Grand Opera

701 It was a theatre built on land that had once belonged to the church – a Convent Garden – given at the time of the dissolution of the monasteries by Henry VIII to the Duke of Bedford.

702 *King Lear*.

703 Franco Alfano.

704 The name by which the Paris Opéra (or Académie de Musique) was affectionately known. Verdi especially refers to it as such in his correspondence.

705 On the Viennese critic Eduard Hanslick, who disliked Wagner's music. Wagner originally was going to call the character Hans Lick.

706 Literally the Italian for realism. The term used to describe the realistic or naturalistic school of Italian opera as typified by Mascagni, Leoncavallo, Giordano and Puccini.

707 It began with *Siegfried*, so that the great German tenor Max Alvary could make his London début in his favourite role.

708 In Cilea's opera, *Adriana Lecouvreur*, in which the character is called Michonet.

709 They are all tenors; they are all Spanish characters; and they are all loved by a Leonora.

710 Leonard Warren, the American baritone, who collapsed during a performance of *La Forza del Destino*; the tenor Aroldo Lindi who collapsed and died in San Francisco during a performance of *Pagliacci*.

711 Opéra comique is the French term for operas with spoken dialogue, generally a light subject, though this is not a necessity; Opéra-Comique is the name of a theatre in Paris, originally the home for French musical pieces with spoken dialogue.

712 Rossini's *The Barber of Seville*.

713 Arrigo Boito.

714 Richard Strauss's *Die Schweigsame Frau* (The Silent Woman).

715 *Oberto, Conte di San Bonifacio* (1839).

716 They are all heard off-stage before they make their entrance.

717 In Mozart's *Marriage of Figaro*, Figaro and Marcellina use the words *I Masnadieri* (The Robbers) in Act 3.

718 Maria Callas and Joan Sutherland respectively.

719 She sings a piece by the French composer Grétry.

720 Walther von der Vogelweide (or the Birds) according to Walther, in his song to the Masters.

General Knowledge 13

721 The Dunkirk evacuation plan (26 May – 4 June 1940)

722 Henry II or Richard I or John. (The early Plantagenet kings from Henry II to John. Henry II (1154–1189) was the son of Matilda (daughter of Henry I) and Geoffrey Plantagenet, Count of Anjou. John lost Anjou in 1204.)

723 Moslem (Islamic, Muslim or Mohammedan). (The year began 25 January 1974 and contained 354 days – year 1395 began 14 January 1975.)

724 Holland. (The Royal Dutch Airline KLM was established in 1919 and flew a passenger service between Amsterdam and London from May 1920. A holding company of SAS, the Danske Luftfartelskab, was founded even earlier, in 1918, but their scheduled service ran only between August 1920 and 1946.)

725 *La Boutique Fantasque.* (Choreography Massine; music Rossini; arranged Respighi.)

726 Clement Attlee.

727 Bishop James Ussher. (It was accepted as the basis of Biblical chronology into the early 20th century. He was Archbishop of Armagh.)

728 John Bunyan.

729 Leucippus. (5th century BC. It was elaborated by his pupil Democritus.)

730 Casquets Lighthouse (or Caskets).

731 Chess – he held the title for 28 years.

732 A calf. (Used especially in cheesemaking, rennet occurs naturally in the stomach lining of calves. Rennet is also used to make junkets. It can also be a type of apple or a farrier's tool.)

733 D. W. Griffith.

734 Zug.

735 *Béatrice et Bénédict*. (Berlioz wrote the libretto himself – the opera was first produced in Baden-Baden in 1862.)

736 Francis Drake's *Golden Hind*. or *Pelican*.

737 Ballistic Missile Early Warning System.

738 1848 (often called 'the year of revolutions').

739 Island of Staffa (Inner Hebrides).

740 Orang-outang.

History of World Theatre

741 Aristophanes (the only comic writer: the others all wrote tragedies).

742 Christopher Marlowe and Johann Wolfgang von Goethe.

743 Henrik Ibsen, the Norwegian dramatist.

744 John Heminge and Henry Condell.

745 Henry Fielding (it was, of course, only abolished in 1968).

746 *The Playboy of the Western World*.

747 Antonin Artaud.

748 Kurt Weill.

749 Jean-Louis Barrault.

750 John Gay's *The Beggar's Opera* (staged by the theatre manager John Rich in 1728).

751 The American playwright Clifford Odets (not to be confused with *Waiting for Godot* by Samuel Beckett).

752 The Shaw Theatre (Euston Road).

753 Sir John Gielgud.

754 The Living Theatre.

755 Chester, Wakefield (or Townley), York, Coventry.

756 The Theatres Royal, Drury Lane and Covent Garden ('theoretically', because there were many ways in which the monopoly could be evaded).

757 Tommy Steele.

758 George Devine.

759 Eduardo and Peppino.

760 Joseph Grimaldi.

19th-Century English History

761 Corrupt Practices Act, 1883.

762 Lord Palmerston (1865).

763 Don Pacifico.

764 £20,000 a year.

765 Lord Cardwell.

766 Free sale; Fair rent; Fixity of tenure.

767 7d in the £ on incomes over £150 per annum.

768 Cowper-Temple. (Under the terms of the 1870 Education Act the clause proposed by W. F. Cowper-Temple granted this right.)

769 Grand Old Man; Murderer of Gordon (Gladstone).

770 Richard Cross (Disraeli was Prime Minister).

771 It listed financial abuses of the Church of England, pluralities, stipends, etc.

The Iliad and the Odyssey

795 Xanthus.

796 A sea horse having two forefeet and a body that ends in the tail of a dolphin or fish.

797 Milman Parry.

798 Well before 1200 BC. Representations date from the 15th and 16th centuries BC.

799 After 750 BC, 750–675 acceptable.

800 Iris.

General Knowledge 14

801 He was the Regent of Hungary.

802 Thomas Henry Huxley.

803 Tara (County Meath).

804 The mho (ohm spelt backwards).

805 Simone de Beauvoir. (She won the Goncourt prize in 1954.)

806 Execution of Admiral Byng.

807 Martha. (By Edward Allbee.)

808 Castor and Pollux.

809 Agrippa (M. Vipsanius Agrippa). (Later rebuilt by Hadrian.)

810 English (Robert Malthus, 1766–1834).

811 Pounded almonds and sugar.

812 Goonhilly Downs, Cornwall. (Although the television communication was the most dramatic aspect of the work at Goonhilly, the GPO's main concern was with radio-telephone communications.)

813 Gerard Manley Hopkins (1844–89).

814 *Pilgrim's Progress* (written by John Bunyan in 1675).

815 There was a riot after two drawn games between Celtic and Rangers.

816 After King Sisyphus in Greek legend who was condemned to roll a huge rock eternally uphill but when it reached the top it fell back.

817 Elektra (or Electra).

818 New Zealand (it is the NZ portion of Antarctica).

819 Konrad Lorenz. (Translated from the German by Marjorie Kerr Wilson.)

820 Otto Rank.

Classical Mythology

821 Saturday (Saturn).

822 Poseidon.

823 Polyphemus.

824 Tyre.

825 A tree nymph.

826 The Phaeacians or Phaeaces.

827 Ajax.

828 Calliope.

829 Cadmus.

830 Children of the primeval marriage of heaven and earth.

831 Theogony.

832 Hyacinthus.

833 Thyestes.

834 Amphiaraus.

835 Virgo.

836 Psyche.

837 Arachne.

838 Zeus.

839 She forced Zeus to appear in his true shape.

840 Artemis.

Arthurian Literature

841 Sir Bedwere, or Bedivere (in the French *Vulgate* it is Sir Girflet).

842 Sir Bors, Sir Percival, Sir Galahad.

843 Igrayne, duchess of Cornwall (other versions have Ygaerne and Igerne).

844 Mons Badonicus, or Mount Badon.

845 Emperor, or Procurator, of Rome allegedly killed by Arthur.

846 The twelfth.

847 The sixth.

848 Sir Balin (or Balain).

849 Sir Bertilak (or Bercilak) de Hautdesert.

850 Speak to him unless addressed.

851 Lancelot had killed his brothers Gareth and Gaheris (or, in the *Vulgate*, his brother Gaheriet).

852 An adder. (A knight drew his sword to kill it, so that both sides suspected treachery.)

853 Mordred was the son of Arthur and Morgawse, Arthur's half-sister. The relationship was therefore both father and son, and uncle and nephew.

854 Sir Mellyagaunce (or Meleagant, or Meliagrance).

855 Ron.

856 The Welsh *Gododdin*.

857 King Pellinore's.

858 To stand by the mad goshawk Cully, till the bells ring three times.

859 It belonged to the Fair Maid of Astolat, Elayne le Blanke.

860 He is 'a blooming boy' in knight's armour.

General Knowledge 15

861 *The Origin of Species*. (On the Origin of Species by means of Natural Selection, or the Preservation of Favoured Races in the Struggle for Life.)

862 Uncle Remus.

863 Harry S. Truman.

864 Nitrogen.

865 Rorschach.

866 Cuckoo.

867 The Devil.

868 Grendel.

869 56.

870 Brezhnev and Kosygin.

871 Caustic soda or caustic potash or lye.

872 Scheherazade, by telling him a story (*The Arabian Nights*) each night.

873 Laser.

874 Henry Moore.

875 He was thrown through a window.

876 Mountains or hills.

877 Republic of South Africa.

878 Winston S. Churchill.

879 Dr Samuel Johnson.

880 Ergotism.

Kings and Queens of England

881 James II.

882 Henry V.

883 Her 'Golden Speech'.

884 Emperor Henry V and Geoffrey of Anjou.

885 William Rufus.

886 Yea-and-Nay (Oc e No – meant he kept his word).

887 Fontevrault (in France).

888 A blank sheet of paper with a royal signature.

889 George V.

890 Francis I of France (Field of the Cloth of Gold).

891 Lucy Walter.

892 Porphyria, a disturbance of the porphyrin metabolism
     – the process producing pigments in the blood.

893 Housing.

894 Her grandmother had been Henry VIII's sister (and
     Mary Tudor had been declared illegitimate by Henry).

895 Her nickname for John Whitgift, her last
     Archbishop of Canterbury.

896 When Princess Beatrice was 21 (in 1878) at Osborne

897 Queen Anne.

898 He would give them Buckingham Palace.

899 Born 'in the purple', when the father was king.

900 John.

Shakespeare's Plays

901 Rosalind (*As You Like It* I, iii, 127).

902 Edgar as Poor Tom (*King Lear*, III, iv, 118).

903 *Timon of Athens*.

904 Petruchio (*The Taming of the Shrew*, IV, i, 93).

905 Of Queen Gertrude, his mother (*Hamlet*, I, ii, 146).

906 *All's Well that Ends Well* (spoken by the Countess of Rousillon).

907 Falstaff (*Henry V*, II, iii, 15).

908 'Britain shall be fortunate, and flourish in peace and plenty' (V, v, 442).

909 Lead (*The Merchant of Venice*, II, vii, 15).

910 Baptista, a rich gentleman of Padua (*The Taming of the Shrew*).

911 Vienna (*Measure for Measure*, IV, i).

912 Bottom (by Titania in *A Midsummer Night's Dream*, IV, i, 36).

913 *Two Gentlemen of Verona* (IV, ii, 40).

914 Yorick (*Hamlet*, V, i, 202).

915 Dogberry (*Much Ado About Nothing*, IV, ii, 88–93).

916 Figs (*Antony and Cleopatra*, V, ii, 234).

917 Hamlet (*Hamlet*, V, ii, 371).

918 Don Adriano de Armado (so described in the dramatis personae of *Love's Labour's Lost*).

919 The crown of the King of England (*Henry IV Pt 2*, IV, v, 22).

920 A simple constable.

MASTERMIND
BOOK THREE

General Knowledge 1

1 Before entering Sandhurst, which school did Sir Winston Churchill attend?

2 What was the country of origin of the dance, the Gavotte?

3 Who was the portrait painter who became the first President of the Royal Academy in 1768?

4 In 1950, the French statesman Robert Schuman lent his name to a plan. What was this plan?

5 In which county are the rivers Taw, Torridge and Teign?

6 With which musical instrument is Leon Goossens particularly associated?

7 Born in 1759, his first play was *The Robbers*, his last was *William Tell*. Who was this German author?

8 The Duke of Norfolk is the Premier Duke and Earl of England. What is his family name?

9 In Greek mythology she was the daughter of Aesculapius and was the Goddess of Health. Who was she?

10 What is the SI unit of time?

11 Who was the MP for Jarrow who became the first woman Minister of Education?

12 A hallmark containing an anchor indicates that an article has been assayed at which provincial assay office?

13 Who was the Milesian woman, celebrated for her talents and beauty, who lived at Athens as Pericles' mistress?

14 Where is the Chester Beatty Library?

15 Who described patriotism as 'the last refuge of a scoundrel'?

16 What name was given to the Roman road running from London to York via Lincoln?

17 Name one of the two physiologists who were jointly awarded a Nobel prize in 1932 for their work on the nervous system.

18 Aboard which American warship did the surrender ceremonies take place that marked the formal ending of World War II?

19 The Irish writer, Edward Plunkett, is better known by another name. What is it?

20 In 1936 he wrote *General Theory of Employment, Interest and Money*, and was an adviser to the Treasury in both World Wars. Who was he?

The Stuart Kings and Queens, 1603–1714

Set by John D. Bareham

21 Queen Mary II died in her thirty-third year. What was the cause of her death?

22 William of Orange, making his bid for the throne, landed in Torbay. Where did he set up his headquarters?

23 What argument did the Speaker use when Charles I asked him to point out the Five Members he wanted to impeach?

24 In substance, what is Charles II reputed to have said when he read the Earl of Rochester's lines about him, 'He never said a foolish thing, nor ever did a wise one'?

25 Which of the Stuart kings had chronic asthma?

26 What vital tax did Charles I levy illegally after 1626?

27 Who was Robert Harley's cousin, woman of the bedchamber to Queen Anne?

28 How did William III die?

29 Who was Charles I's court portrait-painter?

30 Who stayed in the oak tree with Charles II in Boscobel Wood?

31 What horse race did Charles II win in 1671 and again in 1674?

32 Of what did James I remark, 'I am surprised that my ancestors should have permitted such an institution to come into existence'?

33 Why did James I call George Villiers his 'Sweet Steenie'?

34 What was the £25,000 deal that Charles I made with the Duke of Mantua?

35 The Duke of Monmouth's father was Charles II. Who was his mother?

36 Who said, of Charles I, 'a mild and gracious prince, who knew not how to be, or be made, great'?

37 What was the Great Contract which Salisbury failed to obtain from Parliament for James I in 1610?

38 What did Marlborough do with the letter of dismissal he received from Queen Anne in 1711?

39 What was the proper title of the so-called *Kings Book* which showed how Charles I wanted to be presented to the world?

40 What was the political happening that some people, including Arbuthnot writing to Swift, blamed for shortening Queen Anne's life?

Life and Works of Ernest Hemingway
Set by Frank J. Teskey

41 What was Ernest Hemingway's other christian name?

42 What is the name of the suburb in Chicago where Hemingway was born?

43 In what capacity did Hemingway serve in World War I?

44 In January 1954 Hemingway wished to make his wife a belated Christmas present of a flight to the Belgian Congo. What happened on the flight?

45 In *The Old Man and the Sea*, what kind of fish did Santiago hook?

46 In *Across the River and into the Trees*, who went back to the battlefield after the war and located the exact place where Hemingway had been wounded?

47 What is the title of Hemingway's novel that is a parody of Sherwood Anderson's novel, *Dark Laughter*?

48 Which short-story character had trained himself not to quarrel with women any more, and had learned how not to get married?

49 In *The Snows of Kilimanjaro*, what happened to Harry when he was trying to photograph a herd of waterbuck?

50 In a short story a woman says, 'They look like white elephants.' What looked like white elephants?

51 What is the chief topic of conversation among the three main characters in *Today is Friday*?

52 What reason did Johnny Goodner give for eating green Mexican chilli pepper?

53 In *Fifty Grand*, how did Jack Brennan lose his welter-
weight boxing title?

54 In what kind of operation was Hemingway, with his
fishing boat *Pilár*, engaged during the years 1942–4?

55 During his Paris period, Hemingway's first wife decided
to take his manuscripts to him at Lausanne so that he
could work on them. What happened?

56 What is the name of the hill-top farm where Hemingway
lived for most of his latter years?

57 About which of his novels did Hemingway say that its
point was 'the earth abideth for ever'?

58 Who owned the library of 'Shakespeare and Company'
that Hemingway used when he was in Paris?

59 In *The Killers*, who was the intended victim of Al and
Max?

60 To what kind of racing did Mike Ward introduce
Hemingway?

General Knowledge 2

61 What colour is the pigment chlorophyll?

62 Eohippus and Mesohippus are stages in the evolution of which animal?

63 Wordsworth composed a poem a few miles above which Abbey in Wales?

64 Where did the United Nations Monetary and Financial Conference meet in July 1944?

65 In which mythology were Osiris, Horus and Isis major deities?

66 'Schnauzer' is a breed of what kind of animal?

67 Which former London landmark now stands at Lake Havasu City in Arizona, USA?

68 Of which military incident in 1854 did a French general say, 'It is magnificent, but it is not war'?

69 What is meant by the adjective hircine?

70 Which castle was the birthplace of HRH Princess Margaret?

71 Who became famous in 1893 with his opera *Hansel and Gretel*?

72 In *Alice's Adventures in Wonderland*, who is the character that is always weeping, and shows Alice how to dance the Lobster Quadrille?

73 Who was the French statesman, chief minister of Louis XIII and founder of the French Academy, who figures in *The Three Musketeers*?

74 In astronomy, what name is given to the darkest part of the shadow cast by the earth or moon in an eclipse?

75 What is the fruit of the plant *ananas comosus*?

76 What is the meaning of the Latin *ipse dixit*?

77 Who was the former Royalist soldier who served under Cromwell as Commander-in-Chief in Scotland, and later became an elder statesman of Charles II?

78 In Greek mythology, what was a Thyrsus?

79 Emma Lavinia Gifford and Florence Dugdale were the two wives of which famous writer?

80 The ballet *Les Sylphides* is set to music by which composer?

The City of Rome
Set by Professor J. R. Hale

81 To whom is the cathedral of Rome dedicated?

82 Which is the national church of the Americans?

83 In regard to Rome, what was the boast of the Emperor Augustus, as chronicled by Suetonius?

84 The Spanish Steps are a tourist attraction. How many steps are there?

85 Into which ancient building has the Stock Exchange been installed?

86 In which Gallery is Velazquez's portrait of Innocent X?

87 Why is Santa Maria Maggiore also known as Santa Maria delle Neve?

88 Inscribed on the Pyramid of Caius Cestius is the number of days it took to build. What was the number?

89 Which Roman church is the work of the engraver Giovanni Battista Piranesi?

90 Who said, 'We believe that Rome, though it has not all the qualities to be desired, is undoubtedly the capital that the Italians will choose one day'?

91 What are the 'talking statues of Rome'?

92 The most prominent work of the architect Giuseppe Sacconi is sometimes called 'The Wedding Cake', but it is a monument. To whom?

93 Cola di Rienzo, whom Byron called the 'last of Romans', was lynched in the fourteenth century. What was his political aim?

94 Who escaped from Castel S. Angelo with ropes of torn-up sheets and suffered a broken leg while doing so?

95 Who were the so-called Nazarenes, or Klosterbruder, of early nineteenth-century Rome?

96 In which palace did Mussolini establish his office?

97 If you wrote a letter to 'Il Bambino, Roma', where would it be delivered?

98 In Bernini's Fountain of the Four Rivers, three of the rivers commemorated are the Nile, Danube and Plata. Which is the fourth?

99 The Rome subway runs from the railway station to where?

100 Michelangelo's Pietà is in St Peter's. Where is his Statue of the Risen Christ?

The Spanish Anarchist Movement, 1908–75

Set by Professor J. C. J. Metford

101 Who denounced the Canalejas Ministry of 1910 as 'a democratic flag being used to cover reactionary merchandise'?

102 What event on 26 July sparked off the so-called 'Tragic Week' of 1909?

103 Who said to the firing squad, 'Aim well, my friends, you are not responsible. I am innocent.'

104 What was the *Mano Negra*, or Black Hand?

105 What do the initials CNT stand for?

106 Which Spanish anarchist changed his name to Khordoniev, because of his admiration for the Russian Revolution?

107 The Iberian Anarchist Federation (FAI) was founded in July 1927. Where?

108 Name the anarchists who murdered the Archbishop of Saragossa.

109 With what episode in 1933 during the Second Spanish Republic do you associate the man known as Six Fingers?

110 Who described his experiences in the Spanish Civil War in a book entitled *Homage to Catalonia*?

111 Which woman anarchist, much against her convictions, became Minister of Health during the Second Spanish Republic?

112 Can you name the novel, written by the Basque author Pio Baroja, in which anarchists are the principal characters?

113 In which city did the posters exhorting the public to 'organised indiscipline' first appear?

114 When anarchist communes were set up during the Spanish Civil War, the use of money was forbidden. How were the members paid?

115 What was known as the 'pareo' during the Spanish Civil War?

116 The building-up of agricultural unions during the 1919–20 period was the direct aim of which Spanish newspaper?

117 Who was the leading intellectual who said, 'There is no such thing as an Anarchist war: there is only one war and we must win it'?

118 The anarchist leader, Garcia Oliver, took refuge in France after the defeat of the Spanish Republicans and then fled to which country?

119 Who was mainly responsible for the 'Manifesto of the Thirty'?

120 Where was Buenaventura Durruti killed?

General Knowledge 3

121 Simon, called Peter, and his brother were both disciples of Jesus. What was his brother's name?

122 In 1215 King John sealed Magna Carta. What does the name of this document literally mean?

123 Over which organs of the body do the adrenal glands lie?

124 Fuerteventura, Gomera and La Palma form part of which island group?

125 What name is given to the fruit of the egg plant?

126 If you found 'pinx' and 'pinxit' following a name on a painting what would it mean?

127 To which dynasty did the Plantagenet Kings from Henry II to Richard II belong?

128 Musically, what does 'a capella' mean?

129 Roger Bannister was the first to run a mile in less than four minutes. Who was the Australian who was the first to break this record?

130 The American short-story writer, William Sydney Porter, achieved fame under which pseudonym?

131 By which other name was the Augustinian Thomas Hammerken known?

132 The planet Saturn has ten moons. What is the largest called?

133 This city was the fortress site of the twentieth Legion and was known as Deva. What is it called today?

134 In South Africa, what is a 'stoep'?

135 The territory now called California was ceded to the United States after which war?

136 Which author created the character of Sergeant Cuff?

137 Toucans are indigenous to South and Central America. What are they?

138 With which particular skill is the name Thomas Tompion associated?

139 Whereabouts in Northern Ireland is the new University of Ulster?

140 Which craft is practised by a lapidary?

The Alps
Set by Michael Baker

141 What is the Parsenndienst.

142 What peak stands between the Ogre and the Maiden?

143 In 1931 an Olympic Gold Medal was awarded for what
mountaineering feat?

144 Three of the four great ridges on the Matterhorn are
named the Zmütt, the Hörnli and the Italian (or Arête
du Lion). What is the name of the fourth ridge?

145 What is the name of the mountain in the Hohe Tauerne
which was first climbed in 1841 by the Bishop of Gurk in
a party of 61 people?

146 What transalpine road was financed by the King of
Sardinia, who wanted one carriage road across the Alps
which was not controlled by the Habsburgs?

147 What is the name of the first railway tunnel to be bored
through the Alps?

148 In what alpine connection was Edward Schweitzer (also
known as Captain Spelterini) famous?

149 What event, in 1860, had the effect of transferring some
of the greatest alpine peaks from one country to
another?

150 Who are commemorated in a memorial below the north
face of Triglav in the form of a 16-foot-high piton and
karabiner (or snap link)?

151 Who or what was Tschingel?

152 Dolomite was named after the Marquis of Dolomieu;
he suggested it be given another name in honour of a
famous Genevan alpinist. What was the name?

153 Which Swiss Canton has as its heraldic device 13 stars on argent and gules (silver and red)?

154 What was the significance of the fact that a lady in her seventy-first year climbed her first snow mountain, the Wetterhorn, in 1896?

155 What is the special importance of the 'Pierre à Niton'?

156 What are the Viertausender?

157 Why is the East-North-East ridge of the Dent Blanche known as the Ridge of the Four Asses, or Viereselsgrat?

158 The North-East Face of the Eiger yielded a route in 1932 which is named after a Zurich dentist in the party. Who was he?

159 What is the name of the highest Alpine peak entirely in Italy?

160 Running south-west in the Chamoix Aiguilles are the Aiguille du Fou, the Dent du Caiman, and the Dent du Crocodile. What comes next?

History of the Royal Navy, 1794–1805

Set by Rear-Admiral Edward Gueritz

161 Who was the British Commander-in-Chief at the Battle of Copenhagen in April 1801?

162 In which ship did Nelson fly his flag at the Battle of the Nile?

163 What were the 'Quota Acts' introduced by Pitt?

164 Why was Admiral Cornwallis nicknamed 'Billy Blue'?

165 From which French ship was the musket ball fired which killed Nelson?

166 Which ship was commanded by Captain Collingwood at the battle of Cape St Vincent?

167 Who was the First Lord of the Admiralty at the time of the Mutiny of the Fleet at the Nore in 1797?

168 Who was known as the Admiral of the 'Floating Republic'?

169 How, in the summer of 1797, did Admiral Duncan, in the words of the First Lord of the Admiralty, 'keep the whole Dutch fleet in awe'?

170 In April 1797, Admiral Sir Samuel Hood was Governor of Greenwich Hospital. What was his brother's post at the same time?

171 Admiral Lord Howe (1726–99) was known as the 'sailor's friend'. What was his other nickname?

172 What was the action that Nelson described as 'greater was never fought', and that earned Saumarez the Order of the Bath and the freedom of the City of London?

173 Who commanded the Dutch forces at the Battle of Camperdown?

174 What class of ship was HMS *Amethyst*?

175 In 1799, what did Nelson state in a letter as 'the great object of the war'?

176 Why did Captain Troubridge not play an active part in the Battle of the Nile?

177 What was a 'Prame'?

178 What was the name of the naval commander of the British landing at Aboukir Bay?

179 In what year did the British first capture the Cape of Good Hope?

180 What office did Captain Ball take up in September 1800?

General Knowledge 4

181 What do the French normally call the English Channel?

182 In the Revised Version, what is the first sentence of Psalm 23?

183 *Murder in the Cathedral* is an historical verse play written by whom?

184 Who founded the Young Men's Christian Association?

185 Malta consists of a number of islands; which is the next in size to Malta itself?

186 In Wagner's *The Ring of the Nibelung*, who slays a dragon who is really the giant Fafner?

187 Who, in the early 1920s, united a large number of trade unions to form the giant Transport and General Workers Union?

188 What kind of creature is a bittern?

189 Which author created the fictional detective C. Auguste Dupin?

190 By what name are the Malvinas Islands more commonly known?

191 What does the adjective pluvial mean?

192 Who was the British surgeon who laid the foundation of modern antiseptic surgery in the nineteenth century?

193 *Catching the Thanksgiving Turkey* is one of the paintings by an American who took up an artistic career in her old age. Who was she?

194 Which Italian nobleman in 1858 led a conspiracy to assassinate Napoleon III?

195 What was the old name for concentrated sulphuric acid?

196 Who was the first Negro to hold the heavyweight boxing championship of the world?

197 Roan Barbary is the name of the King's favourite horse in which of Shakespeare's plays?

198 One of the many spectacles of ancient Rome was called a *naumachia*. What was this?

199 On 3 July 1938 an LNER A4 Pacific locomotive, No. 4468, established a world speed record for steam traction of 126 mph. What was the name of the locomotive?

200 What was the Elizabethan fashion known as Euphuism?

The Indian Tribes of North America, 1550–1900

Set by Jacqueline Fear

201 Indians once used 'wampum' for money. What was this?

202 Which present-day state was known officially in the nineteenth century as Indian Territory?

203 What is the vital factor that caused the distinctive change in the way of life of the Plains Indians after the arrival of the Europeans?

204 Why were the Sioux Indians, who were not afraid of death, terrified of being hanged?

205 The Choctaws, Seminoles, Cherokees and Creeks are four of the tribes which were known collectively as the Five Civilised Tribes. What is the name of the fifth?

206 What is the better-known name of the great Sioux chief who was called 'Curly' as a boy?

207 Wovoka was the prophet of the Ghost Dance movement of the 1880s. What was his American name?

208 Quanah Parker was of mixed blood, but he is often acclaimed as the last great chief of which tribe?

209 Among which tribe did the missionaries of the American Board of Commissioners to Foreign Missions work?

210 Under the terms of the Dawes Act of 1887, how many acres of land were to be given to each head of family?

211 What was the name of the Indian who led the Wampanoag in their war against New England between 1675 and 1677?

212 Who wrote *A Century of Dishonour*, the classic statement of American injustice to the Indians?

213 Which American general won the battle of Horseshoe Bend?

214 Where was Sitting Bull killed?

215 For which ceremony did all the bands of the Sioux tribe unite annually?

216 In which state was (and is) the Omaha reservation?

217 What is a kiva?

218 Why did the Black Hills (the sacred lands of the Sioux) become particularly attractive to Americans in the 1860s?

219 What was a Navaho hogan?

220 The Nomadic Indians of the plains transported their possessions by means of a pair of poles attached to the back of a dog or pony. What was this device called?

History of the Church of England since 1530

Set by Professor A. R. C. Leaney

221 The Prayer Book of 1549 aroused opposition. What did West Country people describe as 'but like a Christmas Game'?

222 How did King James I characterise worshipping relics of saints or images?

223 In what church may still be seen marks in the masonry which recall the trial of Cranmer?

224 Who was the famous preacher who published works such as *Of a Late and Deathbed Repentance* and *Practical Catechism*?

225 Who wrote the words of the hymn beginning, 'New every morning is the love . . .'?

226 What were the Marprelate Tracts?

227 What is the importance of Coverdale in the history of the English Bible?

228 What is the title of the famous Tract 80, written by Isaac Williams?

229 The institution of the first Anglican bishop in Jerusalem in 1841 was sanctioned by two authorities. The Archbishop of Canterbury was one. Who was the other?

230 Which Archbishop presided over the first Lambeth Conference in 1867?

231 Two famous authors of children's classics were among the founders of Christian Socialism in the Church of England. Name one of them.

232 What was the importance to the Church of England of the Papal Bull of 1896 *Apostolicae Curae*?

233 What was Queen Anne's Bounty?

234 Archbishop William Temple wrote *Mens Creatrix* and *Christus Veritas*. What was the other philosophical work he wrote, but with an English title?

235 Why is the Prayer Book as proposed in 1928 not the statutory Prayer Book of the Church of England?

236 Crowther Hall, in the Selly Oak Colleges, acknowledges in its name an important 'first'. In what way was Crowther an important 'first'?

237 Who was the first Bishop of New Zealand?

238 Who was the author of the hymn 'Rock of Ages'?

239 What was the theme of the Oxford Assize sermon by John Keble that gave the Oxford Movement impetus?

240 Which Archbishop officiated at the coronation of King George VI?

General Knowledge 5

241 What name is usually given to the mounted herdsmen or cowboys of the pampas of South America?

242 In the Bible, which sea is said to have closed in upon the Egyptian Army pursuing the Israelites?

243 Which element has the chemical symbol 'K'?

244 Cowboys often wear 'chaps'. What are they?

245 Of whom did Ben Jonson ask, 'Drink to me only with thine eyes'?

246 Of which country is Bratislava a major river port?

247 The *Washington Post* reporters, Carl Bernstein and Bob Woodward, wrote an account of the Watergate scandal, which was published in 1974. What was the book called?

248 The Communist Information Bureau was created in 1947 and dissolved in 1956. By what abbreviated title was it usually known?

249 In proof-reading, the sign ∧ indicates that something is to be inserted. What is this mark called?

250 The traditional Scottish kelp industry was based upon which type of plant?

251 By which treaty was Gibraltar formally ceded to Great Britain in 1713?

252 What kind of creature is a vendace?

253 The Elgin Marbles were originally part of the frieze of the Parthenon in Athens. By whom were they designed?

254 The Borstal system used in dealing with juvenile crime took its name from the village of Borstal. In which county is this village?

255 In what part of the body would you find cells called rods and cones?

256 Who was the South American revolutionary leader who, in 1819, was named President of a new republic known as Gran Colombia?

257 Born in Liège, his piano compositions include 'Prelude, Chorale and Fugue'. Who is this composer?

258 Together with his brother John, he edited *The Examiner* from 1808. Who was he?

259 In the context of gardening, what are dannocks?

260 How is the Queen portrayed on the 1977 Jubilee crown?

Ancient Egypt, 2700–2339 BC
Set by Cyril Aldred

261 Where in Egypt were found the only surviving examples of royal statues of the Old Kingdom, fashioned in copper?

262 In which dynasty was the Palermo Stone carved?

263 Who was the excavator of the tomb of the mother of Kheops at Giza?

264 What, apart from its shape, renders the Rhomboidal Pyramid unique among the other pyramids of Egypt?

265 What is the name given by Egyptologists to that chamber of the tomb in which statues were housed during the Old Kingdom?

266 In whose pyramid does one find the earliest Pyramid Texts?

267 What monument lies in ruins at Abu Gurab?

268 Where were the quarries located that provided the fine limestone used for encasing the great monuments of the Pyramid Age?

269 A child was buried in an alabaster coffin lined with six-ply wood. Below which pyramid was this coffin found?

270 From whose pyramid does the name of the ancient city of Memphis derive?

271 What exceptional scene of human misery is depicted in a relief from the Causeway of King Unas?

272 Who was the vizier, son-in-law of King Tety, who owned a fine mastaba tomb?

273 In which museum is the pair-statue of King Mycerinus and his queen now found?

274 Where, apart from Sakkarah itself, is there a monument
of the builder of the Unfinished Step Pyramid at
Sakkarah?

275 What monument, unique for the Old Kingdom, has
been found in the mortuary temple of King User-Kaf?

276 According to the granite stela between the front paws of
the Great Sphinx, what did Prince Tuthmosis dream
that he was promised?

277 What kind of stone, transported from Nubia, was used
for the statues of Kheops and Khephren in Giza?

278 What confirmation is there for the traditional belief that
Imhotep designed the Step-Pyramid complex for King
Djoser?

279 What was the Heb-Sed?

280 What was it that caused the young King Pepy II, in a
state of high excitement, to write a letter to Harkhuf, the
Governor of Aswan?

Lady Members of the House of Commons
Set by Dr David Butler

281 Who was the first woman Liberal Member of Parliament?

282 An Act of Parliament in 1945 was seen as a triumph for one woman member, Eleanor Rathbone. What was the Act?

283 Two women have been in the full Cabinet simultaneously on two occasions. Who was the same on each occasion?

284 A woman MP has held the same ministerial office on three separate occasions. Which ministerial office is this?

285 There is no age limit for MPs. Who was the oldest woman to sit in the House of Commons?

286 The Duchess of Atholl gave up the party whip over the India policy. What event brought her back into the fold?

287 The limitations on the franchise have led to some incongruous situations. Which MP was elected when she was too young to vote?

288 Lady Davidson was MP for Hemel Hempstead between 1937 and 1959. What was significant about her election in 1945?

289 Margaret Herbison resigned from the Cabinet in 1967 in protest against what?

290 What was the notable 'first' achieved by Mrs Harriet Slater in 1964?

291 The Duchess of Atholl was the first woman to hold ministerial office. What was this office?

292 What was the family event that made it possible for Lady Astor to become the first woman to take her seat in the British Parliament?

293 Who, according to her testimonial, was the 'thoroughly smart business young person' who was an apprentice in a draper's shop in Brighton but became a Cabinet Minister?

294 Ellen Wilkinson was the daughter of a trades unionist. What was the trades union post to which she was appointed in 1915?

295 Two women took over the seat when their husbands succeeded to a peerage. Lady Astor was one; who was the other?

296 To date, who has held ministerial office for the longest total period?

297 Two women who entered the House of Commons in the 1920s were also there in the 1960s. Jennie Lee was one; who was the other?

298 Mrs Runciman was MP for St Ives in 1928. Who followed her as MP for this division?

299 Who became Secretary of State for Employment and Productivity in 1968?

300 For what purpose did the Duchess of Atholl resign her seat in the House of Commons in 1938?

General Knowledge 6

301 The Mazurka is a traditional dance. What is its country of origin?

302 Coalbrookdale in Shropshire is associated with whose famous ironworks?

303 The colour of human skin and hair is mainly due to what pigment?

304 In a British military context, what do the letters TAVR stand for?

305 Who wrote 'I love any discourse of rivers, and fish, and fishing'?

306 What name has been given to the riots in London, in 1780, to compel the Commons to repeal the Bill passed for the relief of Roman Catholics?

307 Metric crown, metric demy and metric royal are different sizes of what commodity?

308 Pinchbeck is an alloy of copper and what else?

309 By what name is the Russian city of Stalingrad now known?

310 In Greek mythology, who is the Muse of History?

311 In which of Puccini's operas do the characters Rodolfo and Mimi appear?

312 Which American dramatist wrote *Who's afraid of Virginia Wolf?*?

313 In the early 1790s, Pierre Charles L'Enfant drew up plans which formed the basis of which North American city?

314 In Troy weight, how many grains are there in a pennyweight?

315 Which river rises in Plinlimon and flows into the Severn near Chepstow?

316 Hever Castle in Kent was the childhood home of a Queen of England. Which one?

317 What name is sometimes given to the legislative assembly of a country that is derived from the Latin word for old man?

318 In February 1940 British naval forces entered Norwegian waters to rescue prisoners from a German ship. What was the name of the ship?

319 What is the connection between the author of *Brief Lives* and the Holes on the outer perimeter of Stonehenge?

320 Of which Scottish district is Haddington the principal town?

Children's Literature

Set by Boswell Taylor

321 What was the name of the horse that shared the stables with Merrylegs and Ginger at Birtwick Park?

322 What was the question to which the Elephant's Child in Kipling's *Just So Stories* wanted the answer?

323 In *Jabberwocky*, Lewis Carroll's hero had to *beware* the Jabberwock and the Jubjub bird. What did he have to *shun*?

324 Who was the pirate captain who went to his death murmuring 'Floreat Etona'?

325 In Hans Andersen's story, *The Tinderbox*, what appears every time the soldier strikes the tinderbox once?

326 What was the remarkable thing that started off Tom's adventure in *Tom's Midnight Garden*, by Philippa Pearce?

327 How did the Phoenix arrive in W. Nesbit's *The Phoenix and the Carpet*?

328 In *The Lion, the Witch and the Wardrobe*, by C. S. Lewis, what is the name of the fairy-tale world?

329 To what country was Dorothy Gale blown by a cyclone from her Uncle Henry's farm in Kansas?

330 What was the menu for the wedding feast for Edward Lear's Owl and Pussy Cat?

331 In the terms used by Kathleen Hale, who is Orlando?

332 What is the present title of the book that Beatrix Potter originally called *The Roly-Poly Pudding*?

333 In which English county has Alan Garner set his *Weirdstone of Brisingamen*?

334 What is the name of the railway company 'in the top left-hand corner of Wales' that Oliver Postgate created for Ivor the Engine?

335 In his poem, Robert Browning says that the Pied Piper's 'quaint attire was much admired'. How was he attired?

336 What is the promise that Mary Poppins makes to children who beg her to stay for ever?

337 Where is the *original* home of Mary Norton's *Borrowers*?

338 In *The Silver Sword*, what does Jan agree to do to get the silver sword?

339 One of the characters in J. R. R. Tolkien's *The Hobbit* is known by the sound he makes. What is this onomatopoeic sound?

340 According to Hans Christian Andersen in *The Little Mermaid*, what is the lifespan of a mermaid?

The Roman Revolution, 60 BC–AD 14

Set by Robin Seager

341 Who was Julius Caesar's wife at the time of his death?

342 Who wrote the final book of Caesar's *Gallic War*?

343 Where was the so-called first triumvirate renewed in 56 BC?

344 What event in 60 BC decided Pollio to place the origins of the civil war in that year?

345 What blow did the alliance of Pompey and Caesar suffer in 54 BC?

346 Labienus was one of Caesar's greatest commanders; what surprising action did he take at the outset of the civil war?

347 What was the function of the *vigiles* created by Augustus?

348 Who was chiefly responsible for the suppression of the Pannonian revolt?

349 Why did Caesar abandon his claim to a triumph in 60 BC?

350 Where is the principal surviving copy of Augustus' record of his achievements, the *Res Gestae*?

351 What was the alleged reason why Curio went over to Caesar in 50 BC?

352 Where was the alliance between Antony and Octavian renewed in 40 BC?

353 What was Augustus' full formal name during most of his reign?

354 What was the Latin name given to the defeat that Rome suffered at the hands of Arminius?

355 How long did Gaius Caninius Rebilus act as consul under Caesar's dictatorship?

356 Where was Decimus Junius Brutus besieged by Antony?

357 Why was there popular pressure on Octavian to make peace with Sextus Pompeius?

358 On what date in AD 4 did Augustus die?

359 What was Augustus celebrating when he erected a triumphal arch in 20 BC?

360 What power, held by Augustus, did Tacitus call the 'symbol of supreme power'?

General Knowledge 7

361 What is an endemic disease?

362 Who was the Flemish painter who came to England in 1632 and was knighted by Charles I?

363 According to *Revelations*, where were the Kings of the Earth gathered together for battle?

364 Who was the first husband of Catherine of Aragon?

365 If, in France, you asked for *pamplemousse*, what would you get?

366 In addition to Lawn Tennis, which sport is represented in the full title of the All England Club at Wimbledon?

367 Who was the author of the novel *The Riddle of the Sands*?

368 Who holds the title of Earl of Merioneth and Baron Greenwich?

369 In geometry, what do the letters QED at the end of a theorem stand for?

370 Who was the Dominican monk whose sale of indulgences provoked Luther to publish his Wittenberg theses?

371 In Greek mythology, what was the name of the Cyclops who imprisoned Odysseus and his companions in a cave?

372 In which country is the Koruna a unit of currency?

373 In which Shakespearian play do Hermia and Helena both appear?

374 On which river is the city of Leningrad situated?

375 What famous declaration was made in Scotland in 1320?

376 For which particular commodity is Orrefors in Sweden renowned?

377 Of which family of plants are the following genera? *Opuntia* and *Cereus*?

378 What name is given to an issue of bank notes that is not backed by precious metal?

379 What does a phillumenist collect?

380 Which is the premier Livery Company of the City of London?

Instruments of the Symphony Orchestra

Set by Dr Stanley Sadie

381 Which town is the home of violin making?

382 What was original about the trumpet used in Haydn's Trumpet Concerto?

383 Who invented it?

384 Of which instrument are the curtal, the dulzian and the pommer principal ancestors?

385 Berlioz used a 'Jingling Johnny' in his *Symphonie Funebre et Triomphale*. What is it?

386 In that symphony, what other more standard instrument in the orchestra is featured?

387 The 'fiauti d'echo' is a virtually unknown instrument except in one well-known work by Bach. Which work?

388 In which symphony did Mozart first use clarinets?

389 What is 'scordatura'?

390 Beethoven used three trombones in Symphonies Five and Nine. In which symphony did he use only two?

391 What was the instrument used in *Don Quixote* which Strauss suggested should be played off-stage, otherwise the audience might laugh?

392 How many timpani are required in the Berlioz *Requiem*?

393 For the shepherd's pipe in Wagner's *Tristan*, what Hungarian instrument was used by Mahler in Vienna and subsequently at Bayreuth?

394 What is the purfling of a violin or any other stringed instrument?

395 What instrument has an Italian name that means a 'bundle of sticks'?

396 What instrument represents Till Eulenspiegel in Strauss's symphonic poem?

397 Who is the man credited with the invention of the clarinet?

398 What important part of the modern violin was completely missing from the Baroque violin?

399 What instruments did Bruckner introduce to symphonic music in his late symphonies?

400 Who was the great reformer of flute fingering?

History of the Zulus, 1816–79
Set by Antony Brett-James

401 Who was given the title of 'The Black Napoleon'?

402 From whom did the Zulus derive their name?

403 What was the ruler of the Umtetwa who was largely responsible for Shaka's selection as a ruler of the Ama-Zulu, although not the rightful heir?

404 Who was the Bishop of Natal who was called Sobantu, 'Father of the People', by the Zulus?

405 Who was the kindly man of peace who, in 1840, succeeded the cruel Dingaan as King of the Zulus?

406 Who remarked, after the death of the Prince Imperial in 1879, 'A very remarkable people, the Zulus: they defeat our generals; they convert our bishops; they have settled the fate of a great European dynasty'?

407 What did Shaka say when he was attacked by his two brothers Dingaan and Mhlangana in 1826?

408 What does the Zulu word Impi mean?

409 Theophilus Shepstone was Secretary for Native Affairs in Natal. What essential part did he play in Cetshwayo's accession to the throne?

410 Who was the Boer leader who went to see Dingaan in November 1837 to solicit a grant of land?

411 Who became Shaka's European doctor in 1824?

412 Why did no Zulu sit on a chair during the reign of Dingaan?

413 What was the name given to the clan or faction which supported Cetshwayo?

414 How were Port Natal residents saved from massacre when the town was pillaged in April 1838?

415 What is the link between the Battle of Blood River and the town of Pretoria?

416 When Pieter Retief led the Boers into Natal, what was the river that the Zulus recognised as the boundary of Zululand proper?

417 What was the concession that came from the visit to Shaka in 1824 of Lieutenant Farewell and Dr Fynn?

418 What was the name of the river that was the scene of the Battle of Blood River?

419 Shaka appointed James Saunders King, a Natal settler, as his emissary in charge of a mission for what purpose?

420 Mosilikatze, Shaka's general who incurred his wrath, was not of the Zulu tribe proper. What did he and his followers style themselves?

General Knowledge 8

421 Between the fourteenth century and the Revolution of 1830, the eldest sons of the Kings of France were known by what title?

422 What is the distinctive smell of hydrogen-cyanide?

423 Who succeeded Sir Robert Mark as Commissioner of Police of the Metropolis?

424 Which French sculptor created the group *The Burghers of Calais*?

425 Austin is the capital of which of the United States of America?

426 Gustav Holst composed a symphonic poem based on a description of a Dorset landscape by Thomas Hardy. What is the composition called?

427 According to the New Testament, who was the father of John the Baptist?

428 What was the name of Sir Ernest Shackleton's ship that was trapped and crushed by the polar ice in 1915?

429 Which is the third largest ocean in the world?

430 What did John Keats call
      'Thou still unravish'd bride of quietness,
      Thou foster-child of silence and slow time'?

431 How is an isosceles triangle usually defined?

432 What is the Haus der Kunst in Munich?

433 Which piece of equipment has parts called headpiece, cheekpiece, browband and throatlash?

434 Which famous singer made her operatic début in New York in 1859 in the role of Lucia?

435 What is spindrift?

436 Which battle, fought on 2 July 1644, was considered to be the turning point of the English Civil War?

437 What is the official publication for all State proclamations, diplomatic and service appointments, orders in Council, etc.?

438 Which yacht race is the final event in the Admiral's Cup competition?

439 What is the popular name of the garden flower *Tropaeolum*?

440 The Scotsman, James Moffat, is famous for which particular work of translation?

History of London from Roman Times

Set by Francis Sheppard

441 Who said, '... when a man is tired of London he is tired of life ...'?

442 Who does the Venerable Bede record as being responsible for the building of the original church of St Paul?

443 The reigning monarch cannot enter the City on state occasions until what has been complied with?

444 Which Scots poet wrote of London, 'London, thou art the flower of cities all!'?

445 Where in the Tower of London does the resident Governor of the Tower reside?

446 Who was the cartographer who published a large-scale map of London in the 1790s?

447 What was the name of the house in which the British Museum was first established?

448 To which saint is the Chapel in the White Tower of the Tower of London dedicated?

449 When Aethelred II died in London in 1016, the Witan outside London elected Knut for king. Whom did the Londoners choose?

450 The Pantheon, where a 'Marks and Spencer' store now stands on the south side of Oxford Street, saw many changes. What was it originally?

451 The first proclamation of a new monarch is read from which building in London?

452 Piccadilly Circus was named after Piccadilly Hall, a house nearby. Why 'Piccadilly'?

453 Who were the owners of Covent Garden Market in the eighteenth and nineteenth centuries?

454 The first Chairman of the London County Council in 1889 later became Prime Minister. Who was he?

455 Who was the leader of a rebellion against Henry VI, that defeated the King's troops at Sevenoaks and marched upon London?

456 Under which tower in the Tower of London is the Traitor's Gate?

457 London was famous for its Music Halls. Whereabouts was Collin's Music Hall which opened in 1862?

458 Who was the first Lord Mayor of London?

459 Why did Dr John Snow have the street pump in Broadwick Square, Soho, chained up in 1854?

460 What was the service conferred on London by George Shillibeer?

Old Testament
Set by Professor A. R. C. Leaney

461 Who was the mother of Solomon?

462 According to Genesis four rivers flow from Eden. Which one shares its name with a spring near Jerusalem?

463 According to Genesis, how many kings on both sides were involved in the battle of the Valley of Siddim?

464 Where, according to the First Book of Kings, did Elijah triumph over the prophets of Baal?

465 What is the importance of the Cyrus cylinder for Old Testament history?

466 Where did fugitives from Jerusalem take the prophet Jeremiah?

467 What was the name of the King of Judah taken into captivity by the Babylonians in 597?

468 Jonah was swallowed by a great fish: but why was he in the sea?

469 What was the mission on which God sent Jonah when he was swallowed by the great fish or whale?

470 What was the name of the member of the royal house of Darius, regarded as a leader of the returned exiles?

471 What indignity did the Philistines inflict on the headless body of Saul?

472 The Book of Amos dates Amos's activity as two years before what?

473 Hezekiah is said to have prospered in all his works. What is known as Hezekiah's Tunnel?

474 In the battle of Karkar which power was confronted by a coalition of Damascus, Israel and Hamath?

475 What was the capital city of the kings of Israel (the northern kingdom) immediately before Omri moved to Samaria?

476 What king was killed at the battle of Ramoth-Gilead?

477 What figure from the past does the Book of Malachi say will be the forerunner 'before the great and terrible day of the Lord'?

478 How did King Josiah meet his death?

479 According to various authorities Phinehas stayed the plague by 'interposing' or by 'executing judgement' or by 'praying'. What did Phinehas actually do?

480 Who was the governor of Judaea under Artaxerxes I who restored the walls of Jerusalem?

General Knowledge 9

481 What is the name of the country seat in Wiltshire of the Marquess of Bath?

482 Which island, famed for its knitting, is situated midway between Shetland and Orkney?

483 Who was 'The Tiger' of France who presided at the Paris Peace Conference of 1919?

484 *A Shropshire Lad* is probably the best known work of which poet?

485 Jorn Utzon was the architect of which controversial opera house?

486 Alnwick Castle has been the chief seat of which family since the fourteenth century?

487 On a musical score, how is the instruction 'very loud' indicated?

488 Name one of the two countries bound by the Treaty of Tordesillas of 1494?

489 According to the Bible, where did Aaron get the material to make the Golden Calf?

490 Who was the Scottish-born American philanthropist who donated more than $1\frac{1}{2}$ million dollars to build the Peace Palace in the Hague?

491 Some mammals are known as *edentates*. What does this indicate?

492 In French history, what was the *oriflamme*?

493 Who was the President of the USA when Hawaii became a State?

494 Which of Oliver Goldsmith's plays is subtitled 'The Mistakes of a Night'?

495 The IAEA is an agency of the United Nations. What do these initials stand for?

496 Many elections are decided by ballot. What does this word literally mean?

497 In science, what is the Kelvin?

498 A species of ibis was venerated by the ancient Egyptians. What is an ibis?

499 While in Reading Prison, Oscar Wilde wrote a long work to Lord Alfred Douglas which was published after Wilde's death. What was it called?

500 The capitals of Corinthian columns were usually decorated with ornament based on the leaves of which plant?

Life and Work of Vincent Van Gogh

Set by Christopher Brown

501 What was the name of the mining area in Belgium to which van Gogh went as an evangelist in 1879?

502 In May 1890 at St Rémy, van Gogh painted a free copy of a Rembrandt. What was the subject of the original?

503 The first review of van Gogh's work appeared in *De Portfeuille* in August 1889. Who was the critic?

504 Van Gogh sold only one painting during his lifetime. Where exactly did the transaction take place?

505 In the summer of 1890 at Auvers, van Gogh painted the garden of a painter. Who was he?

506 In what positive way did Roger Fry pioneer an appreciation of van Gogh in 1910?

507 In September 1889 at St Rémy, van Gogh painted a Pietà. It was a copy after which artist?

508 At The Hague in November 1882, van Gogh made a lithograph for which the model was his mistress. What was the title?

509 In van Gogh's painting *The Prison Courtyard*, now in the Pushkin Museum, Moscow, which is the London prison represented?

510 A series of English illustrations by Herkomer particularly appealed to van Gogh. What was the subject of this series?

511 Who were van Gogh's employers during his career as an art dealer?

512 Lying on the table in front of L'Arlésienne are two books. One is by Dickens, what is the other?

513 What was the work by Charles Bargue which van Gogh studied assiduously when training to be a painter?

514 When he was living with Theo in Paris, van Gogh attended a studio where life study was taught. Whose studio was it?

515 Early in 1887 van Gogh organised two exhibitions, one of Japanese prints and the second of his own work and that of his friends. Where?

516 In June 1876, van Gogh set out by foot from Ramsgate to visit his sister Anna. Where was she staying?

517 In September 1889, van Gogh began a portrait of Trabu. Who was Trabu?

518 When van Gogh first arrived in Arles, where did he stay?

519 In October 1875 van Gogh preached a sermon with the text, 'I am a stranger on the earth, hide not thy commandments from me'. Where, in England, did he preach this sermon?

520 In *Still-life with an Open Bible*, painted in 1885, there is a candlestick with an extinguished candle, an open bible and a novel by Zola. Which novel?

France in the Seventeenth Century

Set by Professor Douglas Johnson

521 What is the first and most important principle of Descartes' philosophy?

522 Cardinal Richelieu created a famous institution which still exists. What is its name?

523 Who assassinated Henry IV of France in 1610?

524 What did Louis XIV aim to do when he repealed the Edict of Nantes?

525 Who was the character in a play by Molière who discovered that he had been speaking prose all his life?

526 Why was the birth of the future Louis XIV thought to be almost miraculous?

527 What action of Mazarin, in August 1648, brought the Paris mobs into the streets?

528 There were civil wars in France between 1648 and 1653. What were they called?

529 In the novel *Clélie*, Mlle de Scudéry describes an allegorical landscape or map. What is this?

530 Why were the circumstances of Molière's death particularly ironical?

531 What was the nickname of the famous bishop and orator, Bossuet?

532 Who was the chief designer of the gardens of Versailles?

533 In 1662, there was a revolt against the royal authority around one of the Channel ports. Which port?

534 What happened in 1661 which led Louis XIV to announce that he would be his own chief minister?

535 With which religious movement do you associate Pascal?

536 A novel called *L'Astrée*, by Honoré d'Urfé, was published in several parts from 1607 onwards. What is it about?

537 Louis XIV enjoyed ballet and opera. Who was his favourite musician?

538 The War of Devolution was sometimes called the War of the Queen's rights. Who was the Queen?

539 When Molière married, it was said that he had married his own daughter. How did Louis XIV show his disapproval of this rumour?

540 Racine stated that it was not necessary to have blood and death in a tragedy. To which of his plays was he referring?

General Knowledge 10

541 Traditionally, at which battle did the Black Prince 'win his spurs'?

542 What is the traditional Japanese martial art of Kendo?

543 Which sea lies between New Zealand and Australia?

544 In Russia, what is a kolkhoz?

545 Keats wrote of a nightingale and Shelley of a skylark; of which bird did Edgar Allan Poe write in his famous poem?

546 The Queen's Award to Industry was replaced in 1975 by the Queen's Award for Export Achievement and which other award?

547 What kind of substance is Osmium?

548 Who was the great American orator who spoke at Gettysburg immediately before Lincoln delivered his famous Address?

549 In show-jumping there is sometimes an event called *Puissance*; what does this word literally mean?

550 Which Shakespearian character spoke these lines, 'Cowards die many times before their deaths. The valiant never taste of death but once'?

551 Who developed and directed the British operation to block the port of Zeebrugge in 1918?

552 Who composed the symphonic poem *Don Juan*?

553 Who was the only Englishman to become Pope?

554 During daylight, hares crouch in shallow depressions under cover. What are these resting places called?

555 Cato the Elder ended every speech in the Roman Senate with the phrase *Delenda est Carthago*. What does it literally mean?

556 The character, Archie Rice, is a music-hall comic in which of John Osborne's plays?

557 Who was the sculptor whose work *The Gate of Hell* was commissioned in 1880 as a door for the Musée des Arts Décoratifs in Paris?

558 What is the name of the Observatory located on Mount Hamilton, California?

559 Who became the first President of the Republic of Korea in 1948?

560 What kind of wind is graded no. 12 on the Beaufort Scale of Wind Force?

Shakespeare's English Kings

Set by Professor T. J. B. Spencer

561 Which of Shakespeare's kings expresses a desire to
retire to live the life of a shepherd?

562 What title does Henry VIII bestow upon Anne Bullen as
the first mark of his favour?

563 Which King disinherits his son?

564 Mistress Quickly reported that Prince Hal broke
Falstaff's head for insulting the reigning king. What did
Falstaff liken the King to?

565 What does Richard II recommend his Queen to do after
she has been deported to France?

566 Which king is reported to have proclaimed Edmund
Mortimer as heir to the throne?

567 How did the prophecy for King Henry IV's death come
true in a most unexpected way?

568 What is Richard of Gloucester doing when
Buckingham, backed by London citizens, pleads to him
to accept the crown?

569 Whom does Henry V send as ambassador to demand the
crown of France from Charles VI?

570 What is the Greek myth cited by King Henry VI
immediately before he is stabbed to death by Gloucester
who'll 'hear no more'?

571 Which of Henry V's officers compares Henry's life to
that of Alexander the Great?

572 According to Richard of Gloucester, later Richard III,
how had Queen Elizabeth and Jane Shore marked him
with their witchery?

573 When Richard III married Anne, she was a widow. What happened to her husband?

574 Whom does Henry VIII appoint as Lord Chancellor after his dismissal of Cardinal Wolsey?

575 What was the token that King Henry V exchanged with Michael Williams?

576 What card game was Henry VIII playing with the Duke of Suffolk during the night when Princess Elizabeth was born?

577 Where, according to Talbot in *Henry VI Part I*, was the heart of Richard I, Coeur-de-lion, buried?

578 Who crowned Henry VI in Paris?

579 Which King is described by Hotspur in *Henry IV Part I* as 'that sweet lovely rose'?

580 Two English kings appear as ghosts or apparitions in *Richard III*. Name one of them.

The Life of Captain William Bligh

Set by Philip Snow

581 What was Captain Bligh's post on Cook's last voyage?

582 Bligh and Fletcher Christian were together on two ships before they sailed on the *Bounty*. Name one of them.

583 Christian was never appointed Sailing Master. Who was Bligh's Sailing Master on the *Bounty*?

584 On Admiralty instructions Bligh obtained breadfruit from the Society Islands. For whom was this cheap new food intended?

585 Bligh's ship was originally the *Bethia*. Why was it renamed the *Bounty*?

586 Which other post on the *Bounty*, besides that of captain, did Bligh occupy?

587 Whom on the *Bounty* did Bligh consider 'a Drunken Sot', and was to die on the voyage, in Bligh's opinion, from 'intemperance and indolence'?

588 Bligh promulgated a number of rules for his crew before arriving at Tahiti. 'To gain esteem of the natives' was one of them; how were they to achieve this?

589 When the mutiny occurred, off which island was the *Bounty*?

590 In Bligh's narrative, he conjectures the reason for the *Bounty* revolt. What was it?

591 Bligh evacuated the convict settlement of Norfolk Island in 1853. What was the ironic link with Bligh in the island's later history?

592 In identifying Christian, what was the physical characteristic that Bligh mentions in addition to tattoos?

593 How many, of the nineteen who were cast off the *Bounty* into an open boat for the 3600-mile voyage to Timor lasting forty-one days, died at sea on that voyage?

594 What anniversary was commemorated by the name Bligh gave to the first island inside the Great Barrier Reef on which the open boat landed after its historic voyage?

595 What was the specific action by Bligh that began the Rum Rebellion?

596 Which Archipelago was known as 'Bligh's Islands' on early maps and recognises Bligh as its principal European discoverer?

597 What was the name of the ship in which Bligh returned to Tahiti, this time successfully, to transplant the breadfruit trees?

598 In which ocean is 'Bligh's Cap'?

599 Who said, after a sea-battle, 'Bligh, I sent for you to thank you; you have supported me nobly'?

600 For what services was Bligh elected a Fellow of the Royal Society?

General Knowledge 11

601 Theatre stages sometimes have an arch framing them. What is this arch called?

602 Aboard which ship did Lord Kitchener lose his life in 1916?

603 To what family of birds does the Ptarmigan belong?

604 Who was the bellows-mender in *A Midsummer Night's Dream*?

605 According to the Bible, who gave Adam's wife the name of Eve?

606 Who was the American composer of such popular songs as *Stardust* and *Georgia on my Mind*?

607 What is the title of Picasso's work that depicts the bombing of a Basque town during the Spanish Civil War?

608 Which English king's marriage added Poitou and Guienne to his dominions?

609 What word is used by French theatre audiences when requesting an encore?

610 Aganippe was a fountain of the Muses. Where was it situated?

611 Of which British Dependency is Hamilton the capital?

612 Coal gas is *mainly* composed of two gases. Name one.

613 Charles I, King of France, was known as 'the Bald' and Charles II as 'the Fat'. What was Charles III nicknamed?

614 Who created the American comic strip character Li'l Abner?

615 The Organisation of African Unity (OAU) was founded in 1963. Where?

616 What was the pen-name under which Charles Lamb wrote his *Essays* for the *London Magazine*?

617 Bobolinks are known to make lengthy journeys. What kind of creatures are they?

618 Which English tenor is particularly associated with the leading role in Benjamin Britten's opera, *Peter Grimes*?

619 Who surrendered his army at the Battle of Saratoga in 1777?

620 The short play, *Krapp's last Tape*, was written by whom?

Science Fiction

Set by Tom Shippey

621 Which epic novel begins with this sentence: 'Two thousand million or so years ago, two galaxies were colliding ...'?

622 Which story ends with mass panic at the appearance of the stars?

623 What was the 'wild talent' of Wilson Tucker's Paul Breen?

624 Which science-fiction periodical appeared for the first time on 5 April 1926?

625 Hal Clement's imagined planet, Mesklin, had a gravity of 3g at the equator. What was the gravity at the poles?

626 In H. P. Lovecraft's books, who or what waits dreaming in his house beneath the sea at R'lyeh?

627 In Orwell's *1984*, what does it mean if a girl is wearing a scarlet sash?

628 Which author created the magician-detective pair, Lord Darcy and Sean O'Lochlainn?

629 Who wrote *L'Autre Monde ou Les États et Empires de la Lune*?

630 In whose stories would you find Earth infested by erbs, deodands, pelgranes and grues?

631 What was the name of Olaf Stapledon's super-intelligent dog?

632 What can Lucan Hutchman's device do in Bob Shaw's *Ground Zero Man*?

633 How would you go about making a triffid temporarily safe?

634 What did Ixtl do to people?

635 In Kurt Vonnegut's *Cat's Cradle*, who wrote, 'All of the true things I am about to tell you are shameless lies'?

636 What is the uniquely valuable product of Cordwainer Smith's imagined planet, Norstrilia?

637 What did Duke Leto Atreides do in the end with his tooth?

638 Why was Tom Blaine alarmed when he came back to life in Robert Sheckley's *Immortality Inc.*?

639 In Clifford Simak's *Way Station*, what was the strange thing about Enoch Wallace?

640 Why did the ape-men in Conan Doyle's *The Lost World* spare the life of Professor Challenger?

The Vikings

Set by Professor Peter Foote

641 Which Norwegian king in the Viking Age was brought up at the court of King Athelstan of Wessex?

642 The Irish called one group of Vikings 'Dubhgaill'. What country were these 'Black Foreigners' said to come from?

643 What celebrated object provides the model for the animal figure typical of the Viking Age decoration known as the Mammen style?

644 Who is our chief eye-witness source concerning the siege of Paris by Vikings in 886?

645 Name any object, found on the site excavated at Lance-aux-Meadows in north Newfoundland, which has persuaded scholars that this was a Viking Age Norse settlement.

646 What were ice-skates usually made from in the Viking Age?

647 What was said to be the purpose of the god Odin in gathering dead warriors in his Val-hall (or Valhalla)?

648 The last attack on England that could be called a Viking raid was made by King Eystein of Norway in the reign of Stephen. Some said it was an act of vengeance: what for?

649 By which Russian river did Ibn Fadlan observe the funeral rites of a Viking chief in 922?

650 What Irish author described the Faroe Islands round about 820 as deserted by Celtic anchorites on account of Norse freebooters?

651 What object tells us that eleventh-century Swedes reached the island of Berezanj, off the mouth of the Dnieper in the Black Sea?

652 What was the usual technique of sea-fighting employed by Vikings?

653 How was the Trelleborg camp laid out?

654 Whose expedition to the lands of the Baghdad caliphate is recorded on more than twenty rune-stones in central Sweden?

655 Where, in 850, did a Viking force first winter in England?

656 What is the name of the process by which Norse swordsmiths gave blades a marbled appearance?

657 What is thought to be the origin of the name 'Varangians' used of Norse traders and mercenary soldiers in Russia and the Eastern Empire in the Viking Age?

658 What did Adam of Bremen, writing about 1070, say was the occupation of the men whom the Danes called Vikings?

659 Which important Viking township was visited by St Ansgar in the ninth century?

660 Where in Denmark has recent underwater archaeology brought several Viking Age vessels to light?

General Knowledge 12

661 At which castle did the Investiture of the Prince of Wales take place in 1969?

662 Of which country was Ismet Inonu a soldier and statesman?

663 Regina is the capital of which Canadian province?

664 The films, *A Streetcar Named Desire* and *The Wild One*, were two of the successes of which American actor?

665 With which English county is the regiment 'The Green Howards' particularly associated?

666 What did G. K. Chesterton describe as 'the devil's walking parody'?

667 What great catastrophe occurred on 24 August, AD 79?

668 Queen Victoria lived to see her Silver, Golden and Diamond Jubilees. Which one was celebrated in 1887?

669 The *Coffee Cantata* is the name of a humorous cantata composed by whom?

670 In the field of industrial relations, what do the initials ACAS stand for?

671 Of what nationality was the painter Edvard Munch?

672 What kind of soil is tolerated by plants known as halophytes?

673 Who was the first Archbishop of Canterbury to visit the Vatican since the Reformation?

674 What is the name of the Italian city that stands on the River Po and was once capital of the Kingdom of Italy?

675 Wenonah was his mother and the West Wind (Mudjekeewis) was his father. Who is this literary character?

676 In astronomy, what do Miranda, Ariel, Umbriel, Titania and Oberon have in common?

677 What kind of person do the French describe as 'sans souci'?

678 What was the last major battle fought on *English* soil?

679 What Roman poet wrote four books on agriculture known as *The Georgics*?

680 What is the name of the instrument used for measuring the pressure of gases?

Life of Mary Queen of Scots

Set by Nigel Tranter

681 What was the name of Walsingham's agent who persuaded Mary to send her secret correspondence at Chartley in beer-barrels?

682 A special English parliamentary sanction was passed to bring Mary to trial at Fotheringay. What was it called?

683 What was the ruse adopted by the poet Châtelard in order to secure a private audience with the Queen at Burntisland Castle?

684 On 6 March 1565 the 'Dancer' married the 'Lusty'. The 'Lusty' was Mary Livingstone. Who was the 'Dancer'?

685 Henry Stewart, Lord Darnley, had an English monarch for a great-grandfather. Who was this King?

686 Who was executed in the Queen's presence in 1566 for having tried to abduct her?

687 Mary was besieged by dissident nobles in Borthwick Castle after her marriage to Bothwell. How did she escape?

688 Who was Gilbert Curle?

689 What was the social occasion that kept Mary away from Kirk o' Field on the night of the murder of Darnley?

690 What was the real cause of Darnley's death?

691 Who was one of the murderers of Rizzio who later married John Knox's widow?

692 James V said on his deathbed, 'It cam wi' a lass and will gang wi' a lass!' Mary was the lass it would 'gang wi'. Who was the lass with whom it came?

693 The Kirk o'Field plot is traditionally said to have been concocted beneath a yew tree. Where?

694 Who was reputedly 'the handsomest man in Europe' who visited Mary in her captivity at Tutbury?

695 Mary's body now lies in Westminster Abbey. Where was she first buried?

696 What had these three men in common with Mary: James, Earl of Moray; Robert, Earl of Orkney; and James, Commendator of Melrose?

697 Where was Mary's son James, the future James I of England, born?

698 What is the name of the island to which the Queen was taken for refuge in September 1547?

699 Secretary Davison got Mary's death warrant signed by Elizabeth by slipping it amongst less important papers. How was he rewarded?

700 What were the circumstances that caused Mary to spend a night at Niddry Castle, West Lothian?

Drama in Athens, 500–388 BC

Set by Dr W. Liebeschuetz

701 What was the orchestra in a Greek theatre?

702 Name the son of Creon in Sophocles' *Antigone*.

703 With which trilogy did Aeschylus win his last dramatic victory in 458?

704 In the *Lysistrata* of Aristophanes the women of Athens organise a sex strike. What was their objective?

705 What is the *parodos* of a Greek play?

706 The *Medea* of Euripides is about a woman's revenge. What was Medea's principal grievance?

707 According to one play by Euripides, Helen did not spend the years of the Trojan war at Troy. Where did she spend them?

708 What is the original meaning of the word theatre?

709 What playwright is said to have proved his sanity by reciting part of a recently written play in court?

710 In the *Eumenides* of Aeschylus, Athena gives her casting vote for the acquittal of Orestes. What biased her in favour of a matricide?

711 What politician was satirised as Paphlagon in the *Knights* of Aristophanes?

712 How were the judges chosen for the dramatic competition of the City Dionysia?

713 In *The Clouds* of Aristophanes, a father wishes to send his son to school with Socrates. What was he to learn?

714 What is 'Stichomythia'?

715 Name the tragedy which ends with a scene of sacrifice in which a human victim vanishes to be replaced by a deer.

716 In the *Ecclesiazusae* of Aristophanes, the assembly votes to make all women public property. What was the safeguard against over-use of the pretty ones?

717 What was the theoricon?

718 What is the moral dilemma of King Pelasgus in Aeschylus' *Suppliants*?

719 In *The Frogs* of Aristophanes, Aeschylus advised that it is better not to rear a lion in the city, but if one has been reared he must be humoured. Name the politician alluded to.

720 In *The Bacchae* of Euripides, a mother enters carrying the head of her son under the delusion that it is the head of a lion. Name the mother.

General Knowledge 13

721 What term is applied to a man who makes or repairs wooden barrels?

722 In Greek mythology, what happened to those who drank of the waters of the River Lethe?

723 Of which Empire was Palestine a part until the end of World War I?

724 The bird Pica Pica is fond of bright things. What is its more familiar name?

725 What general physical distinction was common to these literary characters: Pantagruel, Despair and Cormoran?

726 A plant whose Latin name is *Isatis tinctoria* is known to yield a blue dye. What is it called?

727 Which British Prime Minister was assassinated in the lobby of the House of Commons in 1812?

728 Which opera was written for the opening of the Cairo Opera House in 1869, though not performed until 1871?

729 Two volumes of autobiography, *Present Indicative* and *Future Indefinite*, were written by which knight of the theatre?

730 Who was the French chemist who demolished the phlogiston theory and established that oxygen supports combustion?

731 Who was President of France throughout the First World War?

732 Voltaire wrote a poem known as *La Pucelle*. Who was the subject of the poem?

733 Which of the planets has two satellites, Triton and Nereid?

734 What is a viviparous creature?

735 Who founded the model town of Port Sunlight in Cheshire?

736 What event is said to have inspired Chopin's *Revolutionary Study in C Minor*?

737 What do J. B. Priestley's initials stand for?

738 Who discovered the island of Cuba in 1492?

739 Who was the fourth wife of Claudius and mother of Nero?

740 Harper's Ferry, made famous by John Brown's raid in 1859, stands at the confluence of two rivers. Name one of them.

Life and Works of Rupert Brooke

Set by Dr John Kelly

741 What is the first line of Brooke's famous sonnet, 'The Soldier'?

742 Complete the title of this poem by Brooke: 'Lines written in the Belief that the Ancient Festival of the Dead was called . . .'?

743 To whom did Brooke write in 1915, 'I suppose you're about the best I can do in the way of a widow'?

744 What was Brooke's nickname at Hillbrow School?

745 On what occasion did Brooke declare that, 'If you write a poem on Tuesday it begins to die on Wednesday. Some take longer dying than others. That is all.'?

746 After which revolutionary group did Brooke and Hugh Dalton name the society that they founded in Cambridge in 1906?

747 Who wrote of Brooke,
     'A young Apollo, golden-haired,
     Stands dreaming on the verge of strife'?

748 What is the last line of the poem 'Heaven'?
     'And in that Heaven of all their wish, . . .'?

749 To which Society in Cambridge did both Tennyson and Brooke belong?

750 In May 1904 Brooke wrote, 'I have met a real live poet'. To whom did he refer?

751 Who was 'Mamua'?

752 Where did Brooke get the idea for his poem, 'Second Best'?

753 What was the original title of Brooke's sonnet, 'Libido'?

754 What is it that 'Unkempt about those hedges blows . . .'?

755 Who is it that
    '. . . will come and go
    On lissom, clerical, printless toe . . .'?

756 Where did Brooke first meet Virginia Woolf?

757 Why did Brooke nickname his mother 'The Ranee'?

758 In Brooke's play *Lithuania*, a prodigal son returns
incognito to his impoverished family. What happens?

759 Of which famous writer did Brooke record that 'he was
incredibly shrivelled and ordinary, and made faintly
pessimistic remarks about the toast'?

760 Of which painter did Brooke say that God, certainly,
does not paint like him 'but it is probable that the
archangels do'?

Political History of China since 1911

Set by Dr Raymond Dawson

761 Which British naval vessel was trapped in the Yangtze by advancing Communist forces in 1949?

762 How was the last Emperor of China employed under the People's Republic?

763 Who adopted the reign-title Hung-hsien (meaning Grand Constitutional era)?

764 Complete the following quotation: 'Let a hundred flowers bloom...'

765 Which important statesman was kidnapped at Sian in December 1936 by Chinese troops from Manchuria?

766 Where did Mao Tse-tung work when he first went to Peking?

767 What was the name of the former Comintern agent sent to China in 1923 as official representative of the Russian government?

768 Who commanded the Flying Tigers?

769 What is the name of the Canadian doctor featured on a Chinese postage stamp?

770 What is the political significance of Matsu?

771 By what name is the conference of April 1955 known, at which Chou En-lai preached the five principles of peaceful coexistence?

772 What is the name of the commune near Soochow visited by Mrs Thatcher in 1977?

773 What is the name of the mountain range between Kiangsi and Hunan where Mao established a revolutionary base in 1928?

774 Who was the Chinese quisling who headed the puppet government under the Japanese in 1940?

775 What was the three-self movement that began in 1950?

776 Who was Chief Inspector of the Salt Revenue Administration from 1913–18?

777 What famous incident took place in Peking on 4 May 1919?

778 What was the name of the bridge where an incident occurred which initiated a full-scale Japanese invasion of China in 1937?

779 What was Sun Yat-sen's family relationship to Chiang Kai-shek?

780 What Chinese port was under German occupation at the beginning of World War I?

General Knowledge 14

781 Of which country is TAP the national airline?

782 What name is given to the four-cornered cap worn by Roman Catholic and Some Anglican ecclesiastics?

783 'Satyrs' were creatures in Greek mythology. What corresponds to them in Roman mythology?

784 What does the Bessemer Process produce?

785 Which English king was the natural son of Robert, Duke of Normandy, by a tanner's daughter?

786 The FAO was the first of the United Nations' specialised agencies. What do its initials stand for?

787 In *Gulliver's Travels* who were the Houyhnhnms?

788 Septuagint is the name given to which translation of the Old Testament?

789 Who was the art critic the first volume of whose *Modern Painters* is said to have rescued the artist Turner from obscurity?

790 Which sea battle took place on St Valentine's Day, 1797?

791 Which part of the body would be affected by a cutaneous disease?

792 Name one of the two Belgian cities linked by the Albert Canal?

793 Who is the 'illiterate loiterer' and clownish servant of Valentine in Shakespeare's *Two Gentlemen of Verona*?

794 What was the name of the exhibition held at Wembley in 1924 and 1925?

795 Where, on the body of a fish, are its pectoral fins?

796 Neil Armstrong was the first man to step on to the Moon. Who was the second?

797 Which country uses the international vehicle registration letters IS?

798 Where do cryophytes grow?

799 In 1927 the Commonwealth Parliament of Australia moved from Melbourne to which city?

800 What name, from the Latin for 'the common people', is given to the direct vote of the whole nation on a specific point?

World War II in Europe

Set by Antony Brett-James

801 What was the name given to the most westerly of the three British beaches on D-Day?

802 Who was Commander-in-Chief of the Polish Army in 1939?

803 Which German city was the target of the first 'thousand-bomber' raid?

804 Who replaced General Gamelin as Commander-in-Chief of the French General Staff on 9 May 1940?

805 What was the code-name given to the operation of which Hitler said to General Guderian, 'Whenever I think of this attack my stomach turns over'?

806 What did Lieutenant Prien's U-boat achieve on 14 October 1939?

807 Which of the airborne landings in September 1944 secured the crossing of the River Waal?

808 Who commanded the 2nd French Armoured Division which liberated Paris in August 1944?

809 Of which operation did Churchill write, 'I had hoped that we would be hurling a wildcat ashore, but all we got was a stranded whale'?

810 In RAF jargon, what was 'window'?

811 Where did the Americans secure their first bridgehead across the Rhine on 7 March 1945?

812 What was the name the Germans gave to their line of defence that ran from the coast near Pisa to the Adriatic at Pesaro?

813 What was the single-word answer that Brigadier-General McAuliffe gave the Germans at Bastogne when called upon to surrender?

814 Two German battle-cruisers escaped in the 'Channel Dash' in February 1942. *Scharnhorst* was one. What was the other?

815 With which battle do you associate the defence of 'Pavlov's House'?

816 Who was awarded a posthumous VC as leader of the Royal Naval attack on German destroyers in a Norwegian fjord in 1940?

817 Who, on Hitler's order, led the spectacular rescue of Mussolini from prison in the Gran Sasso after his fall from power?

818 A desperate battle was fought for Primosole Bridge in July 1943. What area did it give access to?

819 Who was the leader of the Yugoslav Chetniks?

820 Whom did Hitler appoint to head the relief of General Paulus's Sixth Army trapped in Stalingrad?

Salvation Army History
Set by Lt-Col. Cyril Barnes

821 What was the pop song of the day that convinced
William Booth of the value of singing religious words to
the tunes of theatre songs?

822 Who first used the title 'Captain' in the Salvation Army?

823 What invention by Major Frank Maxwell attracted the
attention of Mahatma Gandhi?

824 In the 1880s, when the Salvation Army was persecuted,
who was the Captain's wife left for dead in a Hastings
street?

825 Where did Catherine Booth, co-founder of the
Salvation Army, give her last public address?

826 What disease in England was the Salvation Army
largely responsible for stamping out at the turn of the
century?

827 Complete the phrase coined by Bramwell Booth which
described the Army's internationalism, 'Every land is
my fatherland ...'.

828 Who was the Armenian cobbler in San Francisco who
hammered rivets into the soles of shoes to spell out
'saved from sin' and similar phrases?

829 Why was Captain Charlotte Stirling imprisoned for a
hundred days in 1889 in the Castle of Chillon in
Switzerland?

830 Who was the officer who worked among the Chinese
sailors in Limehouse, London, from 1914?

831 What was the initial proposal by Major John Carleton
that inspired the introduction of Self-denial Week in
1886?

832 Why did William Booth and his followers in Whitechapel move into a dancing academy for their Sunday meetings in September 1865?

833 In which English city was the first Salvation Army brass band formed?

834 What change in the Law came about in 1885 as the result of a campaign conducted mainly by the Salvation Army and William T. Stead?

835 'My ambition is the souls of men.' Where did William Booth inscribe that line?

836 Which was the first country to issue a Salvation Army postage stamp?

837 Who was the first Salvation Army convert among the Zulus?

838 Two emigrant converts, a railwayman and a builder, began the Salvation Army movement in Australia. Name one of them.

839 Why was a stylised sun on the Army flag changed to a star in 1882?

840 On what ship was the Canadian Staff Band lost in 1914?

General Knowledge 15

841 Thursday is named after which Scandinavian god?

842 What is the name of the acid that was first prepared from red ants?

843 On which river is Balmoral Castle situated?

844 Where are the permanent headquarters in London of the National Youth Theatre?

845 Giant oil tankers are sometimes referred to by the abbreviation VLCC. What do these letters stand for?

846 Name one of the two bridges under which the Oxford and Cambridge Boat Race crews pass during the race.

847 As a result of the Franco-German war of 1870–1, which provinces did France lose to Germany?

848 A drama based on the 'Archer–Shee' case was first produced in 1946. What was it called?

849 In an orchestra, which is the smallest of the woodwind instruments?

850 In which English county would you find the Langdale Pikes?

851 On the pre-decimal penny, Britannia is depicted holding a trident and a shield. In which hand does she hold the shield?

852 'Phiz' illustrated some of Dickens' works. What was his real name?

853 In which palace did Queen Elizabeth I and Mary Tudor spend many years of their childhood?

854 The Poet Laureate, Sir John Betjeman, wrote the words of the Jubilee Hymn. Who composed the music?

855 Of which country was Dr Urho Kekkonen elected President in February 1956?

856 Of which Order of Chivalry is the Gentleman Usher of the Black Rod an officer?

857 What name is given to the parliament that Edward I of England called in 1295?

858 In which Shakespeare play would you find the character Launcelot Gobbo?

859 Which English contralto sang the name part in the first performance of Benjamin Britten's *The Rape of Lucretia*?

860 Where is the legendary city of Ys believed to be situated?

The Operas of Benjamin Britten

Set by Harold Rosenthal

861 In *Peter Grimes*, who was going to water his roses now the sun was down?

862 Again in *Peter Grimes*, what was the coroner's verdict on the death of William Spode?

863 Name one of the two nursery rhymes that Britten introduced into *The Turn of the Screw*.

864 What does Flora call the lake in the garden in *The Turn of the Screw*?

865 Who, in Britten's operatic version of *Midsummer Night's Dream*, first created the role of Bottom?

866 In *Billy Budd*, what was *The Rights of Man*?

867 How does Britten depict musically the interview between Captain Vere and Billy Budd before Billy's court martial?

868 In *Let's Make an Opera*, who is always grumbling about her poor feet?

869 Why did Emmy and the schoolchildren in *Albert Herring* have an extra holiday?

870 What does Aschenbach in *Death in Venice* find 'soft, musty and over-ripe'?

871 In one scene in *Gloriana*, Queen Elizabeth contrives to embarrass Lady Essex during a dance at court. How does she do this?

872 On what did Eric Crozier base the story of 'The Little Sweep' in *Let's Make an Opera*?

873 Who conducted the first performance of *The Rape of Lucretia*?

874 Describe briefly the scene in *Albert Herring* in which Britten quotes musically from *Tristan and Isolde*.

875 Sir Frederic Ashton choreographed *Death in Venice*, but he had already been the producer of another Britten opera. Which one?

876 In *Peter Grimes*, why does Mrs Sedley, who 'has never been in a pub in her life', go to 'The Boar'?

877 After the prologue of *The Turn of the Screw*, the orchestra plays a theme which then serves throughout the opera as the subject of how many variations?

878 In *The Rape of Lucretia*, who curtsies with 'that rude politeness at which a servant can excel'?

879 What was the name of the Nó play on which *Curlew River* is based?

880 What is the connection between Shelley's *Queen Mab*, and the character Owen Wingrave, in the opera of that name?

History of Singapore, 1819–1969
Set by Dr John Bastin

881 The first Referendum to be held in Singapore took place on 1 September 1962. What was it about?

882 Raffles Statue was unveiled on the Esplanade, Singapore, on 27 June 1887 to mark an important occasion. What was it?

883 The King of Thailand visited Singapore in 1871. How was his visit commemorated in 1872?

884 What was the title of the literary work that took as its subject the disaster of 12 February 1847?

885 What was the name of the first mail steamer to arrive in Singapore?

886 A well-known Singapore memorial was unveiled in 1954 by Sir Charles Loewen. Whom does it commemorate?

887 What important change was made in the currency of Singapore and the other Straits Settlements in 1903?

888 One of the pioneers of the Malaysian rubber industry became Director of the Singapore Botanical Gardens in 1888. Who was he?

889 What is known as the Transfer?

890 Who was the architect responsible for the design of the first St Andrew's Church and other well-known nineteenth-century buildings in Singapore?

891 Which nineteenth-century British official in Singapore was known as 'Butter-Pot the Great'?

892 Stamford Raffles and Husain Mahummud Shah (of Johore) were two of the three signatories of the Treaty of 6 February 1819. Who was the third?

893 The first bank was established in Singapore in 1840. What was its name?

894 What was the name of the first newspaper published in Singapore?

895 The foundation stone of an important Singapore building was laid in 1823. What was it?

896 Who was the first British Resident Governor of Singapore?

897 Who was the last British Governor of Singapore?

898 What is the main musical contribution of Zubir Said to Singapore's history?

899 During the 1840s, which historic landmark was blown up by the Singapore Surveyor, J. T. Thomson, to widen the entrance to Keppel Harbour?

900 What in Singapore, according to Somerset Maugham, 'stands for all the fables of the Exotic East'?

Supermind

This selection of questions from the 1978 Supermind programme includes:

Section A   *Mastermind* 'Specialist' section – five questions on each of four subjects

Section B   *Top of the Form* – eight questions

Section C   *Forces Chance* – 'Three in a Row' and 'If I'd Been There'

Section D   *Mensa* – five questions

Section E   *Mastermind* General Knowledge

Section A

I. Naval Slang
Set by Boswell Taylor and the Department of Public Relations (Navy), Ministry of Defence

901 What was the origin of the expression 'show a leg'?

902 What did 'to knock the gilt off the ginger bread' refer to in the Navy?

903 What is a 'bumboat'?

904 How did the rum ration get known as 'grog'?

905 A drunk is said to be 'three sheets in the wind'. How is this term derived?

II. Life and Works of John Buchan
Set by Janet Adam Smith

906 John Buchan wrote his first novel while he was still at Glasgow University. What is its title?

907 For which parliamentary constituency was Buchan adopted as a candidate in April 1911?

908 The Trafalgar Lodge is an important rendezvous in one of Buchan's books. Where was it?

909 In *Mr Standfast*, what tune did Mary Lamington whistle in the Château in Picardy?

910 In *The Thirty-Nine Steps*, what was Richard Hannay's first disguise?

III. History of the London Underground

Set by Professor T. C. Barker and Lyndon W. Rowe

911 What role did 'Bumper Harris' play in the history of London's Underground?

912 Who was the originator of the Metropolitan Railway, the first underground railway in the world?

913 In which fashionable road did the Metropolitan erect false fronts to hide the railway?

914 Which uncompleted section of railway was used as an aircraft component factory during World War II?

915 Which line in London formed the world's first tube railway, but was later closed?

IV. The Life of General Robert E. Lee

Set by Professor D. K. Adams

916 A popular novel by Victor Hugo has been suggested as the origin of a nickname for the Army of Northern Virginia. What was it?

917 What was the name of Lee's favourite war horse?

918 To which of the great families of Virginia did Lee's mother belong?

919 What celebrated mission was Lee given by the United States Government in October 1859?

920 How did Lee acquire the nickname 'King of Spades' in the early summer of 1862?

Section B

Top of the Form

921 Two British Prime Ministers held office during the year 1963. Who were they?

922 In Roman mythology, who were the parents of Romulus and Remus?

923 There are two electrodes in a Leclanché cell, one positive and one negative. What are they made of?

924 In the *Divine Comedy*, who were Dante's guides through Hell and Purgatory and through Paradise?

925 Against whom were the British fighting in the Peninsular War of 1808–14?

926 Which canal links the North Sea with the Baltic Sea?

927 More than half the known bird species belong to the order of perching birds. What is the scientific name of this order?

928 In which country is the Jasper National Park?

Section C

I. Forces Chance 'Three in a Row'

Specific Subjects: World Affairs, Literature and Geography

929 Who succeeded Archbishop Makarios as President of Cyprus?

930 Name the title of the book in which Piggy, Ralph and Jack Merridew are among the main characters.

931 The Brenner Pass links two European countries.
Which?

II. Forces Chance 'If I'd been There'

Read the following commentary by Robin Richards and
then answer the questions on it:

'I can see Dinghy Young's "A for Apple" coming in
towards the target. Yes, there're his two spot lights
switched on – visible even in this bright moonlight.

'We've had to send three "Goner" signals already.
With all the trials that Summers did off Reculver, this is
a bitter disappointment. Maybe we'll have better luck at
Sorpe and at the other target, otherwise "Operation
Chastise" will be an utter failure and a big loss of life.

'"232 at 60" have been our orders and we obeyed
them, but it just didn't do the trick. Hopgood did also,
but he's had it. Martin in "P for Popsie" looked a better
bet, but no, it was another "Goner"

'But what's this, a red cartridge sent off Maltby.
Looks as if we've done it. Yes, we've done it. A hole
about 100 yards across and 100 feet deep.

'It's "Nigger" – Hutchinson is tapping it out on his
morse key. Harris back home must be delighted.
Mission accomplished, so far anyway.'

932 What was the event?

933 What was the date?

934 What was the derivation of the code word 'Nigger'?

Section D

Mensa

935 How many different ways are there of making up 4p in coins?

936 Put a word into the brackets that means the same as the word on either side: shrink, (   ), agreement.

937 Insert the word that completes the first word and starts the second: b . . . h.

938 Put the missing numbers into the brackets:
     14641(   )11
     2401 (   ) 7.

939 Historically and geographically, what number and letter follow in this sequence: 46 O, 47 NM, 48 A, 49 A, ?? ?

Section E

Mastermind General Knowledge

Use any of the General Knowledge quizzes from this book.

ANSWERS
to questions in Book Three

General Knowledge 1

1 Harrow.
2 France. The dance originated in the Pays de Gap whose inhabitants were called Gavots. It became popular at the court of Louis XIV.
3 Sir Joshua Reynolds (1723–92).
4 To pool the coal and steel resources of Western Europe. The European Coal and Steel Community came into being in 1952.
5 Devon.
6 The oboe. He is the son and grandson of Eugene Goosens, both conductors; his brother, also named Eugene, is a composer, conductor and violinist and his sisters Sidonie and Marie are both harpists.
7 Johann Christoph Friedrich von Schiller. (His last completed play was *Wilhelm Tell*; he was working on *Demetrius* when he died in 1805.)
8 Fitzalan-Howard. He is also Earl Marshal and Hereditary Marshal of England.
9 Hygiea.
10 The second. SI = Système International d'Unités.
11 Ellen Cicely Wilkinson (1891–1947). She was leader of the 'Jarrow Crusade', and Minister of Education, 1945–7.
12 Birmingham. The hallmark normally comprises the sponsor's mark, assay office mark, standard mark and date letter. The Hallmarking Act of 1973 (effective from 1 January 1975) substituted the sponsor's mark for the maker's mark in certain circumstances.
13 Aspasia. She was a Greek courtesan, born in Miletus, who lived with Pericles from about 440 BC.
14 Dublin, Ireland. Air Alfred Chester Beatty left it to the Irish nation in 1968.
15 Dr Samuel Johnson (1709–84). Believed to have been written to William Strahan, 7 April 1775, and quoted in Boswell's *Life of Johnson*.
16 Ermine Street. The name *may* derive from 'Earningastraet' (the road to Earn's people), a group of Anglo-Saxons who settled near part of its route through Cambridgeshire.

17 Edgar D. Adrian (later Lord Adrian); Sir Charles
    Sherrington.
18 USS *Missouri*, on 2 September 1945.
19 Lord Dunsany (1878–1957). Edward John Moreton
    Drax Plunkett, 18th Baron Dunsany, was a novelist,
    poet and playwright who wrote many plays for the
    Abbey Theatre.
20 John Maynard Keynes (1883–1946), a pioneer of the
    theory of full employment.

The Stuart Kings and Queens, 1603–1714

21 Smallpox. She died 28 December 1694.
22 In Exeter.
23 That he was the servant of the House and could only do
    as the Members required him. Charles I was the first
    monarch to enter the Commons while they were sitting
    (4 January 1641). The five Members he wanted to
    impeach were Pym, Hampden, Haslerigg, Holles and
    Strode – all leading members of the opposition.
24 'That is very true, for my words are my own, my actions
    are my ministers'.'
25 William III.
26 Tunnage and poundage. In 1625 Parliament granted
    Charles two subsidies but no tunnage and poundage.
    The Commons voted it for one year only, instead of for
    life as had been customary since the fifteenth century.
    The Lords refused to pass it in such a restricted form,
    so it fell through completely. Charles, angry, continued
    to have it collected.
27 Abigail Masham (later Lady Masham). She was
    introduced to Queen Anne by Sarah Churchill, her
    cousin, and later became her rival for the Queen's
    affections.
28 His horse stumbled on a molehill and threw him. He
    only broke his collar-bone, but could not take the shock.
    Some days later pneumonia set in.
29 Sir Anthony van Dyck (1599–1641).

30 Major William Careless (or Carles, or Carlos).
31 He rode his horse Woodcock in the Newmarket Plate and won the race both times.
32 Parliament. In 1614, when he dissolved the so-called 'Addled Parliament'.
33 From his supposed resemblance to St Stephen. 'Steenie' was a Scottish nickname. Villiers was the Duke of Buckingham.
34 He bought the Duke's art treasures for that sum.
35 Lucy Walter (Mrs Barlow). She died in 1658. During 1673–80 there were rumours that she had legally married Charles and that the proofs were in a 'black box'. Charles issued three proclamations denying this.
36 William Laud (1573–1645). He became Archbishop of Canterbury in 1633. Impeached for high treason by the Long Parliament, he was executed.
37 The King was to surrender most of his feudal dues in return for a guaranteed annual income of £200,000.
38 He tossed it in the fire.
39 *Eikon Basilike*. The Pourtraicture of his Sacred Majestie in his Solitudes and Sufferings.
40 The furious quarrel between Oxford (Robert Harley) and Bolingbroke at the Council meeting before the Queen in July 1714.

Life and Works of Ernest Hemingway

41 Miller.
42 Oak Park.
43 Ambulance driver in the Red Cross.
44 The plane crashed and Hemingway was seriously injured. The pilot hit a telegraph line with a wing while banking to give his passengers a view of some spectacular waterfalls.
45 A giant marlin.
46 Colonel Richard Cantwell.
47 *The Torrents of Spring*.
48 Thomas Hudson. From *Islands in the Stream*.

49 He got a thorn scratch in his knee; the scratch later turned to gangrene and he died.
50 The hills across the valley of the river Ebro. From *Hills Like White Elephants*.
51 The Crucifixion of Christ. They are Roman soldiers who took part in the Crucifixion and are discussing the event afterwards in a Hebrew drinking-house.
52 It set his mouth on fire, so then he had to cool it by drinking a Tom Collins. From *Islands in the Stream*.
53 He was disqualified for hitting his opponent, Walcott, below the belt.
54 Cruising off the coast of Cuba to destroy U-boats on behalf of the US Navy.
55 They were lost, when the suitcase that held them was stolen at the Gare de Lyon. From *Hunger was a Good Discipline*. Hadley was his first wife.
56 Finca Vigia – at San Francisco de Paula, Havana.
57 *The Sun Also Rises*.
58 Sylvia Beach. It was a bookshop with a library – a meeting place in Paris for writers.
59 Ole Andreson, the Swedish ex-boxer.
60 Bicycle racing. From *The End of an Avocation*

General Knowledge 2

61 Green. Chlorophyll is the generic name for any of several green pigments present in plants.
62 The horse. Eohippus, of the Eocene epoch, was about 11 inches high, and Mesohippus, of the Oligocene epoch, about 24.
63 Tintern Abbey, in Gwent (formerly in Monmouthshire).
64 Bretton Woods, New Hampshire, USA. The International Monetary Fund (IMF) was created as a result of this conference.
65 Ancient Egypt. Isis was the wife of Osiris (identified with the Greek Dionysus), and the mother of Horus, God of Light.
66 The dog. It is a German breed – a kind of wire-haired terrier.

67 London Bridge. It was sold in 1968.
68 The Charge of the Light Brigade. Said by Maréchal
    Bosquet, at the Battle of Balaklava, October 1854.
69 Goatlike, having a goatish smell, lustful.
70 Glamis Castle, on 21 August 1930. The ancient home of
    Macbeth, and now the family home of the Earls of
    Strathmore.
71 Engelbert Humperdinck (1854–1921). It was produced
    in Weimar in 1893 and in London in 1894.
72 The Mock Turtle.
73 Cardinal Richelieu (Armand Jean du Plessis, Duc de
    Richelieu), sometimes known as 'Eminence Rouge'.
74 The umbra. As distinct from the penumbra, the lighter,
    outer edge of the shadow.
75 The pineapple.
76 A mere assertion wholly unsupported, or a dogmatic
    statement resting on bare authority. Literally, 'He
    himself said it'. The 'he' is Pythagoras the master,
    according to Cicero.
77 George Monck (1608–70).
78 A wand (staff) topped by a pine cone and wreathed with
    ivy and vine branches. It was carried by Dionysus and
    the Bacchants.
79 Thomas Hardy.
80 Chopin. The ballet, by Fokine, was originally called
    Chopiniana. Diaghilev altered the title to *Les Sylphides*
    for its presentation during his first Western European
    season in Paris in 1909. It was orchestrated by
    Stravinsky.

The City of Rome

81 St John (i.e. St John Lateran).
82 S. Susanna.
83 He found Rome brick and left it marble. Chronicled in
    Suetonius' *Divus Augustus*.
84 138.
85 The Temple of Neptune.
86 Doria-Pamphili Gallery (or Palace).
87 Because its site was indicated to the founder (generally

said to be Pope Sixtus III) by a miraculous fall of snow in midsummer.

88 330.
89 S. Maria del Priorato on the Aventine.
90 Napoleon, in his Memoirs.
91 Statues to which, from the sixteenth century, political squibs or lampoons were attached. The most famous was that of Pasquino in Piazza Pasquino. Others are Marforio, now in the Capitoline Museum, and Madama Lucrezia in Piazza S. Marco.
92 King Victor Emmanuel II.
93 To subordinate all Italy to Rome again. He was a self-styled Tribune who was supported by Petrarch.
94 Benvenuto Cellini.
95 A group of German painters who settled in Rome then, painting and living in primitive or medieval style.
96 Venezia Palace.
97 To the Church of the Aracoeli. Il Bambino refers to Christ Child of the Crib displayed at the Church at Christmas.
98 The Ganges.
99 The port of Ostia. It is called the Metropolitana.
100 In S. Maria sopra Minerva.

The Spanish Anarchist Movement, 1908–75

101 Señor Moret. In *The Times*, 18 February 1910.
102 A general strike in Barcelona. It was aimed against conscription and rapidly turned into a revolutionary attack on the established order.
103 Francisco Ferrer, a Catalan anarchist who was shot 31 October 1909. He was a theoretical anarchist, known for his anti-clerical work in schools and sometimes called the 'founder of the lay schools' in Spain. He was arrested 31 August 1909, accused of being the chief instigator of the Barcelona Rising.
104 A supposed secret anarchist organisation, allegedly responsible for assassinations, but said to have existed

only in the minds of the police. (After the Anarchist Congress in Seville in 1882 there were fears of violence in the rural areas of Andalusia. The police blamed this secret organisation and made thousands of arrests, but no absolute proof of its existence was ever found.)

105 Confederación Nacional de Trabajo (National Confederation of Labour). An anarchist-syndicalist organisation founded in Barcelona in 1911.

106 Salvador Cordón.

107 In Valencia.

108 The brothers Ascaso. They assassinated Cardinal Soldevila, whom they considered the incarnation of reactionary clericalism. They were sentenced to thirty years in prison, but were released in 1931 on the coming of the Second Republic.

109 The setting up of an anarchist commune, of which he was the leader, in the Andalusian village of Casa Viejas. 'Seisdedos', the nickname of Curro Cruz, and twenty-four other anarchists died when the Civil Guard attacked their house.

110 George Orwell.

111 Federica Montseny.

112 *Aurora Roja (Red Dawn)*.

113 Barcelona.

114 In coupons, the number being based not on the hours of work done, but on the size of the individual worker's family.

115 The execution in Barcelona of victims condemned by the Public Safety committees. The guilty were 'taken for a walk' in the small hours.

116 *La Voz Del Campesino* (The Voice of the Peasant).

117 Diego Abad de Santillán. He urged anarchists, against their principles, to join the Republican governments in Madrid and Barcelona at the outbreak of the Civil War.

118 Mexico.

119 Angel Pestaña.

120 Before the Model Prison, Madrid, in the fighting of 21 November 1936.

General Knowledge 3

121 Andrew.

122 Great Charter.

123 The kidneys. Adrenal means adjacent to the kidney.

124 The Canary Islands. The other main islands are Tenerife, Gran Canaria, Lanzarotte and Hierro.

125 The aubergine or binjal.

126 It refers to the authorship of the original picture. It is Latin for 'he (or she) painted it'.

127 Angevin (derived from 'Anjou'). The Plantagenets ruled England from 1154 to 1399. They descended from Matilda, daughter of Henry I, and Geoffrey, Count of Anjou. Geoffrey was nicknamed Plantagenet because he wore a sprig of broom (genet) in his cap.

128 Literally, 'in the chapel style). It refers to unaccompanied choral singing.

129 John Landy. On 21 June 1954 he ran the mile in 3 minutes 57 9 seconds.

130 O. Henry (1862–1910). In 1896 he was imprisoned for three years for embezzlement. While there he began writing short stories under a variety of pen-names, including Oliver Henry and S. H. Peters. His collection *Cabbages and Kings* was published in 1904.

131 Thomas à Kempis. The name is taken from Kempen, the town near Düsseldorf where he was born in 1379 or 1380.

132 Titan.

133 Chester.

134 A veranda in front of a house. (It is also sometimes at the side of a house, and may be just a raised platform.)

135 The Mexican War of 1846–8. By the Treaty of Guadeloupe Hidalgo (February 1848), Mexico renounced her claims to Texas, recognised the Rio Grande frontier and, in return for 15 million dollars, ceded New Mexico and California.

136 Wilkie Collins in *The Moonstone* (1868). Cuff is the detective and part-narrator of the book.

137 Birds. Of the family *Ramphastidae*, there are about 60 species. They are brightly coloured with huge bills.

138 Watch- and clock-making. He was the leading watchmaker at the court of Charles II. With Robert

Hooke he made, in 1675, one of the first English watches with a balance spring. He also made barometers and sundials for William III.

139 Coleraine, in County Londonderry. It opened in 1968.

140 The cutting, polishing and engraving of stones, especially precious stones or gems; a collector, expert, or dealer in precious stones.

The Alps

141 The rescue and safety organisation at Davos.

142 The Monk (or Mönch) which is between the Eiger (Ogre) and the Jungfrau (Maiden).

143 The first ascent of the North Face of the Matterhorn by the Schmid brothers.

144 The Furrgen (south-east) ridge.

145 The Gross Glockner (12,641 feet).

146 The San Bernardino.

147 The Mont Cenis Tunnel, opened in 1871, also known as the Fréjus Tunnel. It joined Modane and Bardonecchia and went under the Pointe de Fréjus.

148 He was a pioneer of alpine ballooning.

149 Savoy was ceded by Italy to France, with the result that certain of the peaks in the Mont Blanc Massif became French.

150 The Yugoslav Partisans who fell in the Second World War.

151 A dog given by the guide, Christian Almer, to the Rev. W. A. B. Coolidge, a great alpinist.

152 Saussure (after Horace Bénedict de Saussure).

153 Valais.

154 The occasion was the Golden Wedding anniversary of the lady and her husband, the guide Christian Almer, who had guided Alfred Wills on the first ascent of the Wetterhorn.

155 It is a huge granite block in the Lake of Geneva (Lac Léman) used for many years since the first mapping of Switzerland (1820) as the base for altimetry.

156 The peaks of the Alps of a height exceeding 4000 metres (13,111 feet).

157 The guide, Ulrich Almer, said of a party of four climbers
that they were nothing less than four asses (Vieresels, in
German) to have climbed the mountain by that
particular ridge.
158 Hans Lauper. The route is called the Lauper route.
159 The Gran Paradiso (4061 metres). (Monte Rosa is in
Switzerland as well as Italy).
160 The Aiguille du Plan.

History of the Royal Navy, 1794–1805

161 Admiral Sir Hyde Parker.
162 HMS *Vanguard*.
163 Each county and large town had to provide a number of
men for the Navy, its quota fixed according to its
population.
164 When forced into harbour, he kept the Blue Peter
always at the masthead. This was the signal for
immediate sailing. It warned that at the first favourable
turn in the weather the fleet would be making back to
Ushant.
165 The *Redoutable*.
166 HMS *Excellent*.
167 Lord George Spencer.
168 Seaman Richard Parker, hanged for his part in the
mutiny of the fleet at the Nore.
169 Duncan only had four ships because the others were
immobilised by the Mutiny. He pretended he was
commanding a large fleet, sending messages and
assuming different commands for himself.
170 Commander-in-Chief of the Channel Fleet at the time of
the mutiny at Spithead. He was Admiral Lord Bridport
(Alexander Hood).
171 'Black Dick'. Gainsborough's portrait of him shows his
swarthy complexion.
172 The action off Gibraltar, 12 July 1801, sometimes
referred to as the Battle of Algeciras.
173 Admiral de Winter.

174 A frigate.
175 'Down, down with the French.' (To Lord Spencer, First Lord of the Admiralty, late in 1799, when Nelson attempted to justify his failure to obey Lord Keith.)
176 His ship, HMS *Culloden*, went aground during the approach.
177 A gun-vessel, ship-rigged, mounting twelve 24-pounder guns, and capable of carrying 100 soldiers, plus a crew of 32.
178 Admiral Lord Keith. (August 1798, the Battle of the Nile.)
179 1795. From the Dutch.
180 First British Governor of Malta. This was a naval appointment. Sir Alexander John Ball was originally a captain with Nelson and a great friend of his. He took part in the blockade of Malta, after contributing to Nelson's success in the Battle of the Nile. He was governor from 1800–9, when he died. Malta was vitally important as a naval base during this time.

General Knowledge 4

181 *La Manche. Manche* is French for sleeve. *Les Iles de la Manche* are the Channel Islands.
182 'The Lord is my Shepherd; I shall not want.' (The *Living Bible* version is 'Because the Lord is my Shepherd I have everything I need'; the *New English Bible* version is 'The Lord is my Shepherd; I shall want nothing'.)
183 T. S. Eliot, in 1935. It is based on the death of St Thomas à Becket.
184 Sir George Williams, in 1844. He was at that time a clerk in a London drapery. He was knighted in 1894.
185 Gozo. Malta is 95 square miles, Gozo 25, and Comino 1. There are some other uninhabited islets.
186 Siegfried. Fafner guards the Ring and the Rhinegold.
187 Ernest Bevin.
188 A bird of the heron family (Ardeidae). It is renowned for its strange call or 'boom' which can be heard up to three miles away.
189 Edgar Allan Poe.

190 The Falkland Islands. Malvinas is the Argentinian name for the islands, which were colonised by the UK in 1833.

191 Rainy, appertaining to rain, or caused by rain. From the Latin *pluvia*, meaning rain.

192 Joseph Lister (1827–1912). He introduced carbolic acid as an antiseptic in the 1860s. It dramatically reduced the mortality rate of those dying of septicaemia.

193 Grandma Moses (Anna Mary Moses, 1860–1961). She painted this picture in 1943.

194 Count Felice Orsini, on 14 January 1858. Both Napoleon and the Empress were unhurt, but two people were killed and 100 wounded. Orsini regarded Napoleon as a traitor to the Italian cause.

195 Oil of vitriol (or vitriol).

196 Jack Johnson (1878–1946). He won the championship from Tommy Burns in 1908.

197 *Richard II* (Act V, scene 5).

198 A naval battle shown as a spectacle (on an artificial lake constructed specially).

199 *Mallard*.

200 An elaborate and exaggerated fashion in writing and conversation. It derived its name from John Lyly's *Euphues: The Anatomy of Wit* (1579), which was characterised by exaggerated Baroque refinement and artificiality of style.

The Indian Tribes of North America, 1550–1900

201 White, purple or black beads made from shells from the Atlantic coast which were cut, drilled and strung to make strands or belts. Their colours stood for certain things: white for health, peace and riches; purple and black for sorrow or sympathy.

202 Oklahoma.

203 There were no horses in America. The horse was essential to Plains culture. The Indians got their first horses from the Spanish.

204 Because they believed that the soul of a dead man escapes from his body through his mouth.

205 The Chickasaws. The 'Five Civilised Tribes' settled in Indian Territory.

206 Crazy Horse (1844?–77). A great chief of the Minneconjou band of the Oglala Sioux Indians, he led the battle of the Little Bighorn (Custer's Last Stand). He voluntarily surrendered in 1877 and was killed by a soldier when being forced into a jail cell.

207 Jack Wilson. Wovoka was a Paiute Indian, born in Nevada. As a boy he was adopted by David Wilson, a white settler, and was then known as Jack. He founded the ghost dance religion of the western American Indians.

208 The Comanches. He was the son of a Comanche chief named Nokoni and Cynthia Ann Parker, a white captive. He surrendered to the US Army in 1875.

209 The Sioux tribe. Also known as Dakota and Lakota, meaning allies, they roamed the northern plains of North America.

210 160 acres. And each single person over eighteen received 80 acres.

211 King Philip (Metacomet). He became chief of the Wampanoag Indians in 1622 and led them in King Philip's War, an attempt, which lasted three years, to massacre the white settlers.

212 Helen Hunt Jackson (1830–85).

213 Andrew Jackson (1767–1845). He became President of the USA in 1828. The battle took place in 1814.

214 Standing Rock Agency or Reservation, Dakota Territory (South Dakota).

215 The Sun Dance.

216 Nebraska. Omaha city took its name from the Omaha Indians.

217 A secret ceremonial place of the Pueblo Indians used for religious rites and as a gathering place for the men.

218 Because gold was discovered there.

219 The typical Navaho dwelling – a low, domed-shaped structure of logs and mud, covered with earth, with an opening in the centre of the roof for a smoke hole.

220 Travois. The word is really only the pronunciation of 'travails' which was the original word used.

History of the Church of England since 1530

221 The Prayer Book's form of Holy Communion.
222 'I must account it damnable idolatry.'
223 St Mary the Virgin Church, Oxford. Cranmer was chained to a pillar in the church.
224 Henry Hammond, the Caroline Divine.
225 John Keble.
226 A series of Puritan tracts violently and vulgarly attacking bishops in the reign of Elizabeth I.
227 He produced, in 1535, the first *complete* Bible in English.
228 'Reserve in Communicating Religious Knowledge.'
229 The King of Prussia, Frederick William IV.
230 Archbishop C. T. Longley.
231 Charles Kingsley or Thomas Hughes.
232 It condemned Anglican Orders as invalid.
233 A fund formed by the tithes confiscated from the church by Henry VIII and surrendered to the church by Queen Anne, to assist the poor clergy.
234 *Nature, Man and God.* (He was Archbishop of Canterbury, 1942–4.)
235 It was rejected by Parliament.
236 Samuel Crowther was the first black African bishop in the Church of England.
237 George Augustus Selwyn.
238 Augustus Montague Toplady.
239 'National Apostasy.'
240 Cosmo Gordon Lang.

General Knowledge 5

241 Gauchos. They are natives of mixed European and Amerindian blood.
242 The Red Sea (*Exodus* xiv).
243 Potassium (K = *Kalium*, its Latin name.) It was discovered in 1807 by Sir Humphrey Davy.
244 Leather or sheepskin protective leggings. They are usually seatless and worn over normal trousers. The

word is an abbreviation of *chaparejos* (Mexican Spanish).

245 Celia. (Song: *To Celia*.)

246 Czechoslovakia. It is 30 miles east of Vienna, on the river Danube.

247 *All the President's Men.*

248 The Cominform. It took the place of the Comintern (Communist International), which was formally dissolved in 1943.

249 A caret. (Latin for 'there is lacking'.)

250 Seaweed. Kelp is the name of some seaweeds, as well as of the ash resulting from burning them to extract iodine and potassium compounds.

251 The Treaty of Utrecht. The cession was confirmed by the Treaty of Paris (1763) and the Treaty of Versailles (1783).

252 A freshwater fish. (From the old French *vendese*, meaning dace.)

253 Phidias.

254 Kent. Two miles south of Rochester.

255 In the retina of the eye. Rods are cylindrical cells assisting vision in dim light. Cones are conical or flask-shaped and enable perception of colour and detail in bright light.

256 Simon Bolivar. The republic roughly included present-day Venezuela, Panama, Colombia and Ecuador.

257 César Franck (1822–90). 'Prelude, Chorale and Fugue' was composed in 1884.

258 Leigh Hunt (1784–1859). An article on the Prince Regent, in which he described him as 'a fat Adonis of fifty', led in 1813 to Hunt being fined £500 and imprisoned for two years.

259 Hedging gloves. A regional word, used in the east of England (particularly Norfolk) for thick, untanned, leather hedging gloves.

260 Riding a horse.

Ancient Egypt, 2700–2339 BC

261 At Hierakonpolis in Upper Egypt.

262 The fifth. Probably in the reign of Ni-user-re.
263 Dr George Reisner, of the Boston–Harvard Egyptian
     Expedition. The tomb of Queen Hetep-her-es was found
     in 1925.
264 It has two separate entrances.
265 The serdab (Arabic for cellar).
266 On the walls of the vestibule and burial chamber of the
     pyramid of King Unas (Wenis) at Sakkarah.
267 The sun-temple of King Ni-user-re.
268 At Tura (on the east bank of the Nile in the Mukattam
     hills).
269 In a chamber beneath the Step Pyramid of King Djoser
     at Sakkarah.
270 Pepy I. The name of the pyramid is Men-nefer.
271 Enfeebled, emaciated people dying of famine.
272 Mereru-ka.
273 The Museum of Fine Arts, Boston, Mass.
274 In the Wady Maghara (Sinai peninsula). There is a relief
     of King Sekhem-khet smiting an enemy, on the rock of
     the wady.
275 The head, about thirty inches high, of a colossal seated
     statue of the King in granite. It is now in the Cairo
     Museum.
276 How, worn out with hunting, Prince Tuthmosis (later
     King Tuthmosis IV of the XVIIIth Dynasty), fell asleep
     in the sphinx's shade and dreamt that it promised him
     the kingdom if he would release it from the sands which
     covered it.
277 The diorite stone (*anothosite gneiss*), used for the statues
     and other monuments of the Kings of the IVth Dynasty.
278 His name and titles, as builder and sculptor, appear
     together with those of the King on a statue-base of
     Djoser, excavated among the ruins of the Step-Pyramid
     enclosure.
279 A ceremony in which the Pharaoh celebrated his Jubilee
     after a certain period of rule, usually thirty years, and
     which had as its main feature a re-enactment of his
     coronation rites.
280 The news that Harkhuf was bringing him a pygmy, a
     Deng, from tropical Africa, who could execute sacred
     dances. The letter from the king is reproduced in the
     inscriptions in the tomb of Harkuf at Aswan.

Lady Members of the House of Commons

281 Mrs Wintringham. MP for Louth in 1921.
282 The Family Allowances Act.
283 Barbara Castle. With Judith Hart, November 1968 to October 1969; with Shirley Williams, March 1974 to April 1976.
284 Minister of Overseas Development. Judith Hart, 1969, 1974, 1976.
285 Dame Irene Ward. She was 78 when she retired in 1974.
286 Mussolini's declaration of war on Abyssinia.
287 Jennie Lee. Women had to be thirty to vote until May 1929, but she was elected for North Lanark at the age of twenty-four. She later married Aneurin Bevan.
288 She was the only woman Conservative MP to survive the landslide.
289 The Social Services Policy.
290 She was the first woman to serve as a Government Whip.
291 Parliamentary Secretary to the Ministry of Health (1924–9).
292 Her father-in-law died in 1919, so her husband had to resign his seat in the Commons on becoming a peer. She thus stood for the Sutton division of Plymouth.
293 Margaret Bondfield, Minister of Labour, 1924.
294 National Woman Organiser for the Amalgamated Union of Co-operative Employees (later the Union of Shop, Distributive and Allied Workers).
295 The Countess of Iveagh in 1927.
296 Patricia Hornsby-Smith, from 1951 to 1962.
297 Lady Megan Lloyd George.
298 Her husband, who was MP for Swansea, 1924–9.
299 Barbara Castle.
300 To fight a by-election as an independent. She was unsuccessful.

General Knowledge 6

301 Poland. Originally from the Province of Masovia.

302 Abraham Darby's (1677–1717). He established the Coalbrookdale ironworks in 1709.

303 Melanin. It is actually in the skin and its quantity determines skin colour from yellow to black.

304 Territorial and Army Volunteer Reserve.

305 Isaac Walton. From *Compleat Angler. Epistle to the Reader*.

306 The Gordon riots. Named after Lord George Gordon who headed them. Many Catholic buildings were set on fire and 450 people died.

307 Paper (for book production).

308 Zinc. Named after Christopher Pinchbeck, an English jeweller who invented it *c*. 1725.

309 Volgograd. Originally Tsaritsyn, the town was named Stalingrad in 1925. Following Stalin's posthumous fall from favour, it was renamed Volgograd. It lies on the west bank of the Volga river.

310 Clio.

311 *La Bohème*

312 Edward Albee. It was first performed in 1964.

313 Washington, DC. L'Enfant was a French military engineer.

314 24. A pennyweight is 1/20th of a troy ounce. Troy weight is used for weighing precious metals.

315 The Wye.

316 Anne Boleyn (1507–36). Her father was Sir Thomas Boleyn and her mother Elizabeth Howard, daughter of the Duke of Norfolk.

317 The Senate. Senex is Latin for old man.

318 The *Altmark*.

319 John Aubrey was both the author of *Brief Lives* and discoverer of the Aubrey Holes at Stonehenge in 1666.

320 East Lothian.

Children's Literature

321 Black Beauty (or Darkie). *Black Beauty* by Anna
Sewell. He was called Darkie when he arrived at Squire
Gordon's home at Birtwick Park, but Mrs Gordon gave
him his new name in the first few days.

322 What does the Crocodile have for dinner?

323 'The frumious Bandersnatch'.

324 Captain James Hook. In *Peter Pan* by Sir J. M. Barrie.

325 A dog with eyes like saucers. (Struck once, the dog with
eyes as big as saucers (or teacups) appears. Struck twice,
the dog with eyes as big as wheels (or millstones)
appears. Struck three times, the dog with eyes as big as
the Round Tower in Copenhagen appears.)

326 The clock struck thirteen.

327 It came as an egg wrapped up in the new carpet which
replaced the one ruined by fireworks. The egg dropped
into the ashes of a fire, glowed red-hot, cracked – and
out popped the Phoenix.

328 Narnia.

329 The country of the Munchkins in the Land of Oz. From
The Wonderful Wizard of Oz, by L. Frank Baum.

330 '. . . mince and slices of quince'.

331 The Marmalade Cat.

332 *The Tale of Samuel Whiskers*. Published in 1908 in the
original title, it was changed in 1926 to match the
successful *Peter Rabbit* books.

333 Cheshire. Alderley Edge.

334 Merioneth and Llantisilly Rail Traction Company
Limited. (From *Ivor the Engine*, by Oliver Postgate.)

335 'His queer long coat from heel to head
Was half of yellow and half of red.'

336 'I'll stay till the wind changes.' In *Mary Poppins*, and
other books by P. L. Travers. She arrives with the east
wind and leaves with the west.

337 Under the kitchen floor in a large country house.

338 To try to find the children in the Balicki family and to
tell them their father has gone back to Switzerland.

339 Gollum.

340 300 years.

The Roman Revolution, 60 BC–AD 14

341 Calpurnia.

342 Aulus Hirtius. Caesar's seven books, *Commentarii de bello Gallico*, were possibly written in 51 BC, and describe the wars to 52 BC. The eighth book, written by Hirtius, is a supplement covering the events of 51–50 BC.

343 Luca (modern Lucca). Julius Caesar, Pompey and Crassus determined their respective spheres of influence and divided between them the control of the empire.

344 The formation of the coalition ('first triumvirate') of Pompey, Caesar and Crassus. Gaius Asinius Pollio (76 BC–AD 4) wrote a history of the years 60–42 BC, of which fragments remain. He founded the first public library in Rome, *c.* 38 BC.

345 The death of Pompey's wife Julia, Caesar's daughter.

346 He abandoned Caesar for Pompey. It is suggested that he had an over-weening sense of his own importance not recognised by Caesar.

347 To police the city at night and fight fires.

348 Tiberius. In 12 BC.

349 To enable him to hand in his nomination for the consular elections by the proper date. He had earned the triumph for his victories in Spain.

350 Ancyra (Ankara).

351 That Caesar had bribed him by paying his enormous debts. Gaius Scribonius Curio was a tribune.

352 Brundisium (modern Brindisi).

353 Imperator Caesar Divi filius Augustus.

354 'Clades Variana.' Arminius was a German officer in the Roman army. When he returned to his own people, he found them chaffing under the yoke of the Roman governor, Quintilius Varus. He led a rebellion in AD 9, and decoyed the troops of Varus into the Teutoburger Wald, annihilating three legions. Varus killed himself. *Clades* means misfortune.

355 Only for one day.

356 Mutina (modern Modena). Caesar made him Governor of Gaul, but nevertheless he was one of Caesar's

assassins. He resisted Antony, leading one of the republican armies, but was deserted by his soldiers in Gaul. He was betrayed and killed while trying to escape to join Marcus Brutus and Cassius in Macedonia (43 BC).

357 Because Sextus was interfering with the corn supply of Rome and Italy. The triumvirs were obliged to concede to him islands in the western Mediterranean. But Rome pressed for more action, with the result that Octavian picked a quarrel with Sextus and finally overcame him.

358 19 August.

359 The recovery of the standards and prisoners from Parthia.

360 The tribunician power.

General Knowledge 7

361 One that is prevalent in a particular area or people, or that is continually prevalent, as distinguished from an epidemic.

362 Sir Anthony van Dyck (1599–1641).

363 Armageddon. (*Revelations xvi, 14 and 16*).

364 Prince Arthur, eldest son of Henry VII. He died in 1502, only six months after the marriage. She subsequently married his brother, Henry VIII.

365 A grapefruit (or shaddock).

366 Croquet. It is still played there.

367 Robert Erskine Childers (1870–1922).

368 The Duke of Edinburgh.

369 *Quod erat demonstrandum*. 'Which was (the thing) to be proved or shown.'

370 Johann Tetzel. In 1517, Luther nailed his 95 theses to the court church door at Wittenberg. Tetzel published counter-theses, but was rebuked by the papal delegate for his literary extravagance.

371 Polyphemus. Whose single eye Odysseus blinded, so that he and his companions could escape.

372 Czechoslovakia. It is Czech for crown. (1 Koruna = 100 Haleru (Heller).)

373 *A Midsummer Night's Dream*.

374 The Neva.

375 The Declaration of Arbroath (or Independence). This was a letter, prepared in the Abbey at Arbroath after a meeting of the barons of Scotland, to Pope John XXII in Avignon, asserting the independence of Scotland. Nationalist feeling had built up after Robert Bruce's victory at Bannockburn.

376 Glass and crystal.

377 Cactus (*Cactaceae*).

378 Fiduciary Issue. It literally means 'in faith' or 'in trust'.

379 Matchbox labels.

380 The Worshipful Company of Mercers. There are 12 Great Companies. The Mercers were originally a guild of clothes hawkers, then silk merchants. The others are the Grocers, Drapers, Fishmongers, Goldsmiths, Skinners, Merchant Taylors, Haberdashers, Salters, Ironmongers, Vintners and Clothworkers.

Instruments of the Symphony Orchestra

381 Cremona, Italy.

382 It was a keyed trumpet. This was the first concerto to use such a trumpet.

383 Anton Weidinger.

384 The bassoon.

385 A percussion instrument with bells.

386 The trombone.

387 The Brandenburg Concerto No. 4. It is a kind of recorder.

388 No. 31, the 'Paris', K 297 (new numbering, K 300a).

389 Tuning the strings of an instrument in a way different from usual.

390 Symphony No. 6, the *Pastoral*.

391 A wind machine.

392 Sixteen (or eight pairs).

393 A tarogato (a double-reed instrument).

394 The strips of inlaid wood that strengthen and ornament the borders of the body of a violin or any other stringed instrument.

395 The bassoon (*fagotto*).
396 The clarinet in D (small clarinet or high clarinet).
397 Denner of Nuremberg.
398 The chin rest.
399 Tenor or Wagner tubas (tenor tubas in F and B flat).
400 Theobald Boehm.

History of the Zulus, 1816–79

401 Shaka, King of the Zulus.
402 Early in the eighteenth century a chieftain called
    Mandalela settled in the area of the White Umveloosi
    River. When he died, his son Zulu became chief of the
    clan, which adopted his name. They were known as
    Ama-Zulu, 'the people of the Heavens'.
403 Dingiswayo, or 'The Wanderer'.
404 Bishop John William Colenso. He denounced the Zulu
    War of 1879.
405 His brother Mpande, or Panda. Throughout his reign,
    he was at peace with the government of Natal.
406 The British Prime Minister, Benjamin Disraeli.
407 'What is the matter, my father's children?' He was
    wounded by assegais, pushed back his assailants and
    reached the gate of his kraal. There he fell and was
    killed.
408 A body of warriors or armed men.
409 He crowned Cetshwayo and proclaimed him King of the
    Zulu nation in the name of Queen Victoria.
410 Pieter Retief. On a second visit Retief and members of
    his delegation were killed on the orders of Dingaan.
411 Dr Henry Francis Fynn.
412 The only chair in Zululand was Dingaan's 'throne',
    carved from a single block of wood. Any commoner
    sitting on a chair, even squatting on a box, was
    considered to be emulating the king and his life would
    thus in all probability be under threat.
413 The uSuthu.
414 They took refuge on board a small coasting vessel, the
    Comet, which arrived opportunely. From the deck they
    watched the looting and destruction.

415 The Boer leader defeated a large Zulu force which attacked his laager. He was Andries Pretorius, and the town of Pretoria was named after him.

416 Tugela (in 1837).

417 Shaka ceded Port Natal to the British for use as a trading centre.

418 The river Ncome.

419 To negotiate a treaty of alliance with King George IV and to bring back macassar oil.

420 Abaka-Zulu.

General Knowledge 8

421 Dauphin.

422 Bitter almonds, or a bitter nut-like smell.

423 Sir David Blackstock McNee. He was formerly Chief Constable of Strathclyde Police.

424 Auguste Rodin (1840–1917). The work was commissioned by the town of Calais as a monument. A bronze casting of the group is in the gardens of the Houses of Parliament.

425 Texas. Houston is the largest city.

426 Egdon Heath. The piece, subtitled 'Homage to Thomas Hardy', was based on the landscape description in Hardy's *Return of the Native*.

427 Zacharias (or Zechariah). (*Luke*, iii, 2.)

428 *Endurance*. The disaster happened on an Antarctic expedition. The party escaped to Elephant Island, from where they were eventually rescued.

429 The Indian Ocean. The Pacific is 63,986,000 square miles, the Atlantic 31,530,000, the Indian 28,350,000 and the Arctic 5,541,600.

430 A Grecian urn. These are the opening lines of his *Ode on a Grecian Urn*.

431 A triangle with two sides equal, or a triangle with two sides and two angles equal.

432 An art gallery.

433 A horse's bridle.

434 Adelina Patti. (In Donizetti's opera *Lucia di Lammermoor*.)

435 Spray swept across the surface of the sea by a violent wind.

436 Marston Moor. Prince Rupert was decisively beaten by Cromwell.

437 The *London Gazette*. It first appeared as the *Oxford Gazette* in November 1665 (the Court of Charles II was at Oxford to avoid the Great Plague). It became *The London Gazette* in February 1666. It is published by HMSO.

438 The Fastnet Race. The Admiral's Cup is a biennial international competition. The Fastnet race starts on the last Saturday of 'Cowes Week' and is run from Cowes to the Fastnet Rock and back to Plymouth.

439 Nasturtium.

440 The Bible. Moffat (1870–1944) translated the Bible into modern English. His New Testament was published in 1913, and his Old Testament in 1924.

History of London from Roman Times

441 Dr Samuel Johnson. Quoted by James Boswell in his *Life of Johnson*.

442 Aethelbert.

443 The surrendering of the Sword of State at the Temple Bar by the Lord Mayor to the Sovereign, who returns it. It represents the rights of the City Council and dates from 1588 when Elizabeth I went to St Paul's to give thanks for the defeat of the Spanish Armada.

444 William Dunbar (*c.* 1460–*c.* 1530) in his poem 'London'.

445 Queen's House.

446 Richard Horwood.

447 Montagu House, Great Russell St. The museum opened there in 1759. It was founded by Parliament after Sir Hans Sloane had willed his collections to the nation in 1753. The present building replaced Montagu House in 1847.

448 St John the Evangelist.

449 Edmund Ironside, son of Aethelred II (the Unready).

Edmund was king for only seven months, when he died he was succeeded by Knut.

450 A fashionable assembly room, designed by James Wyatt in 1772. Destroyed by fire in 1792, it was rebuilt and used as a theatre, then a bazaar, and then a wine merchant's showrooms. It was demolished in 1937.

451 St James's Palace.

452 The owner was a tailor, Robert Baker, who named his house 'Piccadilly' after making a fortune out of the sale of the starched ruffs or piccadilly collars fashionable at court in the time of James I.

453 The Dukes of Bedford.

454 The Earl of Rosebery (Archibald Philip Primrose).

455 Jack (or John) Cade. He assumed the name of Mortimer and professed to be the cousin of the Duke of York and acting in his name.

456 St Thomas's Tower, which was built by Edward I in the thirteenth century and contains an oratory dedicated to St Thomas of Canterbury. Traitor's Gate lies on the waterfront and was used as a landing place for prisoners who had been tried at Westminster.

457 Islington Green.

458 Henry Fitz Ailwin, Lord Mayor from c. 1192–1212.

459 To prevent cholera being communicated by a contaminated water supply during an epidemic.

460 A bus service. It ran between Paddington and the Bank in 1829. He was London's first bus operator.

Old Testament

461 Bath-Sheba (I Kings i, 17).

462 Gihon (Genesis ii, 10–14).·

463 Nine (four against five) (Genesis xiv, 8–9).

464 Mount Carmel (I Kings xviii, 20).

465 It records Cyrus' conquest of Babylon and his sending the captives of the Babylonians back to their own countries.

466 Tahpanhes in Egypt (Jeremiah xliii, 6–7).

467 Jehoiachin (or Jeconiah or Coniah) (II Kings xxiv, 8–12).

468 At his own request he had been thrown overboard during a storm because he believed his running away from his divinely ordered mission was the cause of the storm. (Book of Jonah.)
469 To preach repentance to the people of Nineveh.
470 Zerubbabel (Haggai i & ii: Zechariah iv).
471 They fastened it to the wall of Beth-Shan (I Samuel xxxi, 10).
472 The earthquake (Amos i, 1).
473 An underground channel which King Hezekiah had cut through the rock to bring water from the Gihon spring to the Pool of Siloam (II Chronicles xxxii, 30).
474 Assyria.
475 Tirzah (I Kings xv, 33; xvi, 8ff.; xv, 23ff.).
476 Ahab (I Kings xxii, 29–38).
477 The prophet Elijah (Malachi iv, 5).
478 He was killed by Pharaoh Necho at Megiddo when trying to stop Necho's progress to the north (II Kings xxiii, 29).
479 He pierced with a spear an Israelite man and Midianite woman who were in a tent together (Numbers xxv, 6ff.).
480 Nehemiah.

General Knowledge 9

481 Longleat.
482 Fair Isle. The art of Fair Isle knitting is said to have been passed on by Spanish sailors from an Armada ship wrecked there in 1588.
483 Georges Clemenceau. Nicknamed 'The Tiger' because of his ruthlessness and caustic tongue.
484 Alfred Edward Housman (1859–1936).
485 Sydney.
486 The Percy family (the Dukes of Northumberland).
487 ff or fff (fortissimo).
488 Spain or Portugal. The Treaty was to settle conflicts arising from Columbus' first voyage. Spain was to have those newly discovered territories west of a line drawn from pole to pole 370 leagues west of the Cape Verde islands, and Portugal those to the east.

489 From the golden earrings of the people (*Exodus* xxxii).

490 Andrew Carnegie.

491 That they have incomplete sets of teeth, or no teethlike parts, or teeth at a low stage of development. They include animals such as the anteater, armadillo and sloth.

492 The royal banner or standard. Possibly derived from the Latin *aurea flamma*, golden flame. Said to have been a crimson flag on a gilded staff, it was last used in the field at Agincourt (1415). It was the standard of the abbey of St Denis.

493 Dwight D. Eisenhower. Hawaii was admitted as the 50th State in 1959. Eisenhower was President from 1953–61.

494 *She Stoops to Conquer*.

495 International Atomic Energy Agency (which came into existence 29 July 1957).

496 A little ball. From the Italian *ballota*. Small balls were put secretly in a box – a method of voting common in ancient Greece and Rome.

497 The SI unit of thermodynamic temperature. The SI (Système International), named after Lord Kelvin, is the system of units now used in science.

498 A wading bird. The Sacred Ibis (*Threskiornis aethiopica*) was the incarnation of the god Thoth, who was pictured as having the head of an ibis. There are 28 species of ibis, including spoonbills.

499 *De Profundis*. Subtitled *Epistola: In Carcere et Vinculis*, it was published in 1905, five years after Wilde's death.

500 Acanthus. And sometimes olive or laurel.

Life and Work of Vincent Van Gogh

501 The Borinage.

502 An etching of the Raising of Lazarus.

503 J. J. Isaacson.

504 At the shop of Julien Tanguy in the rue Clauzel, Paris.

505 Charles Daubigny.

506 He included his work in an exhibition at the Grafton Galleries.

507 Eugène Delacroix.
508 *Sorrow.*
509 Newgate.
510 *Heads of the People drawn from the Life.*
511 Goupil and Company.
512 Harriet Beecher Stowe's *Uncle Tom's Cabin.*
513 *Cours de Dessin, Exercices au Fusain.*
514 That of Fernand Cormon.
515 The Café Tambourin in Paris.
516 Welwyn, Hertfordshire.
517 The head attendant at St Paul's Hospital, St Rémy.
518 The Café de L'Alcazar, Place Lamartine.
519 At the Methodist chapel at Richmond.
520 *La Joie de Vivre.*

France in the Seventeenth Century

521 I think, therefore I am. The statue of Descartes at Tours
    has the inscription 'Je pense, donc je suis'. The
    quotation comes from his *Discours de la Méthode.*
522 The Académie Française.
523 François Ravaillac. He began life as a valet de chambre.
    He became fanatical after an unsuccessful application to
    join the Society of Jesus, and conceived the idea of
    assassination after hearing rumours that the king
    intended to make war on the pope.
524 To prevent the Protestants (Huguenots) from practising
    their religion, in order to achieve unity in his kingdom.
525 Monsieur Jourdain in *Le Bourgeois Gentilhomme.*
526 He was born after his parents had been married for 22
    years – in 1638.
527 He arrested the leaders of the 'Parlement'.
528 The Frondes.
529 It is called *La Carte de Tendre*, a map which shows the
    nature, degrees and paths of love. It is in Arcadia, where
    the river of Inclination waters the villages of Billet
    Doux, Petits Soins and so forth.
530 He died after performing in his play *Le Malade
    Imaginaire*, in which he mocks at doctors and those who
    put themselves in their hands.

531 **The eagle** of Meaux. Fellow-students at the college of Navarre in Paris also nicknamed him *Bos suetus aratro* (an ox broken in to the plough).

532 André Le Nôtre.

533 Boulogne.

534 The death of Cardinal Mazarin.

535 Jansenism, the religious principles laid down by Cornelius Jansen in his *Augustinus*, a digest of the teaching of St Augustine.

536 The nature and psychology of love. Set on the banks of the Lignon in Forez, it is a leisurely romance in which the loves of the shepherd Céladon and shepherdess Astrée give a picture of contemporary French high society in the fifth century. It is regarded as the first French novel.

537 Jean Baptiste Lully. An Italian composer, who wrote the first significant French operas, he became a clever and unscrupulous courtier at the court of Louis XIV.

538 Marie Thérèse, elder daughter of the king of Spain and wife of Louis XIV.

539 By being the godfather of their first child. Molière married Armande Béjard in 1662 when he was 40. The accusation was made by a jealous rival actor, Montfleury.

540 *Bérénice*.

General Knowledge 10

541 The Battle of Crécy (1346). The Black Prince was already a knight, but his father Edward III, on hearing that the Prince was hard pressed, refused to send help saying he 'would that the lad should win his spurs'.

542 Sword fighting. The swords are made of bamboo or wood.

543 The Tasman Sea.

544 A collective farm.

545 'The Raven' (1845).

546 The Queen's Award for Technological Achievement.

547 Metal. Symbol Os, Osmium is the heaviest known substance. It is a metallic chemical element.

548 Edward Everett. Unitarian, clergyman, statesman and orator.
549 Might, power, strength, force. The event is actually to test the horse's ability to jump height.
550 Julius Caesar. (Act II, scene 2.)
551 Vice-Admiral Sir Roger Keyes. On 22–23 April his forces succeeded in sinking three block ships and the mole was attacked and blown up by a submarine packed with explosives.
552 Richard Strauss. It was first performed in 1889 in Weimar.
553 Nicholas Breakspear (as Pope Adrian IV from 1154–9). Born at Langley, near St Albans, among his deeds in office was the giving of Ireland to Henry II of England.
554 Forms.
555 Carthage must be destroyed.
556 *The Entertainer*.
557 Auguste Rodin (1840–1917). He worked on the doors for about thirty years. *Porte de l'Enfer* was unfinished when he died, but many of his other works, *Le Baiser*, *Le Penseur* and others, were originally conceived as part of the design for the doors.
558 The Lick Observatory.
559 Syngman Rhee. He was overthrown in 1960.
560 A hurricane. The name given to winds of approximately 73 mph and above.

Shakespeare's English Kings

561 Henry VI *(3 Henry VI* II, v, 21–54).
562 Marchioness of Pembroke (*Henry VIII* II, iii, 60–5).
563 Henry VI disinherits Henry, Prince of Wales, confirming the crown to the Duke of York and his heirs after his decease (*3 Henry VI* I, i, 171ff.).
564 'A singing man of Windsor' (*2 Henry IV* II, i, 101).
565 To become a nun, to imagine that Richard is dead, and to tell his sad story (*Richard II* V, i, 23, 38ff.).
566 Richard II (*1 Henry IV* I, iii, 145–57).
567 It had been prophesied that he 'should not die but in Jerusalem', and the lodging in which he 'first did swoon'

was named 'Jerusalem' (*2 Henry IV* IV, v, 233–41).

568 He is standing between two bishops and reading a book of prayer (*Richard III* III, vii).

569 His uncle, Duke of Exeter (*Henry V* II, iv).

570 The story of Daedalus who made wings for his son, Icarus, to fly (*3 Henry VI* V, vi, 20ff.).

571 Fluellen (*Henry V* IV, vii, 30).

572 'Behold, mine arm
Is, like a blasted sapling, withered up . . .' (*Richard III* III, iv, 70–4).

573 He was Edward, Prince of Wales, and was murdered by the Yorkists at Tewkesbury (*Richard III* I, ii).

574 Sir Thomas More (*Henry VIII* III, ii, 393–6).

575 Gloves, which they wore in their hats (*Henry V* IV, i).

576 Primero (*Henry VIII* V, i, 6–8).

577 Rouen, in Northern France (*1 Henry VI* III, ii, 80–4).

578 The Bishop of Winchester (*1 Henry VI* IV, i, 1–2).

579 Richard II (*1 Henry IV* I, iii, 175).

580 Henry VI and Edward V (to Richard III and Richmond) (*Richard III* V, iii, 124–30 and 151–8).

The Life of Captain William Bligh

581 Sailing Master. A non-commissioned post on HMS *Resolution*.

582 HMS *Cambridge* or *Britannia*.

583 John Fryer. Fletcher Christian was appointed acting lieutenant, above Fryer, a few days out of Spithead.

584 Plantation labourers in the West Indies (St Vincent and Jamaica).

585 In recognition of George III's bounty, or royal favour, to the West India merchants and planters.

586 Purser.

587 The surgeon, Thomas Huggan.

588 To treat them kindly and never to fire except in self-defence.

589 Tofua or Tofoa, in the Friendly Islands or Tongan Group.

590 That the mutineers had hopes of a happier life among Tahitians, particularly the women, than back in England.

591 Three years later the Pitcairn islanders settled there, and these were the descendants of the Bounty mutineers.

592 Christian was subject to violent perspirations, particularly in his hands, so that he soiled anything he handled.

593 None. One was killed on land in the Tongan Group at the outset.

594 The anniversary of Charles II's Restoration. It was called Restoration Island.

595 Bligh arrested John MacArthur for illegally importing rum stills into New South Wales. MacArthur was a lieutenant in the New South Wales Army Corps and a rich settler. Bligh was the governor of New South Wales.

596 The Fiji Group.

597 *Providence*.

598 In the Indian Ocean.

599 Nelson. After the Battle of Copenhagen.

600 For services to navigation and botany.

General Knowledge 11

601 A Proscenium Arch.

602 HMS *Hampshire*. The ship, bound for Russia, was mined off the Orkneys, 5 June 1916.

603 Grouse (*tetraonidae*). It has black-grey plumage in summer and white in winter.

604 Francis Flute (who was assigned the role of Thisby in the dramatic interlude).

605 Adam himself. Some say it derives from the Hebrew *chavah*, meaning 'living'; others connect it with the Arab word for serpent.

606 Hoagy (Hoagland) Carmichael. He was born in Bloomington, Indiana, in 1899. The lyrics of *Stardust* were by Mitchell Parish, those of *Georgia on my Mind* by Stuart Gorrell.

607 *Guernica* (1937). The painting was a protest against the bombing of Guernica.

608 Henry II. He married Eleanor of Aquitaine, the divorced wife of Louis VII.

609 *Bis*, which means twice. (*Bisser* means to encore.)

610 Mount Helicon. The Muses had two chief seats, Mount Olympus and Mount Helicon. Their favourite haunts were the springs or fountains of Castalia (Parnassus), Aganippe and Hippocrene.

611 Bermuda.

612 Hydrogen and methane. The proportions vary, but an average is hydrogen 48–50 %, methane 30–35 %. Carbon monoxide is 6–8 %, nitrogen 6 %, and other hydrocarbons etc. make up the rest.

613 'The Simple.'

614 Al Capp. Alfred Gerald Caplin, born in Connecticut in 1909, began *Li'l Abner* in 1934.

615 Addis Ababa (Ethiopia).

616 Elia. Lamb used the pen-name because his brother John still worked as a clerk in South-Sea House, the subject of the first of the Essays. The first series of *The Essays of Elia* appeared in 1820–3, and the second series in 1824–5.

617 Birds. The North American song bird (*Dolichonyx oryzivorus*).

618 Sir Peter Pears. The singing of Peter Pears inspired Britten's finest work for solo voice and dominates the operas. *Peter Grimes* was Britten's first opera.

619 John Burgoyne. A British General, he surrendered his entire force to the American General Horatio Gates on 17 October 1777. It is also called the Battle of Bemis Heights.

620 Samuel Beckett.

Science Fiction

621 E. E. (Doc) Smith's *Triplanetary*, the first of the 'Lensman series'.

622 Isaac Asimov's *Nightfall*.

623 Telepathy, He could read minds.

624 *Amazing Stories*. Founded by Hugo Gernsback, this was the first pulp magazine – which in the USA have been closely associated with science fiction.

625 700g.

626 The dead god Cthulhu.

627 That she is a member of the Junior Anti-Sex League.
628 Randall Garrett.
629 Cyrano de Bergerac, in 1657. It was an early science-fiction work.
630 Jack Vance's. (In *The Dying Earth* and *Eyes of the Overworld*.)
631 Sirius. (In the novel of the same name.)
632 Instantaneously detonate every nuclear device on Earth. It is also called a neutron resonator.
633 You would dock its sting. Triffids were plants with long flexible poisonous stings, in John Wyndham's *The Day of the Triffids*.
634 Laid his eggs inside living human bodies, which the Ixtl-larvae then devoured.
635 Bokonon, the philosopher.
636 The immortality drug Stroon.
637 He bit into it, releasing poison gas, which he then exhaled (unsuccessfully) at his enemy, Baron Harkonnen.
638 Because he no longer recognised his body. His mind had been transferred into another man's body.
639 He appeared not to grow old. Because he was running an interstellar transport station, and time only affected him while he was outside it.
640 Because Professor Challenger looked just like an ape-man.

The Vikings

641 Hákon, son of Harald Finehair.
642 Denmark.
643 An iron axe-head with silver inlay from an excavation at Mammen in Jutland (Denmark).
644 Abbo, Monk of St Germain des Prés.
645 A loom-weight and a pin of distinct Norse type, and a smithy for making iron from bog-ore have been found there.
646 From long bones of animals, smoothed on the underside and cut away on the upper.
647 To fight on his side at the 'Doom of the Gods'

(Ragnarok), the last battle to be fought against giants and other monsters.
648 For the death of King Harald (Hardraade) Sigurdsson, killed at the Battle of Stamford Bridge in 1066.
649 The Volga.
650 Dicuil.
651 A rune-stone there.
652 Each side roped their ships together and concentrated the fighting about the bows. Missiles (stones, arrows, darts) were freely used.
653 There was a protecting bank, perfectly circular in shape, pierced by four gateways on the main axes. The buildings were placed symmetrically in the four quadrants.
654 Ingvar's.
655 On the Isle of Thanet.
656 Pattern-welding.
657 It is formed from a noun *varar*, meaning oath, pledge, derived from the goddess Var, and it indicates a body of men bound together by mutual vows.
658 Piracy (sea robbery).
659 Birka.
660 Skuldelev, Roskilde Fjord.

General Knowledge 12

661 Caernarvon. On 1 July 1969.
662 Turkey. He was Kemal Ataturk's Chief of Staff, 1919–22. Born Ismet Paza, he adopted the surname Inonu, the name of the town where he twice defeated the Greeks in battle. After Ataturk's death in 1938, he became President of Turkey until 1950.
663 Saskatchewan.
664 Marlon Brando.
665 Yorkshire. The regimental HQ is at Richmond in Yorkshire.
666 The donkey (in a poem with that title).
667 The eruption of Vesuvius, causing the destruction of Pompeii, Herculaneum and Stabiae.
668 Her Golden Jubilee.

669 Johann Sebastian Bach. It was composed *c*. 1732, and alluded to the contemporary craze for coffee.
670 The Advisory, Conciliation and Arbitration Service. Set up under the Employment Protection Act, 1975.
671 Norwegian (1863–1944).
672 Salty or alkaline soil. Halophytes are to be found on the shores of river estuaries, and can tolerate immersion in the sea at high tide.
673 Lord Fisher. He was Archbishop of Canterbury from 1945–61 and visited Pope John XXIII in 1960.
674 Torino (Turin). It is capital of Piedmont (once a principality, but now a province of Italy). It was the Kingdom's capital from 1861–5.
675 Hiawatha. From the poem *The Song of Hiawatha*, by Henry Wadsworth Longfellow.
676 They are the five satellites of Uranus. Named from characters in plays by Shakespeare and a poem by Alexander Pope. Titania and Oberon were discovered by Herschel in 1787, Ariel and Umbriel by Lassell in 1851 and Miranda by Kniper in 1948.
677 Happy-go-lucky, carefree or easygoing. Literally, without worry.
678 The Battle of Sedgemoor, 1685. It marked the end of Monmouth's rebellion against James II. Monmouth fled from the battlefield, where his troops had been defeated.
679 Virgil (Publius Vergilius Maro). Also called *The Art of Husbandry*, it is a didactic poem on agriculture, the care of domestic animals and the keeping of bees. It appeared in 30 BC.
680 A manometer. There are several types. They measure positive pressure, vacuum and differential pressure.

Life of Mary Queen of Scots

681 Gifford.
682 The Act of Association (1584).
683 He slipped into her bedroom when it was empty and hid under the bed. He died for it later, at the hands of Moray.

684 John Sempill, son of Lord Sempill.

685 Henry VII.

686 Sir John Gordon of Findlater. He had attempted to abduct the Queen and marry her. She had to attend his execution to give the lie to rumours that she had encouraged the handsome young lord in his matrimonial schemes.

687 She disguised herself as a man (probably a page) and escaped out of the castle by night, let down from a window on a rope. She went to the home of the Wauchopes at Cakemuir Castle where Bothwell joined her. The couple then made their way to Dunbar.

688 One of Mary's secretaries in her captivity, 'the melancholy but charming Gilbert Curle'. The other secretary at the time of her arrest was Claude Nau. Both men were implicated in the Babington Plot.

689 She wanted to be present at a masque given in honour of the wedding of her favourite valet to Christiana Hogg.

690 He was strangled. Bothwell and eight others blew up Kirk o'Field in February 1567. Darnley escaped out of the provost's lodging before the explosion. With his servant, and in his nightgown, he attempted to cross the gardens to safety. Douglas' men pursued them and strangled them.

691 Andrew Ker of Fawdonside.

692 Marjory Bruce. The Stuarts gained the throne of Scotland through the marriage of Marjory Bruce, only daughter of Robert I, with Walter, the High Steward. James feared that the birth of Mary would end the direct line.

693 Whittinghame Tower, East Lothian.

694 Patrick, Master of Gray.

695 In Peterborough Cathedral (for 25 years).

696 Their father was James V. They were the illegitimate half-brothers of Mary.

697 In Edinburgh Castle. On 19 June 1566.

698 Inchmahome, on the lake of Menteith. She was only five years old at the time. She was sent to the island between 11–18 September while the English were at Leith.

699 He was tried for having abused the Queen's confidence, deprived of his office, confined to the Tower and fined. However, he was released after one year, the fine having

been remitted and his conditions of imprisonment meantime improved.

700 She sought sanctuary there after her escape from Loch Leven.

Drama in Athens, 500–388 BC

701 The circular dancing place of the chorus.

702 Haemon. Creon was the King of Thebes, who was defied by Antigone. Haemon was her lover and killed himself by her side.

703 The *Oresteia*. The trilogy consisted of *Agamemnon*, *Choephori* and *Eumenides*. Aeschylus won victories in 484, 472 and 458.

704 Peace between Athens and Sparta.

705 The entrance song of the chorus, which entered through a side passage (parodos).

706 Jason was about to desert her to marry Glauce. For revenge, Medea sent a poisoned garment to Glauce which burnt her to death and killed her own two children which she had had by Jason.

707 In Egypt. The play is the *Helen*.

708 A place for seeing (originally only the auditorium).

709 Sophocles. The play was *Oedipus at Colonus*.

710 She was born without a mother since she sprang from the head of Zeus.

711 Cleon. He was considered a vile, unprincipled demagogue.

712 By lot, one from each tribe. The City Dionysia were festivals held at Athens in honour of Dionysus, the God of Wine.

713 The unjust argument; how to plead a bad case and win.

714 A dramatic exchange in which each actor speaks one line.

715 *Iphigenia at Aulis* by Euripides.

716 Old and ugly women were entitled to claim precedence in love-making.

717 The fund from which Athenian citizens received grants to watch the dramatic festival.

718 He had to choose between a breach of hospitality and war with Egypt.

719 Alcibiades. A leading politician and head of a war party
     that was accused of attempting to overthrow the
     Athenian constitution.
720 Agave. The son was Pentheus, who was driven mad by
     Dionysus and then torn to pieces by his own mother and
     her two sisters who in their drunken frenzy thought he
     was a wild beast.

General Knowledge 13

721 A cooper.
722 They forgot their past lives. Lethe was one of the six
     rivers of the underworld. Souls gathered on its shores to
     drink and so forget their past, before they could be born
     again.
723 The Ottoman Empire
724 The magpie.
725 They were all giants. Pantagruel was the son of
     Gargantua in Rabelais' book; Cormoran was a Cornish
     giant killed by Jack the Giant-Killer; Despair was a
     giant in *Pilgrim's Progress*.
726 Woad. Dyer's woad yields a good and very permanent
     blue dye, now largely superseded by indigo.
727 Spencer Perceval. The only British Prime Minister to
     have been assassinated, he was shot by John
     Bellingham, a bankrupt with a personal grievance
     against the government.
728 *Aida*, by Verdi. The performance was delayed because,
     owing to the Franco-Prussian war, the scenery and
     costumes could not leave Paris.
729 Noël Coward. The first volume was published in 1937
     and the second in 1954.
730 Antoine Laurent Lavoisier (1743–94). Phlogiston was
     supposed to be a substance liberated from a material on
     burning. By weighing materials before and after
     burning, Lavoisier found that a substance *gained* on
     burning and later showed it to be oxygen.
731 Raymond Poincaré (1860–1934), President from
     1913–20.

732 Joan of Arc. Published in 1755, its full title is *La Pucelle d'Orléans*. *Pucelle* means maid, or virgin.

733 Neptune. Triton is 3000 miles across and has a circular orbit. Nereid is approximately 150 miles across, and travels in an extremely elliptical orbit.

734 One that gives birth to live young (as distinct from laying eggs).

735 William Hesketh Lever (1851–1925). In 1888.

736 The capture of Warsaw by Russia in 1831.

737 John Boynton.

738 Christopher Columbus.

739 Agrippina (or Agrippinilla).

740 Potomac or Shenandoah.

Life and Works of Rupert Brooke

741 'If I should die, think only this of me . . .'

742 Ambarvalia. This was a joyful procession round the ploughed fields in honour of Ceres, the goddess of corn. The Romans held two such festivals, one in April, the other in July.

743 Ka (Katharine) Cox. The letter was written on 10 March 1915 and was to be sent in the case of Brooke's death. She would therefore have received it in early May 1915.

744 Oyster. Hillbrow was his first school. Subsequently he went to Rugby.

745 On the occasion of his paper, 'Democracy and the Arts', given to the Cambridge University Fabian Society, 10 December 1910. Brooke was then President.

746 After the *Carbonari* (the Charcoal Burners), a nineteenth-century Italian revolutionary group.

747 Frances Cornford, in a poem called 'Youth'. She later regretted the poem as giving the wrong image of him.

748 'There shall be no more land, say fish.'

749 The Apostles. A self-selecting Society to which many distinguished writers and thinkers have belonged.

750 St John Welles Lucas-Lucas. A minor poet and novelist who affected the mannerisms of the Decadents.

751 Brooke's Tahitian mistress, Taatamata, possibly the

daughter of the chief of Mataia village. She appears in
Brooke's poem, 'Tiare Tahiti'. He met her in Tahiti
during his stay there from January to April 1914.

752 From a poster in the rooms at Trinity College,
Cambridge, of the Fabian, Frederic (Ben) Keeling. The
poster depicted the workers of the world surging
forward with fists clenched above the inscription,
'Forward the Day is Breaking'.

753 'Lust'.

754 'An English unofficial rose . . .' From 'The Old Vicarage,
Grantchester'.

755 'Curates – long dust . . .' From 'The Old Vicarage,
Grantchester'.

756 On the beach at St Ives, Cornwall, during a family
holiday in April 1899. He was nearly twelve, she was
seventeen.

757 Because at one time there had been some confusion
about whether or not the Rajah of Sarawak was a
relative of the family.

758 He is murdered for his money by his sister before he can
reveal his identity.

759 Thomas Hardy.

760 Henri Matisse. In his review of the Second Post-
Impressionist Exhibition, held at the Grafton Street
Galleries, autumn 1912.

Political History of China since 1911

761 HMS *Amethyst*.

762 He was a gardener and later a research worker on
historical materials. His name was P'u-i. He was also
known by his reign-title as the Hsuan-t'ung emperor.

763 Yuan Shih-k'ai (who made an abortive attempt to set
himself up as Emperor in 1915–16).

764 'Let a hundred schools of thought contend.' This was
the slogan of the movement for freer criticism of the
cadres and bureaucracy inaugurated in May 1956. It led
to a torrent of criticism which had to be suppressed in
the anti-rightist campaign.

765 Chiang Kai-shek. Pro-Communist generals seized him

and held him prisoner until he agreed on a truce with the Communists.

766 As an assistant in Peking University Library.

767 Michael Borodin.

768 General Chennault. It was an American Air Squadron comprised of American volunteers who fought for the Chinese in 1941–2. In six months, flying P40s, they destroyed about 300 Japanese planes.

769 Norman Bethune, who worked for the Communists in Yenan.

770 An island just off the Chinese mainland, it is still held by the Nationalists.

771 The Bandung Conference.

772 The Evergreen Commune.

773 Chingkangshan.

774 Wang Ching-wei.

775 The movement of the Protestant Church in China after Liberation, for self-government, self-support and self-propagation.

776 Sir Richard Dane.

777 A large crowd of students demonstrated outside the Gate of Heavenly Peace against Japan's Twenty-one Demands on China.

778 The Marco Polo Bridge. It began as a small fight on 7 July, on the bridge.

779 Brother-in-law. Their wives were sisters. Sun Yat-sen was a leader of the revolt in 1911, and was made President of the newly formed Republic in that same year.

780 Tsingtao, in Shantung Province, midway between Shanghai and Peking. The city was built by the Germans who forced China to give them certain privileges there in 1897. In 1914, after the war began, Japan took the city from the Germans.

General Knowledge 14

781 Portugal. The initials stand for *Transportes Aereos Portugueses.*

782 Biretta.

783 Fauns.

784 Steel.

785 William I (the Conqueror). His mother was Arlette (or Herleva) and the tanner was Fulbert of Falaise.

786 Food and Agriculture Organisation. Established in Quebec after the war, its headquarters are now in Rome.

787 A race of horses endowed with virtue and reason and other qualities of man, who inhabit Houyhnhnmland, where they live an ideal existence.

788 The Greek translation. Made by Alexandrian Jews at the request of Ptolemy Philadelphus between 250 BC and 100 BC, from Hebrew texts now lost.

789 John Ruskin.

790 The Battle of Cape St Vincent. Between British and Spanish fleets, following which Sir John Jervis was made Lord St Vincent.

791 The skin.

792 Antwerp and Liège.

793 Speed.

794 The British Empire exhibition. Wembley Stadium was built as the centrepiece of the exhibition.

795 Just behind the gills and in front of the pelvic fins.

796 Edwin (Eugene) Aldrin Junior.

797 Iceland.

798 On snow and ice. Defined as a glacial association of microphytes (the smallest algae or lichens) periodically exposed to ice-cold water.

799 Canberra. The site of the capital city was adopted in 1909, the foundation stone laid in 1913.

800 Plebiscite.

World War II in Europe

801 'Gold'. Centred on the coast between Le Hâmel, just east of the Arromanches, and La Rivière, to the west of Courseulles-sur-mer. The other two beaches were 'Juno' and 'Sword'.

802 Marshal Rydz-Smigly.

803 Cologne. On the night of 30 May 1942.

804 General Maxime Weygand.

805 Operation Citadel. The impending German offensive against the Kursk salient in July 1943. (Kursk is about 400 km east of Kiev.) It was the greatest tank battle of the war, and proved to be a disastrous failure for the Germans.

806 It sank the battleship *Royal Oak*, at anchor in Scapa Flow, with the loss of nearly 800 lives.

807 That made by the 82nd US Airborne Division. Having captured the bridge across the Meuse at Grave, the 82nd eventually secured the strongly defended Nijmegen railway and road bridges across the Waal.

808 General Philippe Leclerc. He was given the rank of Marshal of France after his death in an aircraft accident in November 1947.

809 The landing at Anzio, south of Rome, on 22 January 1944. The American-British corps remained pinned in its bridgehead and failed to push inland and cut German communications leading to the Cassino front.

810 Metal strips which were dropped from aircraft to confuse the German radar.

811 The bridge at Remagen, between Cologne and Bonn (Ludendorff Bridge).

812 The Gothic Line.

813 'Nuts'.

814 *Gneisenau*.

815 The Battle of Stalingrad. Sgt Jacob Pavlov and a dozen other Russian soldiers held this key strongpoint in the centre of the city for more than fifty days, and never lost it. Pavlov was made a Hero of the Soviet Union.

816 Captain Warburton-Lee.

817 Otto Skorzeny.

818 The Plain of Catania in eastern Sicily.

819 Draža Mihailovich.

820 Field Marshal Erich von Manstein. The effort failed mainly because Hitler refused to let Paulus break out to meet the relieving forces.

Salvation Army

821 'Champagne Charlie is my Name.'

822 Elijah Cadman. Once an illiterate sweep and boxer, he rose eventually to take charge of the Army's social services. He died in 1927.

823 A handloom for home-weaving.

824 Mrs Susannah Beaty.

825 The City Temple, Holborn, London.

826 Phossy jaw, or match-maker's leprosy. (Necrosis of the jawbone or teeth, caused by continued inhalation of phosphorus vapours.)

827 'For all lands are my Father's.'

828 Joe the Turk (Joseph Garabedban or Garabed).

829 For having held some meetings for children, thus having broken a law which did not allow such gatherings without the parents' consent. The Captain had been assured that this had been obtained.

830 Catherine Hine. Early in life she had wanted to be a missionary in China, but ill-health had prevented her.

831 He offered to go without his pudding every day for a year and to give the money saved to a special appeal.

832 Because the tent where he had been holding his meetings had blown down.

833 Salisbury.

834 The age of consent was raised from 13 to 16. He revealed the horrors of the 'white slave traffic' and the danger to young girls.

835 In King Edward VII's autograph album in 1904.

836 Netherlands Indies (Dutch East Indies), now Indonesia.

837 Mbambo Matunjwa.

838 John Gore or Edward Saunders.

839 The Army began working among the Parsees in India at this time, and since the sun was a sacred symbol to them, it was changed to avoid offending them.

840 The *Empress of Ireland*. On its way to the Salvation Army's International Congress of 1914, it collided in fog with a Norwegian collier in the St Lawrence river. Over a thousand people were drowned.

General Knowledge 15

841 Thor, the god of Thunder. (Originally 'Thor's Day'.)

842 Formic acid. It was discovered in 1670 by J. Rey (Wray) when he distilled red ants with water.

843 The river Dee.

844 The Shaw Theatre.

845 Very Large Crude (or crude-oil) Carrier.

846 Hammersmith Bridge and Barnes Railway Bridge.

847 Alsace and Lorraine. Under the Frankfurt Treaty of May 1871, Alsace and Lorraine, which had been French for over a century, were made part of the North German Confederation. The provinces were returned to France in 1919.

848 *The Winslow Boy*, by Terence Rattigan.

849 The piccolo.

850 Cumbria (formerly Westmorland).

851 In her right hand.

852 Hablot Knight Browne (1815–82).

853 Hatfield.

854 Malcolm Williamson, Master of the Queen's Music.

855 Finland.

856 The Order of the Garter.

857 The model parliament (the great parliament, or the first complete parliament).

858 *The Merchant of Venice*.

859 Kathleen Ferrier. This was her début at Glyndebourne in 1946.

860 Off the coast of Brittany, France. Ys (or Is) was the capital of Cornouaille in about the sixth century. It was protected from the sea by a dyke. At the request of her lover, the king's daughter opened the sea gate to prove her love. The town was destroyed by the sea. Legend has it that the town was so beautiful that the Lutetia inhabitants, seeking a name for their own town, chose Par-Is ('like Is'), whence the name Paris.

The Operas of Benjamin Britten

861 The Rector, Horace Adams.

862 He died in accidental circumstances.

863 'Tom, Tom the Piper's Son', or 'Lavender's Blue'.

864 The Dead Sea.

865 Owen Brannigan.

866 The name of the merchant ship from which three men, including Billy Budd, were impressed to serve on the *Indomitable*.

867 By a series of slow heavy chords for the orchestra. The stage remains empty for over a minute.

868 The housekeeper, Mrs Baggot.

869 Because their botany teacher, Miss Weaver, with whom they had been camping at Easter, got scarlet fever, and so they were sent home from school.

870 The strawberries he buys on his last visit to Venice.

871 By ordering the ladies to 'change their linen' after a particularly exhausting dance (La Volta), and reappearing wearing Lady Essex's splendid dress herself.

872 'The Chimney Sweeper', from William Blake's *Songs of Innocence*.

873 Ernest Ansermet.

874 Sid laces Albert's lemonade with rum.

875 The original *Albert Herring*

876 To meet Ned Keene the Apothecary, who is going to bring her a fresh supply of laudanum.

877 Fifteen.

878 Bianca, Lucretia's maid.

879 *Sumidagawa*, by Juro Motomasa (1395–1431).

880 Owen reads the verses from that poem which deal with war.

History of Singapore, 1819–1969

881 To decide whether or not the people of Singapore favoured merger with Malaysia. (They did.)

882 Queen Victoria's Golden Jubilee.

883 By the erection in Singapore of a statue of a bronze elephant presented by the King.

884 *The Fire in Kampong Glam*. By the nineteenth-century Malayan, Abdullah bin Abdul-Kadir, or Munshi Abdullah.

885 The *Lady Mary Wood*. On 4 August 1845 en route to Hong Kong.

886 Major-General Lim Bo Seng (1909–44). A Chinese patriot who was tortured to death by the Japanese in June 1944.

887 An exclusively Straits Settlements dollar was introduced, and the old Mexican and other dollars were demonetised.

888 Henry Ridley.

889 The Transfer of Singapore and the other Straits Settlements from the control of the India Office to the Colonial Office in 1867.

890 G. D. Coleman.

891 William John Butterworth, Governor of Singapore from 1843–55.

892 Temenggong Abdul Rahman (of Singapore and its dependencies).

893 The Union Bank of Calcutta.

894 The *Singapore Chronicle*, which began publication in 1824.

895 The Singapore Institution, later known as Raffles Institution.

896 Colonel William Farquhar, Resident between 1819 and 1823.

897 Sir William Goode.

898 He composed the National Anthem, 'Majulah Singapura' ('Let Singapore Flourish').

899 Batu Berlayer, or Lot's Wife – a rock formation.

900 The Raffles Hotel.

Supermind

Naval Slang

901 When women were allowed to sleep on board, they were permitted to lie in and the call 'show a leg' was made to see that it really was a woman who was enjoying this privilege.

902 To damage the gilded and painted carvings on the bows and sterns of the ships.

903 Either a Scavenger's boat removing filth from the Thames, or a boat carrying provisions, such as vegetables and groceries, to ships in port.

904 Admiral Edward Vernon (1684–1757) was known as 'Old Grog'. Grog is short for grogram, the material used for his cloak (a coarse fabric of silk, or mohair and wool mixed with silk). In 1740 Vernon ordered a mixture of rum and water to be served instead of neat spirits for the rum ration.

905 Sheets are the ropes attached to the lower end of the sails. If all three sheets were loosened the ship would reel in the wind.

Life and Works of John Buchan

906 *Sir Quixote of the Moors* (1895).
907 Peebles and Selkirk. He was the Conservative or Unionist candidate.
908 At the top of the 39 Steps at Bradgate on the Kent coast (*The 39 Steps*, chapter 10).
909 Cherry Ripe (chapter 13).
910 He was a milkman (chapter 2).

History of the London Underground

911 He was the man with a wooden leg employed to ride up and down the first escalators installed in 1911 in Earls

Court. The aim was to give the public confidence in the new mode of travel.
912 Charles Pearson, Solicitor of the City of London.
913 Leinster Gardens, Bayswater.
914 Leytonstone to Gants Hill (Central Line).
915 The Tower Subway, linking Tower Hill and the south bank of the Thames. It opened in 1870 as a 2′ 6″-gauge, cable operated line.

The Life of General Robert E. Lee

916 'Lee's Miserables'. Hugo's novel was *Les Misérables*.
917 Traveller.
918 The Carters of Shirley Plantation on the James River.
919 He was sent to Harper's Ferry to suppress the insurrection led by the anti-slavery fanatic John Brown.
920 By ordering the Army of Northern Virginia to dig in before Richmond to block the Union advance.

Top of the Form

921 Harold Macmillan and Sir Alec Douglas-Home.
922 Mars and Rhea Silvia. Mars had surprised the Vestal, Rhea Silvia, daughter of Numitor, king of Alba, while she was asleep.
923 Positive is carbon (graphite). Negative is zinc.
924 Virgil and Beatrice. At the end of Paradise, Beatrice hands Dante over to St Bernard who leads him to his final vision of the divinity.
925 The French (Napoleon).
926 Kiel Canal. Formerly the Kaiser Wilhelm Canal, it is also called the North Sea–Baltic Canal. It is 61 miles long.
927 Passerines or Passeriformes.
928 Canada. In Alberta.

Forces Chance 'Three in a Row'

929 Spyros Kyprianou.
930 *Lord of the Flies*, by William Golding.
931 Austria and Italy.

Forces Chance 'If I'd been There'

932 The attack on the Mohne dam in the Ruhr area of
W. Germany by 617 Squadron (popularly called the
Dambusters).
933 The night of 16–17 May 1943.
934 It indicated the breach of the dam and was the name of
Wing Commander Guy Gibson's dog, which was run
over and killed the day before the take-off for Germany.

Mensa

935 Nine. Two 2ps; one 2p and two 1ps; one 2p and four
$\frac{1}{2}$ps; 2p, 1p and two $\frac{1}{2}$ps; four 1ps; three 1ps and two $\frac{1}{2}$ps;
two 1 ps and four $\frac{1}{2}$ps; one 1p and six $\frac{1}{2}$ps; eight $\frac{1}{2}$ps.
936 (Contract).
937 Oat (boat and oath).
938 (121) and (49). They are the square roots of the left-hand
figures and the squares of the right-hand.
939 50 H. They are states of the USA in chronological order
of joining the Union: Oklahoma (the 46th State), New
Mexico, Arizona, Alaska and Hawaii.